WOMEN, INFORMATION, AND THE FUTURE

Collecting and Sharing Resources Worldwide

edited by
Eva Steiner Moseley

*Proceedings of a conference
sponsored by the Schlesinger Library
on the History of Women in America
and held at Radcliffe College
17–20 June 1994*

Highsmith PRESS

Fort Atkinson, Wisconsin

Published by Highsmith Press
W5527 Highway 106
P.O. Box 800
Fort Atkinson, Wisconsin 53538-0800

1-800-558-2110

© Radcliffe College on behalf of the Arthur and Elizabeth Schlesinger Library on the History of Women in America, 1995.

Editorial Services/Production Coordination: Wordsworth Associates, Grace Olken Sheldrick.

Cover: Design by Frank Neu. Author photo by John Chase. Interior design by Barbara J. Barg.

The paper used in this publication meets the minimum requirements of American National Standard for Information Science — Permanence of Paper for Printed Library Material. ANSI/NISO Z39.48-1992.

Library of Congress Cataloging-in-Publication Data

Women, information, and the future : collecting and sharing resources
  worldwide / edited by Eva Steiner Moseley.
        p.   cm.
  Includes index.
  ISBN 0-917846-67-2 (alk. paper)
  1. Women's studies libraries--Congresses. I. Moseley, Eva
  Steiner.
  Z675.W57W65 1995
  026.3054--dc20   95-8890
                                                       CIP

WOMEN, INFORMATION, AND THE FUTURE

The Schlesinger Library, in the Radcliffe Yard.
Photo by Paula M. Lerner.

This book is dedicated to
the memory of
Patricia Miller King, 1937–1994

Director of the Schlesinger Library, 1973–93
Carl and Lily Pforzheimer Foundation Director
of the Schlesinger Library, 1993–94

Her energy and vision
made this conference possible

Contents

Foreword

Linda S. Wilson

President, Radcliffe College

From time to time an unusual confluence of events, ideas, and people occurs and triggers a transformation. Sometimes such transformations have lasting effects. To sense the potential for such a convergence and to experience it are both rare opportunities. We need to document, celebrate, and learn from such a phenomenon.

The conference on Women, Information, and the Future: Collecting and Sharing Resources Worldwide, held at Radcliffe College and organized by the Schlesinger Library staff and its advisory committee, was just such a strategic coincidence. But it was also something much more. It was a melding of minds and energies focused on the extraordinary power of accessible information to lift the sights and strengthen the efforts of women around the world.

Through this conference we shared our recognition of the remarkable changes that have made knowledge about women and women's access to knowledge and information a societal imperative. And at this conference we made a collective commitment to work together to meet that challenge.

Here, on four very hot days in June 1994, national, racial, and ethnic boundaries became bridges. Commitment to a larger purpose overcame differences and discomfort. And the memory of Patricia King, a champion sadly missing from our midst, served as an inspiration to build a strong and enduring foundation for advancement of society by the advancement of women.

It was a rare privilege to be the host institution for this extraordinary event—and to have the vision of our own institutional mission enlarged and refined by what happened here. As familiar as we were with the plans for the conference, and as convinced as we were that it would be very worthwhile, we underestimated its potential. Now, even months after it occurred, we continue to be deeply impressed by the intensity and depth of exchange that took place and its meaning for our ongoing work. It is our great pleasure to share the proceedings of this transforming experience.

We are very grateful to all who planned, sponsored, led, and participated in this conference. We salute the generosity of spirit and the courage that brought us together.

Preface

Joan R. Challinor

Chair, Schlesinger Library Advisory Committee

It is our privilege, or our misfortune, to live at a pivotal transition in world history. The print era, which spans more than five centuries, is rapidly shifting into a new age in which books are being challenged by electronically distributed texts and images. This revolution will transform every institution and practice—governmental and business, scholarly and popular, public and private.

Believing that libraries are at the very center of this fundamental shift in the ways we acquire, store, and disseminate information and ideas, and wanting to grapple with women's role in the future as well as in the past, the Advisory Committee of Radcliffe's Arthur and Elizabeth Schlesinger Library on the History of Women in America decided to convene an international conference on "Women, Information, and the Future." This conference, the proceedings of which are collected in this volume, was planned as the culminating event of the library's 50th anniversary in 1993–94.

The Schlesinger Library was well suited to hold such a conference: since 1943 the library has collected published and unpublished source materials chronicling the history of women in the United States from before 1800 to the present. During that time, the library has collected papers of prominent and representative women, women's organizations, and families, as well as oral history transcripts, audiotapes, films, microforms, and many thousands of books and periodicals. It has become the foremost center for research on the history of women and their contributions to U.S. society.

The Schlesinger conference had its genesis in an earlier event. In 1991 the Women's Library and Information Center of Istanbul, Turkey, had sponsored the First International Symposium of Women's Libraries. At that meeting, Patricia King, then Director of the Schlesinger Library, offered to sponsor a second conference in 1994. Building on this decision, the Advisory Committee further decided to expand the theme of women's place in the world by considering the challenging issues presented by the Information Age. The 1994 conference was the result.

The conference took place as two further truths were becoming widely acknowledged: that power and information are indissolubly linked and that women have an essential role in sustainable human development. In planning the 1994 conference the organizers wished to explore the ways in which these basic principles interact with one another. If women are to continue to assert their rightful place in the world's evolving social, intellectual, political, and economic systems, they must investigate the issue of their access to and use of the world's growing information base. Also considered in the planning of the conference was the realization that networking among women gathered from every inhabited continent and many diverse backgrounds could generate many insights and engender confidence in their ability to cope with continual alterations to the library and information landscape.

Three fundamental convictions, long promulgated by the Schlesinger Library, inspired the organizers of the conference.

- Women need full and unrestricted access to information if they are to take their rightful place in world affairs.
- Women should be involved in every stage of gathering and disseminating information and should determine what information is to be collected, how, in what form, and how it is to be shared.
- All information gathered by the United Nations and its 185-member countries should include complete data on women; this information should be disseminated in a form accessible to women in every geographic and demographic setting.

The conference organizers agreed that women's information networks should be encouraged, to foster reciprocity and cooperation and to ease communication across national boundaries and geographic divides. Such information networks promote the ability to think creatively and to work collaboratively and will be essential if women are to take their rightful place in the world of tomorrow.

Women possess half the talent and intellectual abilities of the human race. To imagine that we can improve the state of the world without utilizing these largely untapped resources is now impossible. To avail ourselves of humanity's full potential, women must become equal partners with men, not just in access to information but in all facets of world affairs. Time is running out—policies must be put in place that take women as well as men into account. The need to state this fact indicates the mistakes of the past, mistakes that must not follow us into the future, or there will be no future for the world as we know it. The ultimate focus of the 1994 conference was nothing less than the future of sustained human development—and the need to ensure that women are full partners in securing a future worth having.

Patricia Miller King (1937–1994) was Director of the Schlesinger Library for twenty-one years. Her personal as well as professional commitment made the conference possible, for she saw it as a means to bring the work of women's libraries to a broader, more international audience and to further dissemination of information to women around the globe. Tragically, Pat was not able to see her selfless work brought to fruition. She died in May 1994, six weeks before the opening of the conference. We have dedicated the conference and these proceedings to her memory. Pat gave unstintingly of herself to the work of the Schlesinger Library and to furthering its aims and goals. All those who knew and worked with Pat felt privileged, and we share a continuing sense of responsibility to carry on her work with the same devotion and commitment that she exemplified.

Introduction

THE CONFERENCE

Deirdre O'Neill and Karen Philipps

Women, Information, and the Future: Collecting and Sharing Resources World-wide celebrated women's progress in securing access to information. The conference also aimed to further strengthen and facilitate efforts to collect, preserve, and interpret information by, for, and about women worldwide. The international nature of the conference constituted a departure from the Schlesinger Library's traditional focus on the United States.

Women, Information, and the Future was conceived in Turkey, in October 1991, when the Women's Library and Information Center of Istanbul sponsored the First International Symposium of Women's Libraries. Participating in the conference were representatives from the Bibliothèque Marguerite Durand (Paris), The Fawcett Library (London), the International Information Center and Archives for the Women's Movement (Amsterdam), the Center for the Promotion of Women's Studies and Research on Women (Berlin), and the Schlesinger Library. During the Istanbul meeting, Patricia King, then Director of the Schlesinger Library, offered to sponsor the second such conference.

Pat King's personal commitment made Women, Information, and the Future possible. She was dedicated to the conference as a means to bring together not only librarians but also other information workers. Sadly, Pat died of cancer in May. In the six weeks between her death and the conference, efforts were redoubled to make certain that it would be everything she had hoped. Pat unquestionably was present at the conference in spirit and in the hearts of many people there who knew her. Women, Information, and the Future became a memorial to her.

Women, Information, and the Future expanded the scope of its Istanbul predecessor to include many more libraries, grass-roots efforts as well as established institutions. Initially, the Schlesinger Library identified more than 300 women's information centers around the world. They ranged from one woman using a generator-powered fax machine to collect and distribute information, to a new women's archives in Russia, to the U.S. Library of Congress. Word of the conference spread with a life of its own, the mailing list expanded to include more the 900 names, and the preliminary registration list grew rapidly. This enthusiastic and overwhelming response testified to the need for such a conference. The end result was truly international participation, with more than 200 women (and a few men) from more than 40 countries. Efforts were made to secure funding to ensure that at least half the participants would be from countries outside North America and Western Europe. Thus the conference enabled librarians, archivists, documentalists, and information specialists working in diverse settings to share ideas, discuss common problems, and learn from each other's experiences. In general, participants from established institutions provided technological expertise, and participants from grass-roots organizations demonstrated how information can empower women.

Over one hundred participants presented papers. The program was organized into eight "streams," or sequences of sessions focusing on the following themes: grass-roots organizing, institution building, women's studies in established libraries, archival collecting, archival administration, introduction to information technology, advanced information technology, and oral history.

The regular conference sessions were punctuated with keynote addresses. After a welcome from Joan Challinor, Chair of the Schlesinger Library's Advisory Committee, Wangari Maathai from Kenya was the charismatic opening speaker. In 1977 Maathai, with the assistance of the National Council of Women of Kenya, founded the Green Belt Movement, an internationally acclaimed tree-planting campaign. A grass-roots organization comprised mainly of women, the movement has successfully striven to unite and empower rural Kenyans by promoting environmental awareness and activating people for the common goal of protecting and improving their communities.

Arvonne Fraser, then the U.S. representative to the UN Commission on the Status of Women, addressed the second plenary, speaking on "Women, International Information Policy, and Human Rights." Fraser had just returned from a planning conference in Jakarta for the September 1995 United Nations Fourth World Conference on Women in Beijing. She spoke of several issues that she believed would be addressed at that conference as well as the continuing importance to women of the global struggle for human rights.

Dessima Williams, currently a visiting professor at Brandeis University, delivered the closing plenary address. In "Reflections on Returning Home," she inspired the homeward-bound crowd with her passion and fierce determination as an advocate for people struggling for democracy in the Caribbean. Williams's words moved Cynthia Ellis of Belize to lead the conference participants in song.

The papers in this volume can only begin to convey the sense of community that pervaded the conference. Despite uncomfortable heat and humidity, between sessions women gathered in un-air-conditioned rooms or under trees in Radcliffe Yard to talk informally. They continued their conversations late into the night in the dormitory. A visit to a Cambridge women's bookstore was spontaneously organized. Another group went dancing in Boston on Saturday night. Participants also enjoyed dinners in Cambridge homes. Women, Information, and the Future owes much of its success to the patience and good humor of the participants. The sessions were well attended. Every woman filled every minute, generously sharing knowledge and insights.

On the last evening of the conference, participants met in small regional caucuses to discuss the Information Statement (printed at the end of this volume) that Joan Challinor plans to carry to the Beijing conference. Representing nations from all over the planet, the women clustered together in animated debate as sunset brought some slight relief from the sweltering weekend. This image remains as an emblem of the conference. Not only information but also friendship among women was exchanged. Continents, cultures, and differences were bridged by the commonality of every participant's struggle to increase women's access to information.

After two international conferences of women's information centers, a tradition has been born. The International Information Center and Archives for the Women's Movement in Amsterdam has promised to try to sponsor the third conference. Thus the communication networks now established will grow, and the progress manifested in Women, Information, and the Future will continue to be realized.

THE PROCEEDINGS

Eva S. Moseley

The papers given at the conference were to a large extent self-selected. Because the Schlesinger Library had few previous international connections, the Program Planning Committee could not solicit papers from particular people or on particular subjects. It was interesting to see what topics were proposed, to choose among them, and to organize them in the eight "streams" mentioned previously. This scheme worked well at the conference; it has not been maintained in this volume, however, as other categories emerged from the papers selected for publication.

First a word about the selection. Although only about half the presentations are being published, this book contains a very large proportion of the papers submitted for publication. Most of the presentations not included were either demonstrations that relied on computers or visual aids and so could not readily or usefully be written down, or they were informal descriptions—what in the United States is called "show and tell"—of archives or documentation centers in various countries. The Schlesinger Library will preserve as full a record as possible of the conference. In addition to documentation of planning and the conference itself, any papers submitted, and also reporters' notes on many of the sessions, will be available for research use.

The papers in this volume have been divided into four categories. Each article in **Part I** provides an overview of some larger aspect of **Information For**

and About Women. Part I thus sets the stage for the descriptions of particular institutions in **Part II, Information Institutions**. These institutions collect and share documentation by, about, and for women. Some are small, independent, grass-roots efforts, most begun in response to, or as part of, the women's movement of the 1960s and '70s. Some are larger and more firmly established institutions, and some are general academic or other libraries in which (female) staff have taken the initiative to promote collecting on women and to improve cataloging and other means to make these collections more accessible. Although at the conference there was little grouping by location, here, geography is the basis for the arrangement of the papers.

  Part III, Information for Information Workers, consists of articles on various library or information functions: classification schemes, thesaurus construction, preservation, use of automation, and so on, especially as they apply to women's collections. Parts II and III overlap, as usually the author discusses a particular function in terms of its evolution at her own institution. In Part III, however, the focus is on the function rather than on the history or description of the institution.

  The papers in **Part IV, Outside Library Walls**, are directed to the world outside any collecting institution, no matter how grass roots it may be. The articles deal with issues that concern women who may never visit a library or documentation center, and with methods to reach women and girls who may be illiterate or who are burdened by relentless and often menial work.

  One of the discoveries that made this conference so exciting was that not only the women's movement itself, but also many of the issues that arise from dealing with information about and for women, now seem to touch every country of the globe, certainly those represented. A pervasive issue, for instance, is the question of "separatism" versus "mainstreaming." Should women's studies materials be collected in separate institutions or in separate departments of larger institutions (e.g., university libraries)? Or should they be integrated with other materials on the same topics (whether health, human rights, education, or whatever)? Several papers touch on this question, and there is no consensus on the right answer. A related question is whether men and boys should have access to women's collections; again, there is no consensus, and some authors may be said to come down squarely on both sides of the issue, realizing that men and boys need a feminist perspective, while women need spaces of their own.

  Another major theme is the relationship among information, human rights, and women's rights. In every country, including the United States, a women's library is by its nature a political statement. In many countries it is still a very daring statement. One wonders whether it takes more courage to maintain a grass-roots women's documentation center in Asia, Africa, or Latin America, or to challenge the traditional, androcentric administration of a European library founded centuries ago. Both kinds of courage are represented in this volume.

Still another major theme is the need for relevant information, in an appropriate form, for women in developing countries. "Relevant" means information women can use *in* their daily lives and to *improve* their lives. "Appropriate" means that the information must be accessible and must not violate cultural norms. Where literacy is low—and it is evidently everywhere especially low among women and girls—libraries in the traditional sense will be of use to only a small portion of the population. Here is where some of the creative solutions described in Part IV (and also in some papers in Parts I and II) come into play, solutions that rely on radio, posters, and other audiovisual vehicles.

The importance of history for an understanding of the present and the future is more implicit than explicit in this volume. But the posters, memos, newsletters, reports, and audiotapes of today will, or should be, the archives of the future. One hopes that even small, underfunded documentation centers will be able to preserve a record of their work, and of the women in their communities, for the use of future women and men needing to understand the changes of the late twentieth century.

Although most papers are quite short (and virtually all—written for oral presentation—had to be heavily edited, which the authors took with amazingly good grace), the editors have attempted to preserve the different "voices," which reveal not only individuals but also cultures. With a little imagination, one can see the women's library in Nigeria that Helena Hassan describes, or the village women reached by the Radio Pakistan project. Similarly, there is some resonance in reading about German feminists objecting to the use of computers in their documentation centers, seeing this technology as counter to their collective, egalitarian, and feminist way of operating.

There was in fact much interest in automation at the conference, with two of the eight streams devoted to it. As indicated, only papers that do not rely on demonstration of hardware and software are published here. The conference could not have happened, however, nor could these proceedings have been published so quickly, without computers, e-mail, and fax. The German feminists are not alone in having reservations about computers, but nearly everyone would now agree that we need them and must just see to it that they are our servants and not our masters. Several articles discuss existing or planned networks among women's documentation centers; though networks are possible without automation, it makes them much more practical and efficient.

Part I begins with the opening plenary address by Wangari Maathai of the Green Belt Movement. Part IV closes with Arvonne Fraser's plenary address, followed by the Information Statement adopted at the conference for consideration at the Fourth World Conference on Women. The third plenary, the impassioned farewell by Dessima Williams of Grenada and the United States, alas remains only in the memories of those lucky enough to hear it.

Readers will note that there is almost no scholarly apparatus, with only occasional references to published works in the texts of some papers. The choice was made to prepare this volume in time for distribution at the Fourth World Conference on Women in Beijing in September 1995, only fifteen months after the Radcliffe conference. This tight deadline precluded the research and checking that a good bibliography and numerous citations would require. Again, some of this information is available at the Schlesinger Library, and the Internet, available to many in the library, archives, and information fields, provides a quick and handy way to solicit up-do-date bibliographic information.

Finally, the word *information* is used here as a shorthand term to refer to books, periodicals, archives, statistical reports, and other media and formats and their contents. The authors and editors are aware that this word often means facts and figures without context or history or values. But one needs a word that sums up the whole endeavor of collecting and sharing not only information but also knowledge and wisdom. *Information* was the word chosen for the title of the conference and so is stretched in this book as well to include all the kinds of work and collections described in it.

The hope of these proceedings, as of the conference, is that these articles will provide practical advice and useful and inspiring models to those engaged in collecting and sharing information about and for women. Another hope is that the proceedings will demonstrate to information workers, officials of governments and international agencies, and others concerned with information or women's status, the important links among information, empowerment, development, and women's human rights.

ACKNOWLEDGMENTS

In addition to those who spoke at the conference, many people helped make it possible. The Program Planning Committee was chaired by Joan Challinor and included, in addition to Schlesinger Library staff, Joyce Antler, Sherrie S. Bergman, John W. Collins III, Wambui Githiora, Barbara S. Graham, Bessie Hahn, Em Claire Knowles, Paula Mark, Leslie Morris, Sarah M. Pritchard, Diantha D. Schull, Megan Sniffin-Marinoff, Hannah Stevens, Margaret Touborg, and Lucinda Rhea Zoe. From abroad ARROW (Malaysia), CAFRA (Trinidad and Tobago), CIDHAL (Mexico), IIAV (Netherlands), and ISIS International (Philippines) offered advice and ideas.

Grey Osterud, the American editor of the journal *Gender & History* (based at Radcliffe), stepped in as conference coordinator during the last months, when Pat King was no longer able to be in charge. Ms. Osterud and her capable staff—

Aimee Brown, Deirdre O'Neill, Karen Philipps, Julia Soyer—accomplished what seemed for a time impossible, organizing a most successful event in the midst of the grief and disorientation caused by Pat King's death. Others who worked tirelessly behind the scenes were Kate Eastment, Darcy Rodenhiser, and Mary Sullivan, as well as nearly everyone at the Schlesinger Library—while keeping the library functioning as well. Many friends and neighbors of the library provided hospitality.

Funding for the conference came from individuals, corporations, and foundations. Some travel grants were made directly to participants. In addition, the following individuals provided financial support: Barbara Bell, Sherrie S. Bergman, Joan R. Challinor, Dawn-Marie Driscoll, Patricia King, Suzanne Solov Labiner, Mary Eugenia Hartmann Myer, Mrs. Jefferson Patterson, Anne Hazard Richardson, Clara Goldberg Schiffer, Susan Wallach, and Doris Yaffe.

Corporations and foundations that contributed were BayBank, Chadwyck-Healey, Citibank, Faxon Company, Gale Research, Gaylord Brothers, German Marshall Fund of the United States, Highsmith Company, Houghton Mifflin, Knight-Ridder, Inc., Putnam Corporation, Reed Reference Publishing, Research Publications International, Marcia Brady Tucker Foundation, University Microfilms, University of Cape Town Fund, USAir, United States Information Agency, and Wallach Foundation.

The Schlesinger Library and its Advisory Committee are grateful to Highsmith Press for its offer to publish the proceedings, made at the time that Highsmith provided support for the conference. Others who have contributed toward the costs of preparing the papers for publication are Joan R. Challinor, Gale Research, Clara Goldberg Schiffer, and University Microfilms.

PART I

Information For and About Women

Users of the Israel Women's Network Resource Center, Jerusalem, range from members of the Knesset (parliament) to schoolchildren. The coordinator, Yaffa Flissler, is at the left.

Photo: Debbi Cooper, Jerusalem.

Wangari Maathai launched the conference with the inspiring story of the Green Belt Movement, which is largely her own story. The movement has used information to empower women to meet their own needs and those of their families and communities and to stand up to what they saw as an oppressive and corrupt regime. Both Maathai and Valentina Stoeva, who spoke about the artificial information barriers between women in eastern and western Europe, show how individual lives mesh with political events and emphasize the practical and vital role of information in women's lives.

Sarah Pritchard lays out the stages of the development of women's studies, for each stage showing its effect on libraries. Though she focuses on the United States, the culture she knows best, her history and analysis will no doubt find parallels in other cultures.

The article by Isabel Duque and María Soledad Weinstein on organizing a women's documentation center could be seen as the kind of "how-to" article that appears in Part III. Because of its scope, however, it rightly belongs here, as it spells out fundamental issues for new and existing centers and libraries.

Carol Mitchell's paper, too, might be seen as belonging elsewhere: in Part II under *Asia*. But it discusses cross-cultural collecting, which has wider application than the two geographic areas it touches: a U.S. library collecting on Southeast Asia. Many countries have area studies programs for other regions of the world, but probably very few of those programs deliberately and explicitly incorporate substantial information on women in their collecting, teaching, and research. Mitchell lays out some of the problems and discusses solutions developed at her library. Her ideas should encourage others to seek to enrich area studies with women's studies.

Information for Action

Wangari Maathai (Kenya)

INTRODUCTION

I live in a world where the battle for freedom of information and expression is still being fought. The politicians still decide what is good and safe for us to read and, so far, the Bible is one book that has successfully evaded, and indeed impressed, the censors.

So I do read the Bible, a book full of wisdom. Hosea 4:6, for example, says, "My people perish for lack of knowledge." The tree at the center of the Garden of Eden is the tree of knowledge of good and evil; but Eve is warned that if she partakes of it, she will be like God.

I quote these references to knowledge often during our training seminars to emphasize the importance of acquiring knowledge and using it for the common good. During the seminars we read these quotations to remind ourselves that what we need is *correct* information so that we can make the right decisions and take appropriate action. We urge participants not to escape from knowledge by clinging to supernatural powers. We must all seek knowledge and information from the tree of life in the center of the garden of our intellect, our heritage, our libraries, laboratories, and indeed even Mother Nature herself. That is what Eve did: she took action to seek knowledge, never mind what man had to say about it!

Wangari Maathai is a founder of the Green Belt Movement. Much autobiographical information is incorporated in this article.

THE MAKING OF AN ACTIVIST

I am currently working with the Green Belt Movement (GBM). I first collected information in the humble but rich countryside of my childhood, then studied biology at Mount Scholastica College in Kansas. At the University of Pittsburgh, where I earned a master's degree, I learned the embryology and microanatomy of the pineal body of birds and to prepare tissues for microscopic observation. I became interested in anatomy, embryology, and histology and was recruited for the University of Nairobi in Kenya. I learned electron microscopy at the University of Munich, and at the University of Nairobi I pursued a Ph.D. and in the early 1970s became a permanent member of the Faculty of Veterinary Medicine. It seemed as though besides being a wife and mother, I was destined to help produce graduates of Veterinary Medicine who would feed Eastern Africa with livestock products. At that time Kenya's livestock industry was the best in the eastern region. I thought that from then on it would be smooth sailing to old age and eternity. Was I wrong!

I took up research on the parasite responsible for East Coast Fever, a fatal cattle disease. One part of the parasite life cycle is spent in the salivary glands of brown-ear ticks. I collected hundreds of ticks and cut up their salivary glands to produce thousands of slides for microscopic observation. But my life in the university was cut short. Others have continued the work but have not found a cure for the disease, nor fully unraveled the life cycle of the parasite.

While I was collecting ticks I came to recognize environmental degradation in Kenya. The animals from whose bodies I picked the ticks were clearly suffering from hunger. There was little grass or other fodder. The people, too, looked undernourished and poor. Vegetation was scanty, the soils poor, yields low, and famine almost guaranteed.

This information hit me from all angles: from observations as I collected ticks, informal exchanges with women, seminars organized by the National Council of Women of Kenya (NCWK), the press, the newly formed United Nations Environmental Program, and from a group of diligent European and American environmental activists.

From these encounters I realized that the real threat to the cattle industry was not the brown-ear tick but the deteriorating environment, and that not only the livestock industry but also my children, and my entire country, were threatened. The cumulative knowledge I had acquired enabled me to link the symptoms of degradation and their causes, which are now well known: deforestation, devegetation, unsustainable agriculture, soil loss, pollution.

Several years later, I joined the NCWK and attended seminars about women and their problems. At one seminar I was struck by research data indicating that children in the fertile Central Kenya Province were suffering from diseases associated with malnutrition. Women, the researcher reported, were using agricultural residues as fuel and therefore opting for foods that required little energy to cook: such processed foods as bread, maize flour, rice, and tea, rich in carbohydrates but wanting in vitamins, proteins, and minerals. We now know that this changed diet was also a symptom of environmental degradation, as was rampant urban and rural poverty. The people were trapped in a vicious cycle.

We leaders of the NCWK were the privileged few, mostly well educated and successful in our business, professional, or religious lives. Preoccupied with giving each other company and moral support, we were also concerned with the social and economic status of the rural women who were the bulk of the members. We were concerned with such basic matters as water, school fees, and clothing, and we wondered what we could do to ease the burden of those less privileged. After all, rural Kenya is where our mothers and our sisters were, and still are, living.

THE GREEN BELT MOVEMENT

Despite the culture of development aid and an influx of experts from the developed countries, I had learned that it is better to "teach people to fish" than to give them fish. So, through the NCWK, we decided to encourage women to plant trees so that they could meet many of the needs they were expressing at meetings. This was the right idea at the right time.

In 1977, the Green Belt Movement (GBM) was born. GBM has identified a long list of both short- and long-term objectives. The overall objective is to raise the awareness of ordinary citizens on the need to care for the environment so that it may take care of them. We educate them on the links between their own survival and that of the environment in which they live, helping them meet their needs while promoting sustainable development.

The main activity is the planting of tree seedlings, which women raise and share with neighbors. More than ten million seedlings have been planted. But I think that the real success of the movement lies in having demystified the forestry profession and created an accepted category of foresters without diplomas! That has been done by giving women information on afforestation, tree planting, and maintenance and by making the connections between trees and food, fodder, shade, and the beauty of the natural environment. The tree has turned out to be a great sign of hope and source of inspiration.

The women of the GBM took up tree planting to meet such perceived needs as firewood, cash, building and fencing material, fruit, shade, and beauty. In the process they have learned about the causes and symptoms of environmental degradation. They have begun to appreciate that they ought to be the custodians of the environment, to demand it be protected, and to consider the rights of future generations to a healthy environment. They are now foresters without diplomas, and this gives them a great sense of accomplishment. Information and success are very empowering, and these women continue to experience both, in the process improving the communities in which they live.

HUMAN RIGHTS

In sixteen years we have encountered many obstacles, bottlenecks of development such as corruption and the abuse of human rights. We argue that unless they are tackled, development will not be realized in our part of the world. To counter these bottlenecks we must create a strong and free civil society and a democratic national government that is accountable and responsible to the people, who vote for its leaders in free and fair elections. We in the Green Belt Movement never decided to become political, to fight for a more open and democratic civil society, or to become human rights activists. But we found ourselves confronting injustices against ourselves, our members, and the environment. In the beginning it was on a personal level; then it extended to the work place, then to national issues, and finally to the international level.

ASSERTING OUR RIGHTS

As for myself, perhaps it started before birth—I remember very early finding myself asserting my right to be myself. I saw nothing wrong with being a woman, a graduate, a professional, to have an opinion on all manner of issues, to fall in love, to marry, to raise children, and to remain a completely sane woman. But many did. Because I insisted and persisted, I became labeled an activist, a controversial figure, a radical, a rebel. But I still insist that none of that is really me. I am Wangari. I do not need labels. As I broke new ground, I was absolutely certain that it was good for women to pioneer on the basis of the information at their disposal.

Twenty years ago, there were few men or women in Kenya who shared that view. I now believe that the few who did were either too jealous to be sympathetic or too frightened to be publicly associated with such sentiments. Public opinion held that women's place is at the bottom and that there must be something seriously wrong with a woman who aspires to reach for the stars. Many men needed to see such women publicly humiliated to teach all women a lesson. Women who were not sympathetic were comforted to know that they were not alone under the stifling oppression of men. This is the only way I have been able to understand the reactions I used to get from men and women. Today it is a different story, because many believe that asserting my rights was a great inspiration to them and encouraged them to do the same. At that time it seemed I was almost alone; today we are a multitude.

Uhuru Park

Our struggle for human rights and a more democratic, responsible, and accountable government is best exemplified by our efforts to save *Uhuru* (Freedom) Park in downtown Nairobi. Our government was a one-party dictatorship, with greedy and corrupt leaders who used national resources as if they were their own personal property. In 1990, the president of our country decided to take over the only remaining public park in town to build a sixty-two-story skyscraper and beside it a four-story statue of himself! He intended to borrow money on the international market and have the Kenyan government guarantee the repayment of the loans. This was going to be yet another white elephant for the prestige and ego of one man.

When we raised the alarm we were abused and ridiculed at a parliamentary session and reminded that, as African women, we ought to have known that when men speak, women should be agreeably silent. But this time around the women spoke; they disseminated information exposing the greed and corruption of a government that was interested in creating such a grandiose monolith.

The GBM women and the Kenyan people received support from environmental and human rights activists around the world. Fortunately, the potential lenders listened. Financial arrangements were canceled and the project stalled. We believe it may never be built. The park continues to be a haven for ordinary people in the middle of busy Nairobi. This experience was greatly empowering to women and to all who were fighting for democratization and an end to violations of human rights. Once again people saw the power of information in the hands of a small group of determined women.

Mothers' Protest

Another example came in 1992, when mothers of political prisoners walked to *Uhuru* Park and staged a peaceful hunger strike demanding the release of their sons, jailed because they had agitated for democratization and an end to the one-party dictatorship. They were held illegally: the government had already acceded to a change in the constitution allowing the formation of many political parties. The strike was initially planned for three days. The sight of mothers on a hunger strike and sleeping out in the open in a corner of the park, soon to be dubbed "Freedom corner," attracted huge crowds of citizens who supported an end to dictatorship and one-party governance. Many visitors, including leaders of churches and political parties, came to the park to support the mothers and their demands. Survivors of torture and detention-without-trial narrated their stories for the first time. People prayed and held all-night vigils. We shared information, learning and drawing strength from one another.

The government knew that knowledge in the "wrong" hands is a dangerous thing. It reacted to the few peaceful women by sending hordes of policemen to beat them with batons and the butts of guns and blind them with tear gas. The scene was reminiscent of attacks on Black people by state troopers during the civil rights marches of the 1960s in the United States, and more recently in South Africa. The women were furious. Some stripped to expose their nakedness, a traditional way to express utmost disgust, anger, and frustration. This expression of abhorrence is said to place a curse on the attackers. The women who were not taken to hospital were evacuated from the park and driven to their homes by night under police guard. Yet without any prior consultation, the women returned to the city and regrouped in the basement of the nearby All Saints Cathedral of the Anglican church.

Several weeks later the government sent more than 500 heavily armed soldiers to surround the cathedral. The siege lasted about a week. When negotiations between the bishop and the government were over, the soldiers moved out of the church compound, the bishop blessed the church to drive the devil away, and the women were barred from receiving visitors. They were effectively isolated from the rest of the world, yet they continued their campaign in silence. They also published and distributed information about their jailed sons. The government tried to woo them and to bribe them to accept compromises, but most held fast to their ideals.

Almost one year after the mothers staged the strike, fifty of the fifty-one sons were released. The women and many of the sons held a thanksgiving service in the cathedral.

We are now putting up a monument in the crypt where the women lived for almost a year. This monument will honor the mothers and all those jailed for following their conscience. It will remind future generations of the courage of women in the struggle against dictatorship and corrupt leaders and, one hopes, inspire future generations to stand up for justice and the rule of law.

CONCLUSION

In Kenya, information is hidden from ordinary people by the economically and politically powerful. In my personal and professional life I have tried to use information to reach out to my fellow citizens, to empower them so that they can liberate themselves and improve their lives. What we do with information is the challenge to which each of us must rise.

Women Against the Information Borders

Valentina Stoeva (Bulgaria)

The Iron Curtain and the Berlin Wall, one figurative and one physical, were erected after World War II to divide people and clearly distinguish the borders between the two worlds. The Iron Curtain and the Berlin Wall were political structures of patriarchal ideology. They were information curtains, information walls, information barriers, and gaps between the different worlds. When the Berlin Wall was torn down in November 1989, the information border between East and West was torn down.

We, the women of Eastern Europe, have been artificially separated from our Western sisters by the Iron Curtain during the last forty-five years. As a result, we suffer from the lack of a common memory and know little about each other.

What happened to women in the communist countries? One main task of the communist propaganda machine was to create the image of the new communist woman as emancipated, enjoying equal rights, being socially and politically active. But the equal right women in the ex-communist countries had was the right to share the most unattractive and mainly low-paid labor with men. Although women had equal access to higher education, the key positions

Valentina Stoeva was until recently a researcher at the Institute of Sociology, Bulgaria, and is now a free-lance writer. She is the author of *From the Horse's Mouth* (*Ot Purvo Lize*), the life stories of eighteen young women workers. She was researcher and interviewer for a documentary film about Bulgarian women for Belgian TV, is one of the co-founders of the Women's Studies Centre at New Bulgaria University, has held fellowships at the University of Kent (U.K.), and is active in the Women's Union in Bulgaria.

in totalitarian societies were men's jobs and men's responsibilities, as in the so-called democratic and civil societies.

Special attention was paid to the image of the new woman. The masculine woman tractor-driver or the *kolkhoznichka*, the sturdy woman with strong hands and hips, intent on fulfilling her five-year plan, haunted the whole of Eastern Europe. Thus women had to live through a double filter. The first intended to wipe out their identity as women. The second was to deprive them of their national identity and establish the international image of the new communist woman. To the double filter, women put up double resistance. It was considered noncommunist to be elegant, refined, and beautiful; and although it was almost impossible with the empty communist shops, East European women nevertheless managed to be elegant and beautiful.

Communism produced a double standard of values and morals—an official one and a human one. Officially, women were organized in a national women's movement, but an underground women's movement existed at the same time. In Bulgaria its spontaneous emergence was the most significant sign of feminism.

The changes in Bulgaria started with an informal women's movement for clean air. During the totalitarian regime it was dangerous to talk about environmental issues, dangerous to organize protest rallies. Sixty-year-old Maria Varamezova was the first to organize a small group of women in the first environmental demonstration, on September 28, 1987. This was the first unofficial protest rally in Bulgaria since communist dictatorship had been established after World War II. Then, on February 10, 1988, more than 5,000 men and women took part in an ecological demonstration in the town of Rousse. The Public Committee for Ecological Protection of Rousse was set up on March 8, 1988, marking the start of the organized opposition movement in Bulgaria. Later the committee grew into the Ecoglasnost organization. The Committee for Ecological Protection of Rousse and the Committee for Glasnost and Democracy (founded in November 1988) laid the foundations of the future Union of Democratic Forces in Bulgaria. Thus the underground women's movement ushered in the struggle for democracy and other profound changes.

It does not matter whether a country is classed as First, Second, or Third World, developed or underdeveloped, totalitarian, free market, or democratic—all of these different types of societies share one thing in common: the patriarchal order. There are common features that unite women all over the world. The more information we have about each other, the stronger we will be. The more fragile the information curtains between us are, the more powerful we will be. Women have a lot of common experience to share, an experience that goes beyond race, class, national borders, and cultures. The lack of information about each other and the strong, newly established information borders prevent us from organizing ourselves across class, race, and culture, thus keeping women in their specific places.

Global feminism is impossible with information barriers, new iron curtains and Berlin walls. Knowledge about each other requires a strong information wave in both directions—to the East and West. The global feminist voice will differ from the patriarchal voice, in which the bell of the dominant patriarchs rings. The global feminist voice should sound like the orchestra of life itself, where all cultures have a place.

I do believe in the enormous potential of global feminist culture, in its power to destroy information barriers and thus to widen the horizons of the whole of humankind. I do believe in the power of the invisible and still unvalued efforts of the many ordinary women who collect, store, and circulate information about and for women. I would like to encourage all the women who work in such libraries, collecting and storing information about women's history. I think that these women in these libraries are the bravest builders of the new world, a world with fewer information curtains and borders, a world with a human face.

Women's Studies Scholarship

Its Impact on the Information World

Sarah M. Pritchard (U.S.A.)

INTRODUCTION

There is a fundamental connection between feminist thought and the world of information and libraries. Librarianship is concerned with understanding the nature of information or recorded expression, the ways people seek and use it, and thus the best structures and processes for organizing, documenting, preserving, and sharing it. Feminist thought calls into question the values and definitions underlying our very concepts of knowledge, thus also questioning the structures and institutions we have built around those concepts.

In examining information, women's studies, and the fruitful interaction between them over the last twenty years, I use the term *information* in its broadest sense: that is, recorded knowledge, creative writings, the documentation of human endeavor, whatever the subject or the physical format, whether printed books and periodicals, unpublished records, electronic databases, graphic images, broadcast media, or access to information services themselves.

With graduate degrees in French and in Library Science from the University of Wisconsin—Madison, **Sarah M. Pritchard** is Director of Libraries at Smith College in Massachusetts. Previously she was Associate Executive Director at the Association of Research Libraries and the Reference Specialist in Women's Studies at the Library of Congress. In the American Library Association she has served as member of Council, chair of the ACRL Women's Studies Section, and member of the Committee on the Status of Women and the Feminist Task Force. She is the editor of *The Women's Annual 1983–84* (G. K. Hall) and the *RLG Conspectus in Women's Studies* (1990).

In libraries, we analyze the systems for organizing information, starting at its creation: who generates the material, what is produced, who publishes or distributes it, what materials are distributed through what channels and aimed at what audiences, who collects, who controls access, and who may use the material. Further, how can we track materials and information services even if we do not actually own them, and how can we explain all this information and all these access mechanisms? Libraries serve as gatekeepers of culture and learning. In selecting some items and ignoring others, in codifying knowledge through cataloging and classification, in actively assisting users or passively standing by, libraries control access to, and impose a structure and relational value on, all forms of information, creativity, and communication. These activities have implications for women, women's studies, and other topics and users who may not fit into these structures and values.

What has been the impact of women's studies on the way we define and organize information? Although writings by and about women date back to the Greeks, there was no integral body of feminist thought until the nineteenth century, and no "women's studies" before the 1970s. I hope to show how the growth of library collections and services in women's studies has paralleled the growth of the field itself. My analysis of this growth, obstacles encountered by researchers, and the responses of librarians is based on the North American experience; it would be useful to have comparative studies of this development in other countries.

DEFINITION AND ORIGINS

The term *women's studies* is not only difficult to define but also problematic. At the narrowest, it means material about women, their activities, and their characteristics but not necessarily from any particular perspective; at the broadest, it means a gender-based critique of all fields of academic inquiry and social endeavor.

Women's studies—perhaps a better term is *feminist thought*—encompasses the humanities, sciences, and social sciences, historical and contemporary analyses, from scholarly, popular, and activist perspectives. It is international and interdisciplinary and is continually evolving both within itself and as it transforms traditional disciplines. In fact, it challenges the very *notion* of distinctions, whether among disciplines, between teachers and students, or among the academy, the state, and the populace. Feminist thought has posed new theories about the connections between subjects, criticized philosophical notions of objectivity and universalism, uncovered bias in the canon, and questioned the *idea* of a canon. Feminist research has found new value in sources long forgotten or thought to be too subjective or trivial and has forged links among subjects, materials, and perspectives. The "subject" of women's studies is not limited to women but extends to our gender-based culture and its effect on learning, knowledge, and the power that knowledge bestows.

All aspects of women's studies must be considered when organizing and providing information. Feminist critique is particularly crucial to understanding the communication of knowledge, in which libraries and universities play a part. The feminist movement helped create new information, redefine old sources, create new research methods, and critique the traditional ones; it studies women both as participants in and subjects of the creation and dissemination of knowledge. This critique has been applied to women and writing, publishing, mass media, literacy, education, technology, and, of course, libraries. It applies to women as creators, managers, and users of information and raises issues of economics, employment, public policy, and ethics.

WOMEN'S STUDIES IN LIBRARIES

Women's studies in the United States is an outgrowth of the women's movement of the late 1960s and early 1970s. This movement had at least two branches: the more mainstream approach of government commissions, national women's organizations, and women active in public policy debate; and the more radical grass-roots women's liberation movement, which gave rise to a much broader social and political critique. The first official women's studies program was established in 1970. Both separate women's studies programs and courses in existing departments proliferated rapidly. This distinction colors teaching, research, the sources and methods deemed acceptable, and also library and information services.

The 1970s women's movement felt a need for bibliographies, resource materials, and the recovery of "lost" primary documents; thus, many early publications were anthologies, bibliographies, or guides. Women's studies programs and feminist groups created a wealth of books, newsletters, manifestos, self-help publications, conference papers, and other documents. The development of these resources reflects movement concerns: breaking down barriers and hierarchies; accurate and evolving language; revisionist interpretations of academic canons; grounding theory in grass-roots experience; inclusion of perspectives from lesbians, ethnic women, women of color, from diverse ages and classes, and women with disabilities; and women's control over the creation and distribution of their work.

Feminist and women's studies sources are valuable both for their immediate content and as artifacts, evidence of the frameworks of the movement and the discipline. But how much of this material found its way into libraries? It was not brought in through traditional acquisitions channels. Much of "it" did not yet exist in the 1970s, but librarians and scholars began to create it, find it, keep it, consider why it had not been kept before, and investigate whether what *was* in libraries would facilitate new, emerging kinds of research.

The impact of feminism on women librarians and the development of women's studies are two converging trends that affected library resources and services. Over the last twenty years, the drive for equity and equality in the library profession has included, from the beginning, a focus on library resources and services. At least six groups and committees of feminist librarians arose, and still exist, within national U.S. library organizations. A profession that is 85 percent female, librarianship suffers from job segregation, pay inequities, underrepresentation of women in management, lack of flexible employment policies, and the relatively low salaries of the profession. The effort to improve information and services for women and women's studies is all the stronger because it is situated within this context of professional awareness.

The structure and content of women's studies research are broader and more complicated than any one field, issue, or ideology, and the library collections to support it must be as well. Among the important questions librarians need to ask are the following: What information is needed? What sources are available? What is missing from libraries, and why? How do selection criteria and our processing priorities affect access to women's studies information? What is probably in libraries, but obscured by biased interpretation, archaic or sexist language, lack of indexing, or censorship? What sources are thought inappropriate for libraries or are prejudged by traditional standards as being valuable only for certain limited insights? What has been neglected because it was ephemeral, did not seem "academic," was hard to obtain or controversial? What does not seem to exist at all? How should we use the sources and access tools we do have to respond to and educate library users? Most important, who *are* the users, where do they get information, and do they know they can come to the library for help?

PHASES OF WOMEN'S STUDIES INFORMATION IN LIBRARIES

The growth of women's studies information resources can be described by using what women's history scholars call "stage" or "phase" theory, looking at the intellectual evolution of the field and the library resources and responses each stage evoked. The idea of phases is borrowed from such scholars as Gerda Lerner and Peggy McIntosh. The following five phases overlap and coexist, but they help us understand changes in research done, sources used, and teaching in U.S. universities.

"Male" Scholarship

The first phase—"womanless" or "male" scholarship—is the classic, dominant White male Western tradition. It embodies highly exclusionary standards and the assumption that these standards are not only objective but also universal, essential, and unquestionable. Women are not entirely forgotten; there are a few works noting deviations when women step out of their role or praising them for upholding men and the family. But the little information by or about women is peripheral to the way scholarship is conducted and so is easily overlooked, not collected, not listed in bibliographies, not asked for.

When confronted at this stage, libraries and information resources begin a process of recognizing invisibility and developing strategies to overcome it. Researchers and activists may go directly to special collections in organizations or develop their own primary material. Libraries may be seen as worse than useless.

"Compensatory" Scholarship

In the second phase, women are added but only in the roles and standards defined in the first phase. There have in fact been substantive works on aspects of women's history and sociology since the nineteenth century. The advent of women's studies meant the rediscovery of these sources. New questions are asked about old sources—for example, about images of women in existing texts—and there is additional "factual" documentation, such as identifying nineteenth-century U.S. women novelists. But active women are still seen as exceptions, and all women as adjuncts, to the main discourse.

This phase was typified by the Library of Congress subject headings that begin "Women in" or "Women as." Libraries held material on women, especially in literature, travel, domestic manuals, medical works, and religious and educational works aimed at women. A few special collections and archives focused on women's history. Except for famous women, however, there was a dearth of biographical information and little detailed demographic data. Women appeared under their husbands' or fathers' names in census, property, and legal records; author headings on catalog cards listed the surnames of all of a woman's husbands, even if she never used them. There was little information written from women's points of view.

We are still in this phase for many subjects. It continues to generate many academic publications because it is "safe" and libraries will buy the books. But it has not challenged the underlying structures or built significant new tools.

"Bifocal" Scholarship

In the third phase, we start to look at women as a "problem" or anomaly, an absence in history and scholarship, and we identify the barriers that have excluded them and other groups. This "bifocal" phase looks at women as separate and yet as part of the dominant society. The discovery of deep discrimination can generate immense anger, a sense of deprivation, a demand for rights and redress, and a push toward separatism. Scholars and librarians and, one hopes, policymakers begin to challenge the traditional canons and paradigms. Women's studies scholarship in this phase generates a steady flow of research, new journals, and publications from both mainstream and alternative presses, only a portion of which—again, the more acceptable academic work—gets into libraries or is readily found once there.

In libraries, this phase has motivated a highly productive examination of tools, procedures, and the biases and omissions embedded in them. In acquisitions, selection criteria may cause ephemera, small press, and lesbian materials to be ignored; in cataloging, subject headings call for criticism and revision; in bibliography, feminist and women's studies sources are inadequately and inaccurately covered in periodical indexes and reference books; and in public services, outreach to meet the informational and scholarly needs of women is underdeveloped.

Strategies to address these biases and omissions include revising Library of Congress subject headings, getting more periodicals covered in indexes and databases, getting more feminist press books reviewed in traditional library journals, and compiling more comprehensive bibliographies. New ideas for special services for women users include referral files, clearinghouses, and bibliographic instruction for women's studies classes. But these services and integration attempts will be seen as temporary or remedial unless we move to the next phase.

"Revalorizing" Women

The anger and frustration of the third phase lead to the fourth, which looks at women on their own terms, revalorizing them as a group. The focus is on women's lives and experiences, the cultures and values women have created, their ideas and affiliations. Some fear that such a focus may lead to ghettoization; nonetheless, it has resulted in a large body of research and has been a link between academic research and feminism, a link the more conventional forms of scholarship or the more antiacademic branches of feminism cannot establish. A search for new sources of knowledge and documentation has immense implications for libraries, changing the uses of existing sources and pushing us to acquire more and different sources.

Librarians must exercise considerable creativity to support research at this stage. Scholars may be using old sources but employing a revisionist method. New sources needed may include realia, audiovisuals, oral history, elementary textbooks, demographic data, domestic manuals, diaries, and so on. Women's traditional lack of education, power, and access to public institutions resulted in a dearth of historical records and evidence of their daily lives, although there was no lack of prescriptive and didactic writing on what women were supposed to do. Institutions outside the library become very important as information gatherers, so the librarian must maintain an active liaison and referral role.

Librarians are now in a position to review the whole scholarly apparatus for women's studies: creating not just single bibliographies but bibliographies of bibliographies, not just adding periodicals to old indexes but creating new indexes and databases. National and international collaborative projects have produced thesauri, databases, major guides for research, and a "conspectus" for women's studies. The conspectus, a set of guidelines and a classification system for evaluating the strengths of library collections, is being used for all subjects at many major libraries; the addition of women's studies is a major step toward developing resource-sharing agreements, planning preservation programs, dividing acquisitions budgets, and even promoting user education. The resources being linked and documented with these tools may not be new, but the view of them as an integrated whole is, and the services described above are becoming more permanent as the discipline itself is firmly established.

A Multifocal Approach

The fifth phase, the most radical and the most unrealized, implies a multifocal approach to history and to all subjects. It would bring a holism and integration to the study of all areas of human endeavor. At this point we might not need "women's studies" as a separate department, but only because the way we define subjects and departments should by then take into account the critiques emerging from the earlier phases. No information or academic field has fully reached this phase; we will be using the philosophies and strategies of women's studies as a distinct field for some time to come.

FEMINIST ISSUES AND LIBRARY STRATEGIES

Although women's studies and feminist critique cannot be contained within a single department, discipline, group, or issue, there *are* unique central theoretical perspectives. I believe that we will always see two ongoing, interrelated strategies in scholarship, political activism, curriculum, and information services.

In the *mainstreaming approach* we try to get information about women into individual disciplines, ultimately changing their methodological foundations. In a library, we would try to get every subject specialist and bibliographer to include items by and about women. We would make sure that these books are cataloged and classified so that they are spread throughout the stacks, each with related books, and not lumped under the Library of Congress classification HQ. Bibliographic instruction would incorporate women's studies topics in regular sessions for students in history, English, psychology, and so on, as would electronic forms of information.

In the *separatist approach* we continue to maintain a distinct women's studies department and core faculty. We focus on the special needs of women faculty, employees, and students, and those in the community who need educational or information services. The library has a women's studies specialist and perhaps a women's studies reference collection. This ensures that multidisciplinary works, feminist theory that does not fall into any preexisting category, and works that challenge the traditional divisions of format, subject, and genre are acquired and linked with the other creative and scholarly work in women's studies. Separate bibliographic instruction classes, computer training, and similar public services would be tailored to support women's studies and women students.

I strongly advocate that we maintain both approaches, because both have value and because neither one is effective on its own. Both strategies have been deployed through the phases of the discipline's growth. We need to maintain a focus on our topic and its unique aspects, but we also need to integrate it into all collections and syllabi.

THE FUTURE OF WOMEN'S STUDIES INFORMATION

Will women's studies be forgotten once it is no longer trendy or politically "hot"? In the current debate over the academic "canon," will conservative pressures squeeze out the whole subject? A number of issues need to be considered.

LIBRARY PURCHASES   When budgets are tight and materials need to be cut, will we let hardcover academic publications in women's studies predominate at the expense of ephemera and alternative presses? Will we select only "safe" women's studies material? Will we still complain that electronic media replicate many of the old biases? How will we ensure that we get foreign material, when financial constraints, standardized vendor plans, and official policies of national libraries and large publishers may filter out the materials we most want?

CATALOGING PRIORITIES   Even if we can afford to buy all the necessary material, our organizing and cataloging priorities may relegate women's studies sources to the back shelf because they are unbound and raggedy and arrive without cataloging data from the Library of Congress. Sources not listed in a national computer network may be invisible. Similarly, the lower cataloging priority U.S. libraries often give to material in other languages may affect access, just when international women's studies is expanding.

MATERIALS PRESERVATION Given the increased emphasis on preserving library materials, and the reliance on government and foundation funding to accomplish this, an important issue is the selection of items for microfilming, digitizing, or remote storage. Important women's studies historical sources may be lost because they do not fit into the classifications and bibliographies used to plan preservation projects. We may lose much non-U.S. material, as so few countries can afford wide use of acid-free paper. Those countries need technical and financial support to begin preservation programs, and women's information must be included.

ELECTRONIC ACCESS As more and more people gain access to information through computer networks rather than libraries or other intermediaries, nonmainstream information may be lost. Information that is issued only electronically will be unavailable to poor people, most of whom are women. The commercial sector may control more information. Girls and women will need training if computer systems link countries. Librarians, computer systems designers, and information users need to work together to ensure equity in content and access.

The influence of women's studies extends beyond cataloging and collection development for one subject. The greatest potential impact for feminist thought, an impact that may have a longer-lasting effect than many political changes, is in the sociology of knowledge. Libraries are among the concrete mechanisms for transmitting culture and legitimacy. We must mobilize resources to enable writers, librarians, publishers, faculty, students, policymakers, and women in the community to find information and to use it to create new services, structures, and sources.

Organization of a Documentation and Information Center on the Theme of Women

Isabel Duque and María Soledad Weinstein (Chile)

GENERAL BACKGROUND

Documentation has become a key aspect of mass communication and therefore of social organization. It constitutes the focal point in which scientific and technical advances combine with political, social, economic, and cultural needs and the stimulus of social movements.

Documentation is, in a sense, the precursor of information. It implies work with data that must be compiled and processed. The processed data then become information. The problem is that we live in a complex world bursting with data. These data must be converted into useful and relevant information that can be applied to decision making in the areas of economic, social, and cultural development. The relationship between information and decision making is fundamental within information systems, which constitute the basis of documentation work.

Isabel Duque holds a degree in social work from the Catholic University of Chile. She has worked and studied in this field in Canada, Ecuador, and, since 1984, in Chile. She has done advanced studies in cataloging and classification systems for libraries and documentation centers. She joined Isis in 1988 as a documentalist on the Women and Violence project. **María Soledad Weinstein**, a Chilean, has a degree in sociology from the Catholic University of Chile. She conducted research and training programs on agrarian reform at the Center of Agrarian Studies in Santiago (1969–73) and since 1974 has been engaged in women's studies, focusing on women and work. She helped develop a documentation center, DOCPAL, for CELADE, the Latin American Center for Demography. She joined the Isis International Latin American Program in 1984 and is coordinator of the Resource Center and Information Program of the Electronic Communication Program at Isis Internacional.

If information is a fundamental base of support for decision making, then democratization of information becomes a priority. Different segments and groups in society must be given the opportunity to produce information useful to them, creating adequate channels of access according to their needs. This is where the problem of production and distribution of information emerges, and thus the imbalance between those who produce information and those who organize and process it. Latin American documentation centers linked to the social sciences are a good example. In hoping to overcome vertical and centralized structures for the dissemination of information, these centers have a double challenge. On the one hand, they offer and sometimes stimulate the generation of information appropriate to the needs of different users, which implies finding data in a generalized context while at the same time identifying local specifics. On the other hand, they establish channels that favor horizontal communication.

DOCUMENTATION CENTERS SPECIALIZED IN WOMEN'S ISSUES

The emergence around the world and especially in Latin America of documentation centers that specialize in women's issues can be partially explained by the need expressed by women and their organizations systematically to compile information relating to them. This process is indispensable to the advancement of discussions and action and to making women's realities more visible. In this sense, documentation centers have become repositories for the collective memory of women. Together with systematically recording experiences and knowledge, they must create adequate channels for gaining access to and disseminating information, especially that generated by women.

Unique Traits

To understand the dynamics of documentation centers that specialize in women's issues, it is important to point out a few unique traits.

1. The multifaceted nature of the subject, insofar as it deals with widely diverse data, has made the adaptation of selection, processing, and retrieval techniques to the varied needs of the users more complex.
2. Despite an ever-greater volume of information being generated, voids exist in some areas. This situation is aggravated by the fact that documentation centers in Latin America continue to process general data about women without specializing in specific subjects.
3. Adapting instruments and methods developed in other information systems to the specific requirements of women has not been easy. The problem may be the lack of specialized resources, or complicated relations with other information systems. Some United Nations agencies have been

a great help. The Economic Commission on Latin America and the Caribbean (ECLAC), for example, has offered effective instruments with which to analyze information about women.

4. Although documentation centers have become legitimate aids for decision making on women's issues, there is a lack of recognition of how they can help in decision making on other matters, owing in part to inadequate dissemination channels and also because certain subjects—especially those about private life, with which most women's documentation centers are concerned—are highly undervalued.

5. Documentation centers face the challenge of establishing information networks that compile data on different aspects of women's issues and promote exchanges but that also save money and avoid duplication. The most successful information networks in Latin America are subject specific and structured with different levels of responsibility.

6. In recent years, Latin American documentation centers have been profoundly revolutionized by automation.

How the Centers Work

Most centers are in the process of institutionalization. This process has helped to define objectives, users, methodology, guidelines, and channels of communication. However, the lack of recognition concerning their specific contribution has hindered fundraising efforts and has made their work more difficult.

One fundamental parameter guiding the work of the centers is the definition of users (organizations, groups, individuals) to whom the information is oriented. The following factors help define the users:

- **Type of organization** according to the level of decision making power of the potential users (governments, parliaments, labor unions, political parties, universities and the academic world, mass media, women's or youth organizations).
- **Scope of the organization** (international, intergovernmental, government, nongovernment, academic, grass-roots).
- **Geographic scope of potential users** (local, national, regional, international).
- **Subject matter potential users focus on** (education, culture, health, violence, labor, politics, social movements, family, environment, legislation).

The combination of these variables helps pinpoint the universe of information systems users. A user profile can help identify information needs.

Changes are occurring in the information needs from documentation centers geared toward women's issues. There is a greater need for statistical and qualitative information rather than the bibliographic data required in the past decade. There is also an increasing need for systematized information (catalogs, directories, bibliographic files, and the like).

Another change in information needs has resulted from a shift in the type of individuals and organizations interested in women's issues. In the past decade, most information was channeled toward activities related to ideological and organizational development and was used for education and promoting gender identity. Thematic specialization, the automation process, and the increased professionalism of the centers now link them more directly to decision makers and other social sectors that need more integral information from other systems.

ORGANIZATION AND INFORMATION PROCESSING

Documentation centers use certain criteria for establishing organizational methods and processing bibliographic information. Documentary operations that permit the dissemination of this information are related to selection, analysis, storage, and retrieval.

Selection of Information

The selection of information is one of the most complex operations in the entire process. It is intimately related to the objectives and strategies defined by the institution; the profile of potential users of the system; the human and material resources available to process and disseminate information; and relations with other organizations, groups, individuals, and information systems.

The process of bibliographic selection is related to the content of the information, and also to the type of document: monographs, periodicals, nonconventional documents, theses, newspaper articles, or institutional information. The selection of documents is also based on the criteria or policies established by the institution on subject scope, language, and geographic context. Even if the user profile has defined the need for one kind of information, the policies of the organization may require a wider variety of information in the documentation center to enable users to evaluate programs and analyze different realities by using comparative data.

The selection process implies the acquisition of materials through purchase, exchange, and/or donation. Latin American documentation centers most commonly use the exchange method, which stimulates the production of information and encourages the creation of networks.

At Isis International, the criteria for selection and acquisition of materials are closely linked to institutional objectives. Isis is an information and communication service for women, dedicated to the empowerment and full participation of women in development processes through the creation of networks and adequate channels of communication. Concretely, this means gathering, systematizing, and disseminating information on women's issues throughout the world and at diverse human and social levels. The vast quantity and variety of information available demand that more attention be paid to the bibliographic, statistical, and reference material related to an organization's programs and organized to meet the internal and external demands for information. This is done through several means: (1) the Latin American Women's Health Network, the Women and Health Documentation Center Network, and the Latin American and Caribbean Network on Violence Against Women and their publications; (2) publications such as the Isis International Book Series and the quarterly magazine *Mujeres en Accion*; and (3) permanent updating of information. The documentation center receives regular queries on women's issues in Chile and elsewhere, especially from government agencies, parliaments, international organizations, NGOs, universities, information networks, grass-roots organizations, and individuals.

Another selection criterion is the need to keep up to date the production of information on women's issues. The permanent exchange of information between Isis and its network of contacts allows Isis to inform on the condition of women in different parts of the world, while detecting information vacuums and problems pertaining to situations about which only primary sources are available.

Also in the selection process are materials generated at conferences, seminars, and workshops, occasions when organizations share their experiences. The materials express and summarize many theoretical and methodological discussions. In recent years, owing to the increase in information needs of individuals and institutions linked to other social spheres, Isis has begun to include statistical information as well as comparative qualitative and reference information (catalogs, directories). In general, this material serves as a fundamental support for planning, program and project evaluation, legislative and government tasks, and the analysis of different realities using comparative information.

Finally, the acquisition of materials depends on the possibility of gaining access to different information sources, which may require funds or information products that can be offered in exchange. Also important are contacts with other networks and with international or government agencies and NGOs that permanently distribute information on women's issues.

Information Processing

Information processing involves analysis, storage, and retrieval. Through analysis, the selected documents are examined and data are extracted that identify documents in terms of form, presentation, and content. These data constitute sources of information that are stored physically or magnetically. The information can then be retrieved either separately or through cross searching, which is one main advantage of computerized information systems. The data are analyzed and registered using standardized methods and instruments that facilitate the exchange of information. Isis International, for example, has adapted the ECLAC Information System to its own needs.

The fundamental format adapted from the ECLAC system is the work sheet, with certain modifications relevant to Isis needs. The AngloAmerican Cataloging Rules were also adopted, with some modifications, as well as the ISO (International Standards Organization) Codes of Countries and Languages. For subject indexing of material, Isis uses the *List of Descriptors on the Theme of Women* (fifth version).

Content Analysis: Indexing and Abstracting

Content analysis, also done using the work sheet, depends fundamentally on the type of services the center wishes to grant. To retrieve information, however, there must be an index of available material by descriptor, to which indicative or informative abstracts may be added. Indexing indicates the basic concepts and methodology used in a document, translated into controlled vocabularies, such as lists of descriptors or thesauri.

The abstract is another way to analyze content. It is common in documentation systems to assign descriptors on the basis of the abstract. Given that access to direct bibliographic sources is scarce in some countries of the region, Isis uses informative abstracts to increase the circulation of information on women and related subjects, and on methodologies used, time ranges, and geographic reach.

Terminology

One principal task of the Information and Documentation Center has been the development of a conceptual system as a tool to index material on the condition and situation of women throughout the world. Three objectives have been to share an instrument that facilitates the retrieval and exchange of information with groups and institutions interested in women's issues, to find common criteria for the storage of information, and to select the terms that best reflect women in their different fields of activity.

This terminology, which constitutes a specialized database, is presented in an updated version of the bilingual publication *List of Descriptors on the Theme of Women*. This product grew out of discussions between Isis's multidisciplinary staff and women from other institutions and groups, and from comments and suggestions made about different versions of the list. All materials in the databases (which in June 1994 consisted of about 8,000 entries and their abstracts) serve as the basis for the analysis of terminology.

At present, the *List of Descriptors on the Theme of Women* (fifth version) systematizes and organizes 457 descriptors and defines 30 subject categories, each of which has been assigned—for purposes of analysis only—a group of descriptors that characterize it. The content and form of the document to be analyzed determine the selection of descriptors and their relationship with one another.

USE OF COMPUTER PROGRAMS TO PROCESS INFORMATION

The increased communication and dissemination of information on women in recent years are due in large part to the use of computerized techniques. Users' needs can be met quickly, and large amounts of varied information can be handled efficiently.

Choosing computerized processing of information entails many decisions affecting both selection and analysis of the information. For data entry, the following must be defined: the subject, geographic, chronological, and language scope; the bibliographic, referential, or statistical level on which the material will be treated; the indicative or informative content of the entries; the work sheet; the format for data entry and output; the definition of fields; and periodic updating of the database and its backup. The choice of hardware and software is also fundamental.

Most documentation centers in Latin America have adopted the UNESCO CDS-ISIS Program for personal computers to process information. This program offers definition of databases; creation of entries; modification or erasure of existing entries; automatic construction and maintenance of quick access files in each database; retrieval of diverse information using a search language; classification of entries according to needs; and printing of files, lists, catalogs, or partial or complete directories from any database.

CREATING A DATABASE

The CDS-ISIS Program makes it possible to create different databases covering a broad range of information requirements and the entry of different types of information. It has created seven types of databases distinguished by their content and sources of information.

Bibliographic Database

This is made up of documents produced by institutions, groups, and persons working on women or related subjects. In Isis International this database now includes approximately 8,000 entries and their abstracts, from institutions, groups, and people from all over the world, especially Latin America and the

Caribbean. The large subject range this database covers includes health, violence against women, economy and work, culture, policies, legislation, and women's identity. It also informs about international conferences, seminars, and regional or national workshops, programs and projects, studies and research, policies and legislation, and statistics regarding women of different social and economic situations throughout the world. Selected material from this database has been published as the *Base de Datos Mujer—Women's Data Base*.

Reference Database

This contains information on institutions, groups, and people who work on the subject of women from different perspectives. In general, it includes identification, objectives, activities, and publications. Priority has been given to a constant updating of information on members of the Latin American and Caribbean Women's Health Network and the Latin American and Caribbean Network on Violence Against Women.

Descriptors Database

This database is continuously being updated in an effort to standardize the language pertinent to the analysis and processing of documentary or reference material.

Periodical Publications Database

This database includes approximately 700 entries on periodicals related to women and about 500 entries for contextual publications that constitute support material for the information system. Most material is sent by institutions and groups on an exchange basis or by subscription. The database provides a geographic and subject inventory of what is being produced by women in different parts of the world.

Books Database

This database has about 800 entries on books, mainly in history, literature, and philosophy. The entries are selected for their theoretical, methodological, or experiential importance. They are not in the Bibliographic Database because they are considered support material.

Supplementary Database

This database systematizes information on violence against women that does not fit the criteria for inclusion in the Bibliographic Database: for example, newspaper clippings, brochures, pamphlets, manuals, conference programs.

Evaluation Database

A computerized system has been designed to evaluate the users' needs. Information gathered here is being used to determine ways in which Isis's communications channels and distribution system can meet these needs better.

NEW COMMUNICATIONS TECHNOLOGY

Isis has also begun to implement other electronic communication technologies. These include electronic mail (e-mail), which speeds communications and permits the exchange of information and documentation generated in different parts of the world. Isis participates in the Women and Health International Documentation Centers Network; the five member institutions in Latin America, the United States, and Asia regularly exchange documents and information on women's health via e-mail. Isis has also been able to access official and unofficial documents of conferences, such as the Human Rights, Population and Development, and the 1995 Fourth World Conference on Women in Beijing. In December 1993, Isis held its own electronic information conference for the Fourth World Conference on Women. Communication by fax is also widely used in the women's network. WoMeNet (Women's Media Network), for example, was created following a workshop organized by DAWN (Development Alternatives for Women in the New Era) in February 1992 in Barbados. At present twenty-four groups, institutions, and women's communication networks are part of it.

Isis has also acquired a CD-ROM reader that has great potential for storing and retrieving a large quantity of information.

EVALUATION CRITERIA

One problem facing documentation centers is how best to adapt channels of communication to information needs and the type of information available. Such adaptation requires instruments and criteria for evaluation.

The Isis Documentation Center receives many requests, by letter, fax, e-mail, and in person. These requests are important for exchanging experiences, knowledge, policies, legislation, and other materials relating to women. They provide feedback indicating the areas and subjects of interest to different sectors of society or regions of the world, as well as to organizations and groups interested in women's issues. They are also valuable for evaluating institutional activities because they permit a comparison between the types and quality of services offered and the multiple needs for information.

Isis's Evaluation Database systematizes the needs of its users and the services offered by the center. A detailed analysis of the profile and needs of users, and the type and quality of services requested versus those rendered, have allowed Isis to update its center and redefine its strategies and activities. Briefly, these services include

- Bibliographic searches as computer printouts or on diskette.
- Computer printouts of abstracts drawn from the Bibliographic Database in response to specific information requests.
- Preparation of information packets about specific topics, including quantitative and qualitative information from documentary material, directories, studies, laws, news clippings, and so on.
- Assistance to women's groups or institutions in formulating research and other projects.
- Assistance in conference organization.
- Human resource references.
- Training in the organization and implementation of documentation centers on women's issues using new technologies.

All these services imply an exchange of materials, experiences, and information about an institution's activities.

Breaking Boundaries

Area Studies Collects Women's Studies

Carol L. Mitchell (U.S.A.)

INTRODUCTION

Although area studies specialists have been collecting materials on women for some time, those engaged in women's studies have known little about these collections and the research on women derived from them. In the process of internationalizing its focus, the field of women's studies needs to consider a potentially important link in the women's information chain—area studies programs. The artificial boundaries that exist between the two fields need to be broken down.

The barriers between area studies and women's studies stem from their very different historical and political contexts. Although similar in their multi-disciplinary approaches and their marginal positions at discipline-oriented U.S. universities, they are strikingly different in their origins and political agendas.

THE GROWTH OF AREA STUDIES

The phenomenal growth of area studies as a recognized university program coincided with the expansion of U.S. diplomatic and foreign economic policy after World War II. The research and teaching priorities for area studies were originally defined from

Carol L. Mitchell is Southeast Asian Bibliographic Services Librarian at the University of Wisconsin — Madison. She has a master's degree from the School of Library Science at the University of Michigan and a Ph.D. in Southeast Asian Studies from her present institution. She has published articles and reviews in her field and in 1987 traveled to Malaysia on a Fulbright-Hayes award.

35

outside; area programs were intended to serve a broad national and political agenda. Funding has come from a variety of private foundations, the U.S. Department of Defense, and the Office of Education's foreign-education programs. Today area programs are facing significant change brought on by the changes in Eastern Europe and the former Soviet Union, as well as by a number of other factors.

Increasing Role of Feminism in Area Studies

One factor is the increasing number of feminists in area programs. In addition, the increased attention to international issues in *Ms.* and other feminist publications motivates U.S. students to learn about women in other parts of the world.

As the Southeast Asian specialist with the General Library System at the University of Wisconsin, I am responsible for collecting materials from and about Brunei, Cambodia, Indonesia, Laos, Malaysia, Myanmar, the Philippines, Singapore, Thailand, and Vietnam. The women's portion of the collection is one component of the Southeast Asia collection rather than a women's studies collection.

The Southeast Asia collection at the University of Wisconsin began in the mid-1960s. Since its inception, the Center for Southeast Asian Studies and the supporting collection have emphasized popular political and social movements, particularly those in Indonesia, the Philippines, and Thailand.

As in most libraries, women have not been well represented in Wisconsin's Southeast Asian collection; but this is changing. We have exchanged the publications of our Women's Studies Librarian for feminist newsletters from the region. We are also working to ensure the inclusion of the full political range of organizations, not only feminist groups but also such traditional ones as Girl Guides, welfare societies, and women's auxiliaries. At the national level, Southeast Asia collections are attempting to identify and acquire important mass-circulation magazines, including those for women.

Autobiography, an important genre in women's studies, is, in Southeast Asia, much more hagiographic, with none of the confessional overtones of its Western counterpart. Autobiographies of Southeast Asia women are nevertheless important, if scarce, sources for research. Biographical sources are equally scarce. The exception is Thailand, where Buddhist cremation volumes may be the only source of information on a woman whose life might otherwise have gone unrecorded.

SOCIAL CHANGE IN SOUTHEAST ASIA

One measure of the vast social and political changes in Southeast Asia is the tremendous growth of print culture. As part of its effort to document these changes, the library began several "modern culture projects" to acquire and preserve popular culture publications not generally collected by U.S. academic libraries. The result is extensive collections of romances and other genre fiction, mass-circulation magazines, religious materials, cookbooks, books on childrearing, and the like. An impressive number of these materials appear to be intended for women.

In recent years nongovernmental and political organizations in the region have increased their visibility. Their activities range from development work to environmental monitoring to health care provision. Women have played a significant role in these organizations' growth and development, serving both on boards of directors and on the front lines. They have also organized to examine and document their own lives. Women have thus become increasingly visible both in public life and in the printed expressions of mass culture.

INTERNATIONALIZATION OF WOMEN'S STUDIES

The internationalization of women's studies is perhaps best manifested in the explosion of literature on women in development. Much of the research suffers from a lack of deep knowledge of particular languages, histories, and geographies; good research is characterized by familiarity with and concern for the women. The University of Wisconsin's Land Tenure Center collection is of particular interest for research on women in development. Materials about peasant women and their role in rural development provide an added perspective to the vast holdings on land tenure and agricultural development. In gathering such materials the center regularly consults with area studies specialists and so ensures that indigenous voices are represented along with Western research.

Although the emphasis in Wisconsin's collection is on the printed text, other media are also included. Recordings of popular women vocalists have been collected, as well as videos created by women's organizations. These are part of the University of Wisconsin *South and Southeast Asian Video Archive,* which can be accessed on the University of Wisconsin's gopher, *WiscInfo,* through the Internet.

Challenges

The challenges faced when documenting women's lives in Southeast Asia are no different from those for other parts of the world. To collect, organize, and preserve the materials is labor intensive. Identifying organizations involves careful reading of newsletters and pamphlets, as well as regular visits to Southeast Asia to establish and maintain personal contacts. Over the course of a year, we write to dozens of organizations and feel lucky to get two or three positive replies. Changing politics brings changing alliances. Groups may combine to form new organizations, or disappear only to reappear under a new banner. Again, letters and personal contacts help one track these changes.

If NGOs and political groups are difficult to trace, their official counterparts are scarcely better. Most countries lack central control over government publishing, so acquiring government reports and studies requires a knowledge of the bureaucracies. Adding to the difficulty are secrecy and censorship.

Poverty too is an obstacle: cost-saving efforts prohibit many countries from publishing and distributing information; there are no funds for large print runs or overseas postage.

The Future

Much still needs to be done to document the lives of women in Southeast Asia adequately. The most noticeable gap is archival sources—diaries and other papers not only of individual Southeast Asian women but also of Western, colonial wives; missionaries; doctors; and teachers and the anthropologists and other academics who lived and worked in the region.

We who work in the better-funded libraries of the West should not be seeking indigenous women's papers. Rather, we should be working with local women's studies institutes to ensure that such collections are amassed in local institutions. Libraries in Europe and North America should focus on the many Western women who have lived and worked in Southeast Asia. Cooperation between area specialists and women's studies specialists can ensure that we document the work of international women's organizations. Finally, we need to ensure that the lives of refugee women are well documented.

As we set about documenting women's lives in Southeast Asia or other regions, it is important that we not view women's movements as possessing the attributes of our own feminist movements. There is little reason to organize a women's movement in a country where there are few political freedoms, where development policies ignore vast segments of the population, or where people are still struggling for basic human and civil rights. This does not mean that there are not strong women's voices; they may be found in other texts. It is the job of librarians and information specialists to seek texts that record such voices. Finally, as we seek historical documentation, we must remember that colonized peoples had few opportunities to document their experiences. Colonized women are even less well represented in the scarce historical documentation than men. We need to reread the older colonial texts for the information they hold on women.

CONCLUSION

The challenge of breaking down boundaries is to identify projects best undertaken jointly by area studies and women's studies programs. We should begin by examining how we share information about Third World women locally and nationally. Both fields would benefit from the creation of specialized printed bibliographies and guides. Those in area studies need to support the internationalization of women's studies. Those in women's studies need to support area specialists seeking to apply feminist methodology to a wider geography.

PART II

Information Institutions

The experimental national-language library in Caytu, Senegal, conducted by the Senegalese librarian's association and an NGO devoted to basic education.

Readers will find that the papers in Part II do not fairly represent the geography of the world. Europe predominates; East Asia and North America are missing altogether. This imbalance is due partly to the uneven distribution of resources: it is not surprising that more Europeans were able to attend the conference and speak at it than women from some other continents. But Africa, Asia, and Latin America are also represented in the other three parts, and the United States not surprisingly dominates Part III.

While these articles are mainly descriptive, each raises significant issues about the connections between and among information and empowerment, development, feminism, and other aspects of women's lives, their histories, ideas, and needs. These descriptions will give readers a taste of the excitement conference participants felt as they shared stories, problems, questions, and solutions, and as they discovered—despite continuing neglect of women's studies and issues in many quarters—how much activity there is in the women's information field all over the world.

Within each geographical region the articles are arranged alphabetically by country, with the exception of the first two European articles. The first, by Jensen and Nielsen, in addition to discussing a Scandinavian model of women's libraries, ties the different types of women's information centers to the stages of the women's movement, a scheme that helps one understand such centers in other countries of Europe. The second, by Marieke Kramer, describes Europe-wide information-sharing efforts and so looks ahead to a future in which Europeans increasingly transcend their national borders.

Information for Women in Development

The Role of the Information Worker

Buhle Mbambo (Botswana)

INTRODUCTION

The pivotal role of women in implementing development programs has been well documented, as has the important role of information in development. However, literature that links information resources and women in the process of development is scanty.

Besides the role of women and of information in development, useful questions include these: How important is information to development? Is information really power? At what stage in the development process is information useful?

Definitions

The term *development* is used here as it was defined by the World Bank in 1975 and the International Labour Organisation in 1976: as alleviating poverty, meeting basic needs, and achieving certain desirable social objectives. This integrated approach sees development as a process, an achievable goal, and a

---

Buhle Mbambo is currently a Social Science Librarian responsible for the gender and women studies collection at the University of Botswana. She has published "An Annotated Bibliography of the Women's Collection of the University of Botswana" (1992) and "The Gender and Women's Studies Collection at the University of Botswana" in *The Botswana Library Association Journal*, vol. 1, 1991.

tool for empowerment. Although this model is increasingly being superseded by that of sustainable development, here the previous model is preferred.

Harrod's Librarian's Glossary and Reference Book defines *information* as "an assemblage of data in a comprehensible form capable of communication." In this context, *information workers* refers to information disseminators, which includes those who disseminate agricultural, legal, health, literacy, and other information at the grass-roots level. This group includes librarians and others.

Community resource center refers to the rural information centers that take the place of First World–type libraries in developing countries. They generally provide basic development information and basic literacy material.

WOMEN IN DEVELOPMENT

In the first United Nations development decade, 1960–70, women were not seen as a distinct group needing special focus in the development process. The assumption was that populations within each Third World country were a homogeneous whole. When attempts were made to examine any group needs, family needs were preeminent, and the assumption was that the male head effectively expressed these needs. Women's needs were subsumed under family needs. It was also assumed that men were the economic providers while women took care of the family. The consequence was that planners planned with men in mind; women's work of food production, food processing, and family care was given no economic value, and female-headed households were ignored in development planning.

The crucial role of women in development was first acknowledged by the U.N. in the early 1970s. In the second U.N. development decade, some planners realized that mass macroeconomic development could not be achieved while ignoring such other factors of community development as population growth, improved health, and women. The growth of the women's movement led NGOs and the U.N. to realize that development could not be achieved while half the population was ignored.

Over the years, however, there has been a growing realization that considering only the women's position, while remaining silent about the men's, is further polarizing the two sexes. The tendency has therefore been to move to a relatively neutral concept of gender. This move, which has been both political and linguistic, was born from the realization that changes in women's roles necessitate a change in men's roles and attitudes. Society will be better served if the roles of both sexes are changed.

Constraints for Women in Development

Although it is generally accepted that women have an important role in development, statistical information on the actual contribution of women is scarce. Statistics tend to reflect only work that is accorded economic value. Because women's activities in agriculture and the household are usually unpaid and so not accorded any economic value, they are not reflected in social and economic statistics.

Various forms of socioeconomic and legal barriers prevent women from participating fully in development. Women in Botswana, for example, are minors at common law regardless of their age, first under their fathers' guardianship and after marriage under their husbands, Zimbabwe's Legal Age of Majority Act (1982) declared that children of both sexes reach majority at eighteen. The same legislation enabled women to enter into contracts without their husbands' consent. No real change in women's status resulted, however. Few women own real property to use as collateral in obtaining loans to start businesses, and few were even aware of what the act enabled them to do.

In Botswana and Zimbabwe, and probably in most developing countries, women lack managerial and basic bookkeeping skills. Until women are trained in such skills, even those who have the courage to venture into business will not be successful.

Overcoming Constraints

Women cannot effectively participate in development until the socioeconomic and legal barriers that hinder them have been removed:

1. There is a need for statistical techniques that will measure the economic value of work done by women and thereby reflect their true contribution to development.
2. Laws that discriminate against women in education and employment need to be changed.
3. There is a need for a change in outlook—of women as well as men—regarding women's participation in development. The socialization process should incorporate new views of sex roles.
4. There is a tendency for the sexes to be stereotyped in education; girls tend to study social science and the humanities, while boys study the sciences. Teachers, career advisers, and information scientists should work to eradicate stereotyping in education and training, and to inform girls about life alternatives.
5. To make informed decisions, women need information on socioeconomic, legal, political, health, education, and other issues that affect their development and that of their communities.

EMPOWERMENT OF WOMEN

Empowered women determine their own course of action and seek to find their own solutions. Empowerment is not something imposed from outside but a process by which an individual absorbs information and develops a strength of character that changes her from victim to victor. Empowerment is crucial to women's participation in development because it enables them to break through tradition and other barriers and become actively involved in decision making, in efforts to acquire the means of production (land, labor, and capital), and in the implementation of development plans.

In many societies there is a general reluctance to change gender structures. Culture serves as a pretext. Women continue to labor under the misconception that the culture, the status quo, cannot be changed; but it can be.

Empowerment can be encouraged in several ways. First, it is the responsibility of all governments that are signatories to "The Forward-Looking Strategies for Advancement of Women," signed in 1985 at the end of the U.N. Decade for Women. The signatories committed themselves to promoting "an equal share of power" for women "in guiding development efforts" and "measures to . . . bring . . . women into the mainstream of the development process on an equal basis with men." Governments can implement the "Forward-Looking Strategies" by setting up, supporting, and financing units or ministries that encourage women's participation in the nation's affairs. In addition, a change of attitude is needed on the part of government officials, largely male, who may be benefiting from unequal gender relations.

Second, NGOs can team up with development agencies that have a serious interest in women's empowerment and work with those that are not reached through government channels.

Third, oral communication, which is an important means of communication among largely illiterate groups, should be exploited. Speaking empowers the communicator and informs the hearer.

Finally, it is the responsibility of freedom-loving individuals to ensure that in their corner of the world all persons share in the activities of the community. This demands changes in socialization and for women to change their own attitudes toward their situation and aggressively seek information and means of empowerment.

THE ROLE OF INFORMATION

In *Mass Media and National Development* (1964), Wilbur Schramm stated that the role of information is to "bring people into the decisions of development, to give them a basis for participating effectively, to speed and smooth changes decided upon" (p. 38). Schramm identified three roles of information: (1) the role of watcher—to scan the horizon on behalf of society and to inform society, (2) the policy role, and (3) the teacher role—by means of which members of a group are socialized.

Systems of communicating information are as complex or as simple as the society they serve. With increased development comes increased information flow, which in turn brings further increase in development. Information reduces uncertainty while affording people an opportunity to identify alternatives and make decisions on the basis of a synthesis of acquired data and their own knowledge.

THE ROLE OF THE INFORMATION WORKER

Providing information for development is the responsibility of all sectors concerned with development, particularly those trained as experts on information and information handling. Information is increasingly being seen as a powerful resource and a commodity to which all citizens must have access. The power of information in everyday lives lies in its potential to facilitate informed decision making.

On its own information has only latent power, but its power is activated when it is applied to a specific situation as a problem-solving tool. This has implications for information provision techniques. For every population served, information must be provided in such a manner that it can readily be applied to problem situations. To achieve this, information workers need a clear understanding of the environments in which they operate.

User Needs

To serve a population group effectively, information workers must understand its information needs and its information-seeking habits. Information workers should extensively research the information needs of the female clientele in the communities they serve. The role of research in establishing the information needs of women cannot be overemphasized.

The author found only one research study in Africa on women's information needs, conducted in Nigeria: Georgina K. N. Nwagha, "Information Needs of Rural Women," in *Information Development* 8:2 (April 1992): 76–82. In a study of the information needs of rural communities (published in the *African Journal of Library, Archives and Information Science* in 1992), K. J. Mchombu deliberately indicated the gender ratios in the sample of informants; this study is, however, silent at the analysis stage about the information needs of women in the sample. Gender specification was limited to the demographic outline.

Assessment of user needs should not be limited to information needs but must also include the means of transmitting information, which should be based on the served groups' information flow networks. For instance, women's informal and formal networks of communication may be vehicles for information exchange, but an assessment of a community must establish such a method as appropriate.

Information workers must be careful not to impose new and strange ideas on women. Women have rejected new technologies intended to alleviate hard work if these technologies contradict their social values. For instance, in Central Africa a pedal-operated machine for grinding meal was rejected because women had to stand astride the device while using it. This body posture was considered indecent. Introduction of new technology requires education and socialization of potential users, but success in providing new information is highly dependent on conformity to existing norms.

Information for Women

The three roles of information identified by Schramm (1964) apply to women. The role of watcher refers to information that presents alternatives to women. The policy role is information that enables women to plan for their participation in development. The teacher role is information essential for socialization, not to maintain the status quo but to empower women and enable them to determine their own development goals. Information should be provided at all three levels.

Information provision for women in development will require a radical change of attitude on the part of both governments and information workers. As a problem-solving tool as well as an empowerment tool, information ought to be provided at appropriate times. This requires information workers to go beyond providing service in formal buildings; they must deliver information to women at the grass-roots level.

Many socioeconomic, cultural, and religious constraints hinder women's access to and use of information provided in the types of libraries and information centers available in the Third World countries today. Information workers need to understand these constraints so that they can help women clients overcome them.

First, most information essential for development is in print form, while the illiteracy rate among African women in 1993 was estimated at 62.4 percent (United Nations, *Statistical Yearbook*, 38th Issue, 1993). With such a high illiteracy rate, information in print form is obviously of little use unless accompanied by services to interpret it. Among largely illiterate populations, print media play a very small part in information dissemination; oral communication is more effective, including open discussion of new concepts.

Further, in most rural African countries, the literacy rate of women is lower than that of men. So, while libraries exist and are seen as a means of education and self development, they are of little value to illiterate populations.

Information workers must transfer information in print formats to media illiterate women can understand: posters, radio broadcasts, public address notices, and the like. The objective is to reach the targeted group with accessible information.

Second, African libraries stock primarily inappropriate American and European literature that reflects Western culture and has little relevance to development. Even literate women are thus unable to find useful information. Third World libraries need to change their orientation from imitating Western public libraries to becoming community resource centers that, in addition to printed material, include posters and audiovisual materials relevant to the served community.

Third, when development information is available, it is often written in a foreign language (usually that of former colonial masters), which most women in rural areas do not understand, let alone read. Such information should be translated and presented in local languages and in forms accessible to an illiterate end user.

Fourth, it is essential that information workers participate in women's community programs so as to establish close contact with and learn more about the culture of the served community.

Fifth, most women are busy people with multiple roles. Their schedules demand an information-provision technique that enables them to access different types of information at the same time. Information repackaged for them should be presented at places where women gather, such as markets, religious gatherings, festive occasions, and so on.

Finally, information workers who provide information to researchers on women in development often must deal with difficulties arising from lack of bibliographic control, and from a controlled language that may contain inappropriate terms. Networking is just as essential for this group as for groups at the grass-roots level. Networking with women's organizations helps information workers learn about research in progress, while also yielding information on problems that researchers have with information centers. Since the primary role is to provide information to women, the primary consideration ought always to be how best to do it; information workers can learn from each other. They should also closely monitor the processing and use of the information supplied to ascertain whether it is, in fact, facilitating development and empowering women. If not, the information worker must evaluate and improve the information provision project so that it meets stated goals.

Information for Development Planners

On another level, useful and appropriate information on women needs to be supplied by information workers to development planners on issues of concern to women. And library associations should provide guidelines to governments and other interested parties for providing information in rural areas. They can play a leading role in devising means of reaching people.

CONCLUSION

The roles of the information worker can be outlined so as to accumulate a relevant information base, to disseminate information from this base in a readily usable manner, to forge links between women and development information, to conduct research, and to serve as resident information gatekeeper to a local community.

The role of information as a problem-solving agent in the process of development cannot be overemphasized; the critical job for the information worker is to be a catalyst by bringing together women and information.

Library Collections in Women's Development Centers in Africa

The Case of Nigeria

Helena R. Hassan (Ghana)

INTRODUCTION

In recent times worldwide focus has been placed on the development of women. This has come about because the world realizes that women's contributions to national development—which hitherto had been erroneously termed "no contribution"—really count in computing the gross national product, if accuracy of such a computation is the ultimate goal.

In Africa most women have always been the recipients of all the negatives of development: poverty, illiteracy, serving as beasts of burden, social maltreatment. Moreover, their fertility has weakened them, making them dependent on men. This situation was nonexistent before the advent of colonialism. Precolonial African women were involved in governance. But the colonialists' policies set African women back politically, economically, and culturally.

African women have had an arduous task since then, because African men enjoy women's subservient position. Since the launching of the United Nations Decade for Women in 1975 and the international body's directive to countries to put into place measures for the advancement of women, however, there have been some appreciable efforts to develop women in Africa. Today women are in

Helena R. Hassan is a Senior Assistant Librarian at the University of Science and Technology Library, Kumasi, Ghana. With bachelor's and master's degrees in library science, she was the pioneer librarian of the Maryam Babangida National Centre for Women Development Library in Abuja, Nigeria. She has published *A Small Library for the Rural Woman: A Manual, Women on the Move: A Bibliography of the Better Life Programme in Nigeria*, and *Nigerian Womanhood*.

51

the majority in the agricultural sector and, according to the International Fund for Agricultural Development, constitute 85 percent of the labor force but only a negligible percentage (6 percent in Ghana) in decisionmaking and policymaking at all levels of government. Thus there is urgent need for a remarkable improvement in the status of women.

DEVELOPMENT OF WOMEN

During the Decade for Women (1975–85), most African governments set up bodies to ensure that women are in the mainstream of national development. In Nigeria the National Commission for Women (NCW) was established in 1990 at the prompting of the wife of the then head of state. Maryam Babangida had also set up the Better Life Programme for the Rural Woman (BLP) in 1987 and had achieved some success in improving the lot of rural women. The NCW's primary goals are to ensure the full use of women in national development and the welfare of women. The NCW is the supervising body of the women's commissions in the thirty states and the federal capital. NCW activities were for long overshadowed by those of the BLP; the BLP was officially brought under the NCW in 1992.

MARYAM BABANGIDA NATIONAL CENTRE FOR WOMEN DEVELOPMENT (MBNCWD)

The MBNCWD, Abuja, was commissioned in October 1992 to provide a resource center for training and research and to help women attain self-fulfillment and to prepare for leadership roles. The MBNCWD academic wing comprises research, training, and library and documentation departments.

Library and Documentation Centre (LDC)

The Library and Documentation Centre of MBNCWD opened officially in October 1992. When I assumed duty as the "pioneer librarian" in January 1993, I found a handful of books and some furniture in the public area. In addition to the normal functions of a library—to collect, process, and store information for retrieval and dissemination—the specific functions of the MBNCWD Library are to

- develop a data and information base on women, first for Africa and Nigeria and then for the rest of the world
- provide adequate literature on women, which will help identify areas or subjects about African women that have not yet been researched

- assist the NCW and the government, through the MBNCWD, in policy decisions concerning women, by means of materials assembled from countries that are more advanced in women's matters
- provide materials about Nigerian women for foreign clientele and materials about women in other countries for the use of Nigerians

Physical Facilities

The LDC occupies the top floor of the three-story Administrative Block. It is fully sealed from noise from the other floors and fully air-conditioned. The offices of library staff and processing and computer rooms are on the same floor. The concrete floor had to be carpeted to exclude noise from passers-by; the circulation desk had to be reduced in size; and library furniture had to be acquired. Computerization is the ultimate goal, but we had to start with catalog cabinets.

A photocopier is available in the library; telex and facsimile machines are available on lower floors, and altogether the MBNCWD is well equipped as far as modern methods of communication are concerned.

BUILDING THE LIBRARY'S COLLECTION

The library's policy is to acquire all known information in all available forms about women. It also provides basic reference materials: subject and general encyclopedias and dictionaries, almanacs, yearbooks, atlases, and so on. Books, manuscripts, journals, magazines, conference papers, research publications, theses and dissertations, reports, case studies, newspapers, government documents, photographs, drawings, and audio- and videotapes have been or are to be acquired.

The library uses the standard methods of collection development—purchase, exchange, gifts (books or cash), legal deposit, and institutional membership. Interlibrary cooperation is also being pursued. The librarian makes selections for acquisitions and sends them to the chief executive for approval for purchase.

Being in haste to get the library well stocked with all types of material, we had to resort to spending a great deal on postage. Letters were sent to the following people and places:

- International organizations with offices in Nigeria, and their headquarters outside Nigeria, asking for copies of all documents, reports, pamphlets, and other material produced by them on women.
- All foreign missions, requesting all available information about women in their countries.

- Women's organizations. Professional, philanthropic, and social groups were asked for copies of their aims, objectives, and publications. Addresses of foreign ones were supplied by foreign missions.
- Notable Nigerian women were asked for their résumés as the basis for the compilation of a Nigerian women's Who's Who, as well as for their publications.
- Nigerian universities with departments or institutes involved in projects on women were asked for copies of their publications and reports.
- Federal and state government ministries were contacted for copies of their publications, documents, and policy statements on women.
- The NCW and state commissions were asked for copies of publications, speeches, and audio- and videotapes of all activities for and about women.
- Local and foreign booksellers and publishers were asked for copies of catalogs and computer printouts on women; a list will be compiled for later purchases.

With such an extensive solicitation effort, one would have expected the shelves of the LDC of MBNCWD to become filled and the number of pamphlet boxes to become uncountable. On the contrary, only half responded. About 30 percent sent publications or documents. About 20 percent wrote to say that they had nothing to offer. We did not hear anything from the remaining 50 percent. About 20 percent of the respondents put the library on their mailing lists; publishers, booksellers, and authors began sending complimentary copies of their books on women and in relevant fields. Until October 1993, the MBNCWD had purchased only one book—*Webster's International Dictionary*; all others were donated.

Requests for sample copies were made to about fifteen journals. By October 1993 only three had responded; one sent a sample copy, one a year's free subscription, and one an invoice for a subscription.

The library subscribes to twenty daily Nigerian newspapers and nineteen weekly magazines, four of them foreign. Newspaper articles are clipped for the following subject areas: Women and Health; Women and Education; Women and Associations; Women and Motherhood; Women and Crime; Women and Societal Issues; Babies; Children; Food; Health; Education; Family and Marriage; Agriculture; and Environment and Rural Development. Subjects are arranged alphabetically; titles are listed alphabetically within each subject. Wonewdex (Women Newspaper Index) is compiled monthly. Titles, volume, and numbers of magazines are recorded in the periodical catalog. Such information is also indexed according to subject areas and arrangement; that index is called Wodex (Women Index).

Problems in Collection Building

Because the library is still in its infancy, it has some teething problems.

- Women's studies is a comparatively new field in Africa, so few publications are available. One can lay hands only on documents and research reports, which are now gradually increasing in number.
- Lack of funds, a perennial problem, slows the acquisition of basic information sources.
- Lack of response from organizations to our requests deprives us of valuable information. Some were indifferent; others were antagonistic, feeling that women are now getting undue attention.
- Most of the women's organizations, especially local NGOs, do not have well-organized systems of documentation; in fact, most, having been set up by illiterate and semiliterate women, have no written information on their activities. They feel no need to document their activities and care only that their work goes well.
- No comprehensive list of local NGOs is available, so it was difficult to contact them. Occasionally members came to the library and informed us of the existence of other groups, which we later contacted.
- Audiovisual materials relevant to African women are rare. Most women's organizations, lacking knowledge of their handling techniques and usefulness, have not accepted audiovisual media as effective means of storage and dissemination of information.
- The library's staffing situation is inadequate, with only one professional librarian and two inexperienced assistants.
- The library has no clearcut budget. Any amounts needed were taken out of the central fund. This practice made large purchases of equipment and materials difficult, as such expenditures were much larger than those of other departments.

Nonetheless, these problems, major as they are, can be surmounted with a little determination, goodwill, and education.

STEPS FOR FUTURE DEVELOPMENT

- Women's development centers worldwide should work together, not in isolation. Especially in Africa, there should be a regular exchange of information and data—networking to involve existing libraries and to include new ones as they are set up. Proper standards should be set up to ensure the success of such a program.
- The transfer of information technology to Africa must be stepped up. Technology is needed for collecting, processing, storing, and dissemi-

nating information and data on women. The use of computers and modern communication systems is a *must*, not a *may*.

- Sources of primary information acquisition on women are not yet streamlined. They are ad hoc, put together as needed; therefore, there is no guarantee that information collected is complete. A proper information collection system must be set up.
- Each country or agency responsible for women's affairs must have a clearly defined policy on the collection of information on women, as well as appropriate methods of storing and disseminating it.
- Information about women is of paramount interest these days; therefore, enough funds must be specifically committed to the acquisition of information on women. LDCs should have funds set aside for them in their parent agencies' budgets.
- MBNCWD should step up its drive for information from agencies and organizations.
- Workshops or seminars need to be organized for leaders of NGOs to educate them on the usefulness of documenting their activities and to teach them how to do it.
- Research grants should be awarded to carry out studies on women.
- Strong links or liaison with libraries of related organizations worldwide should be of primary concern. This would ensure that current information is easily accessible for dissemination. In effect, library cooperation should be vigorously pursued.

CONCLUSION

The Maryam Babangida National Centre for Women Development in Abuja, Nigeria, aims to be a center of excellence. It wants to be able to provide information about women in Africa in general and Nigeria in particular to foreign and local researchers, as well as information about women in countries outside Africa for African and Nigerian women to use to improve their lives. MBNCWD is a pacesetter in West Africa, in its attention to issues relating to women and in its facilities for housing planned activities. It has modern equipment for communication and processing information. But despite this impressive start, the center needs to give more attention to its Library and Documentation Centre—to enable it to perform its functions creditably, especially in the area of collection development.

Women's development centers in Africa are indispensable vehicles for the improvement of the status and lives of our women. These centers must have *effective* library and documentation centers that will provide adequate information to support women's development activities.

Women's Information Services in Senegal

Mariétou Diongue Diop (Senegal)

INTRODUCTION

Located at the westernmost point of Africa, Senegal is primarily rural. About 36 percent of girls attend school, but the illiteracy rate among women is more than 80 percent.

The country has two university libraries; the one at Dakar University is the more important. Senegal also has several public libraries and other documentation centers. A number of African women's associations are based in Senegal.

This article reports on a survey of Senegal's main libraries, specialized documentation centers, and small information and documentation units attached to governmental and nongovernmental organizations (NGOs) working on women's issues.

INFORMATION AND DOCUMENTATION SERVICES

Institutions

Information services for women exist in three types of institutions.

- Documentation centers within larger organizations, such as research organizations, international agencies, and NGOs, contain some books,

Mariétou Diongue Diop is Chief Librarian of the Department of Exchange and International Relations in the library of Cheikh Anta University in Dakar; President of the Senegalese Association of Librarians, Archivists and Documentalists; and a member of the Classification and Indexing standing committee of the International Federation of Library Associations. She has published studies on access to information for newly literate women, classification and indexing in African libraries, and other library topics.

journals, and videos, as well as limited numbers of audiocassettes, research reports, legal texts, posters, and the like.

- Small information and documentation units attached to women's associations and organizations working on women's programs contain some audiocassettes, and occasionally a few books, journals, and other documents.
- Research and general libraries with significant collections on women that are generally unknown to researchers contain books, journals, official publications, and other documents.

Bibliographic Retrieval

Almost half the institutions surveyed (17 of 37) offer at least partial access to their collections. Only a few, however, use a classified arrangement. Most collections simply use headings, such as Women/Development or Women/ Informal Sector.

Among the thirty-seven institutions surveyed, only ten have subject-heading files, and only eight use a controlled vocabulary. Institutions using subject-headings showed a genuine will to enhance the information available on women. For example, *Woman* is systematically considered as an *entry word*. The various aspects come under topical, geographical, chronological, and other subheadings. In institutions that lack subject-heading files, lists of new acquisitions or periodical indexing may be available.

The institutions surveyed are gradually automating their cataloging; almost half are already equipped with microcomputers for their bibliographic data. Nearly a third provide users with computerized information retrieval systems.

Besides the possibility of searching for local resources, the access to international databases has broadened perspectives. Five institutions possess databases on CD-ROM and have access to international databases. The University Library has very important databases on CD-ROM not only in science and medicine but also in social science.

BARRIERS TO ACCESSING WOMEN'S INFORMATION

The users of the present system are an elite group of professors, researchers, consultants, and postgraduate students. Women in rural areas and those who are lower-class, illiterate, or literate only in African languages are often the subjects of studies kept in libraries but are forgotten in the information system.

Even those who do use the present system face a number of barriers in accessing information:

- Information and documentation services are dispersed, thus making research difficult.
- Relevant information is not visible.
- Statistical data are few, and lack differentiation by gender.
- There are no research results of recent studies on women, legislation, study reports, projects under way, legal texts defining the state's policy toward women, and other such documents.
- Documentation services are not organized: bibliographic services are nearly nonexistent, classification and collection processing are inappropriate.
- Facilities such as reading rooms are not available.
- Accessing primary documents is difficult: home lending is not always authorized but copiers are lacking.
- Coordination and cooperation among the various structures are at present limited to exchanges of publications or lists of new acquisitions. Some agencies have begun to develop a common database, and a network of financial institutions publishes a newsletter entitled *Women and Development*.

Needed Strategies

Several actions must be undertaken for an optimal use of resources.

- Promote cooperation among organizations that produce or disseminate women's information.
- Establish a national database of information and documentation services on women, providing location and fields covered.
- Create a national documentary network on women. The National Women's Information and Documentation Center cannot play the role initially assigned to it because of its limited facilities and staff. The creation of a national women's documentation network would allow pooling of resources, informing members of available publications, and giving each member access to available documents. It could also cooperate with centers with the same mission at regional and international levels.

Potential Users at the Grass-Roots Level

Although women represent the central axis of physical, economic, and cultural life in any society—caring for the elderly, educating children, preserving family life, and contributing to economic development—in Senegal they are ill-prepared to fulfill these tasks for want of appropriate education and training. The major obstacle is illiteracy.

Even women's sector organizations with efficient documentation units lack strategies to disseminate documentation among grass-roots women. Most communication used is oral: interpersonal communication, conversations in native tongues, and occasionally audiocassettes. Only a few women's programs translate and publish information leaflets in African national languages. The number of titles is very limited, as is circulation.

Women need to become literate, and information should be written in African national languages. Women's literacy should be an absolute priority for the state, NGOs, and financial institutions. A number of other things are necessary as well:

- Defining women's information needs as a priority and a national information policy aimed at satisfying these needs. One aspect of such a policy would include the translation of useful documents and legal texts into African national languages.
- Enhancement of traditional knowledge conveyed through the oral tradition by recordings, films, and transcriptions.
- Promotion of newspapers and documents in African national languages.
- Creation of a national network of public libraries to help give grass-roots women access to documents in African national languages.

For example, an experimental national-language library, conducted by the Senegalese librarians' association in collaboration with TOSTAN (an NGO concerned with basic education) at the village of Caytu, is providing services to local women who have become literate through the efforts of TOSTAN. Collections in national languages are made up of novels, tales, short stories, African legends, proverbs, legal and religious documents, and poems. On the spot, we have been able to assess the impact of literacy on women's daily lives and the interest they show in discovering new fields of knowledge through reading. These 200 newly literate women have themselves produced beautiful poems deserving to be collected into a book.

CONCLUSION

Women will be able to get involved in development, in the changing social relations between men and women, and in the real promotion of their own selves only when their access to information is favored, enabling them to assume fully their responsibility as workers, mothers, wives, and citizens.

Information for Change

A South African Perspective

Cathy-Mae Karelse and Jennifer Radloff (South Africa)

INTRODUCTION

In South Africa, information was used, misused, abused, and controlled by the apartheid state to reproduce and sustain a system of discrimination and oppression. Part of the democratic movement's valiant, successful initiatives to combat state propaganda and advance the liberation struggle consisted of the channeling and mediation of appropriate and accurate information.

The two significant features of the apartheid state's strategy of curtailing information flow were the unbalanced provision of services and the active and at times legislated control of ideas. Library and information services (LIS) have been concentrated by and large in White areas; townships, rural areas, and lower-income groups are generally deprived of such services. Services in impoverished communities were likely to be alienated from their constituencies and associated with the apartheid state. However, some information workers appropriated and transformed these services in an attempt to address community information needs.

Cathy-Mae Karelse holds a B.Soc.Sci. in Library and Information Science and is a Lecturer at the School of Librarianship, University of Cape Town. She is currently researching curriculum development in library and information science and completing a master's degree on Alternative Models of Information Provision. **Jennifer Radloff** holds B.A., H.D.E., and P.G.Dip.L.I.S. degrees. She is Education and Resource Coordinator in the Equal Opportunity Research Project at the University of Cape Town and involved in the establishment of a Resource Centre to support the work of the proposed Africa-wide Gender Institute.

The apartheid government also vigorously legislated the censorship of ideas—evidenced through the banning of persons and publications and the raiding of organizations. These strategies, coupled with the lack of services to the majority of South Africans, such as education, housing, and health care, have resulted in highly impoverished yet politicized communities.

RESOURCE CENTERS: APPROPRIATE INFORMATION SERVICES

To counter this skewed state provision, resource centers emerged organically as alternatives to traditional services in an attempt to provide needed information and resource services to communities. Resource centers are often linked to nongovernment organizations (NGOs) and/or civic structures and support traditionally disempowered and (until April 1994) disenfranchised constituencies aiming to build a free, united, democratic South Africa. They are usually run along democratic lines with the purpose of helping their constituencies improve their living and working conditions. The typical resource center occupies a single room and has an eclectic array of materials, a photocopier, and sometimes a fax machine. It often doubles as a meeting room.

The resource center sector is not homogeneous but comprises a range of services diverse with respect to location, target audiences, and style of delivery. This article deals with resource centers concerned with the transformation of South African society. It does not include special libraries attached to corporate structures.

Information flow is crucial in the development process. The Reconstruction and Development Programme (RDP) originated from the African National Congress (ANC) and Congress of South African Trade Unions (COSATU). The RDP, adopted as the development program of the Government of National Unity, calls for a democratic information program and argues that the free flow of information is crucial in equipping people and the government to make informed decisions. Arising from this, a challenge facing information workers in South Africa is to play a more active role in the empowerment of communities through adequate resource provision.

Resource centers contribute to social transformation in a number of ways. They serve to break down the barriers of alienation that users sometimes experience in relation to traditional services. Through their concern with generating a culture of lifelong and resource-based learning, they find creative ways of transmitting information; users are enriched through their interactions with these services. Centers mediate information and resources in appropriate and helpful ways, ensuring that users are able to act on the information provided. Finally, resource centers encourage communities to build on their own experiences.

Within the framework of resource center practices, the classic concepts of borrowers and custodians of information are replaced by interactive information work based on exchanges and interchanges between information workers and user communities. Interactive information work is premised on information services interfacing with other development initiatives that incorporate an information function, such as job creation schemes and health, legal aid, and education services. It emphasizes user-friendliness and is concerned not only with providing appropriate information, but also with the use of information to effect change. By actively mobilizing resources, this approach improves the appropriateness and usefulness of information for consumers.

Services Produced by Resource Centers

A Directory of South African Resource Centers, published by the Educational Resources Information Service (ERIS), lists more than 100 centers. Of these, nine specifically serve rural communities; the rest are urban. Services offered by resource centers include

- free legal advice
- adult literacy programs
- study space for students
- the monitoring, investigation, recording, and publicizing of aspects of the socioeconomic position of people in rural Natal
- a neutral venue for persons dealing with conflict resolution
- promotion of positive and alternative social values and collection of nonracial, nonsexist, cooperative children's resources
- development and circulation of a toy collection designed for children with special needs
- provision of grass-roots control over rural development and training in organizational skills to manage projects related to land, food production, health care, and water supply
- information and resources not found in local libraries

PRACTICAL WORK OF THE RESOURCE CENTER SECTOR

Networking

Given the variations among resource centers and the differing needs of communities, resource center operations inevitably vary. Attempts are made to unify them through emphasizing commonalities. One such initiative is the Western Cape Resource Centre Forum, established to discuss and act on common issues. The Forum addresses the needs of information workers, provides a supportive forum, has created a network for referrals, and is attempting to streamline services.

The many such structures in other parts of the country are all involved in similar activities and in mandating representatives to participate in or observe on forums aimed at transforming library information services. TransLis (Transforming library and information services) is an overarching structure that brings together alternative and establishment Library and Information Services (LIS) groupings.

Indexing and Classification

In many resource centers information is stored in box files and shelved according to a simple indexing system. The classification is arrived at by looking at the main subject areas, defining subcategories of these areas, and allocating either an alphabetic or numeric indexing system. Material is then stored in the box files by subject. The classification number may be written on each document, which is then filed in the appropriate box. Indexing systems vary among resource centers, the common denominators being accessibility, appropriateness, and transparency.

Some centers use the Dewey Decimal Classification System for books but devise unique systems for other material. This is because Dewey is often inaccessible and unsuitable to both users and information workers, the collections are eclectic, and the centers lack clearly defined collection development policies.

Databases and Information Technology

A subgroup on computerization has been established within the Resource Centre Forum to enhance an understanding of the implications of computer technology. Organizations such as the Community Education Computer Society (CECS) offer inexpensive computer training to NGOs and community-based organizations in an attempt to remedy the imbalance in computer knowledge. Some literacy programs use computers, so that as people become literate they are also learning to use computers.

SANGONet (South African NonGovernment Organisation Network) was established by NGOs involved in information provision and capacity building. Its aims are to use information technology to promote a vision of development in South Africa and to achieve justice, sustainability, and inclusiveness. It is used by community-based NGOs and organizations involved in development and social change.

THE PRODUCTION OF RESOURCES AND INFORMATION

For information to contribute to social development and empowerment, it has to be appropriate. Resource centers are in a unique position to know what resources and information their user constituencies want. Information workers must interact and consult with users to understand and determine what is appropriate. They must understand the subject areas, the level of knowledge, and the format in which information should be presented. Resources need to be appropriate to the community, the individual, and their experiences. Resource centers can draw on their umbrella organizations to create appropriate resources.

Despite the strong tradition of struggle, years of apartheid have resulted in a public ill-informed about human rights. A human rights culture can be achieved in part through the provision of appropriate information. Many resources available in South Africa speak of the experiences of other countries. The need now is to produce resources that speak of South African realities, such as the position of women and of Black women in particular. Some resource centers and NGOs have taken up these challenges by producing booklets, pamphlets, videotapes, manuals, and bibliographies.

Print Resources

DEVELOPING JUSTICE SERIES   The Institute of Criminology saw a need to bring to the community level current academic and policy research. It published a series of booklets called the Developing Justice Series to encourage community awareness of and participation in debates on justice issues. The series aims to be accessible to a broad audience, including community and civic organizations, youth groups, service organizations, and social welfare and criminal justice agencies. Each booklet focuses on a specific aspect of access to justice, such as women's rights, lesbian and gay rights, children's rights, rights of the disabled, punishment, policing, and community courts. The booklets examine the current situation, posit a vision for the future, and raise suggestions for the transitional period.

SEXUAL HARASSMENT FACT SHEETS   The interest expressed in the Equal Opportunity Resource Project's collection on sexual harassment led to the generation of fact sheets. Because they combine appropriate format and relevant content, these sheets have proved both popular and useful.

BATTERED WOMEN'S WORKING GROUP   From the experiences of women working on violence against women came a booklet called "Watinti Abafazi— You have struck the women: Stories of four women who were beaten by their husbands." A collective of women calling themselves the Battered Women's Working Group contributed their experiences and published this useful and accessible booklet, which has been translated into Xhosa and Afrikaans.

Audiovisual Media

RADIO   With deregulation of the airwaves and restructuring of the South African Broadcasting Corporation, radio is freer than it has ever been. The early 1990s saw the birth of community radio stations that fulfilled an important need for local information presented by local people. Radio is especially important as a means of communication in areas without access to electricity.

Radio Zibonele, for example, is a community radio station established in April 1993 with a focus on health issues of importance to the local community. Health care workers and interested people from the community decide on the format and content of the programs, which, because of the density of the population, reach an estimated 500,000 people. For a year Radio Zibonele was illegal, broadcasting from under the operating table in the clinic.

VIDEOS   Videos are in great demand from organizations running workshops to educate, inform, or raise consciousness. Coordinated Action for Battered Women (CABW) is one women's organization that makes use of videos. In addition to creating informational booklets on domestic violence and battery, CABW has produced two videos, "Every 83 Seconds" (taken from unofficial statistics on the frequency of rape in South Africa) and "When Love Hurts," on battered women.

WOMEN'S ISSUES

Most resource centers serve a broad spectrum of users, but some specialize in providing information and resources on the struggles and conditions of a particular social sector. For example, the International Labour Research and Information Group (ILRIG) brings workers' experiences from all countries to the labor movement, as well as to women, students, youth, and community organizations in South Africa, through educational workshops, booklets, information packets, and the like. Its international labor collection, which documents workers' socio-political, economic, and cultural experiences, also includes a section on women.

There has been a tendency to understand women's struggles and experiences as only a part of the struggle against apartheid. This has sometimes meant that women's issues are overlooked. South African women have historically organized around women's struggles and the advancement of women's rights. While there are few centers that focus exclusively on women, some incorporate collections on women's experiences within their broader scope. Alongside existing women's collections, such as those held by the Social Justice Resource Project and the Equal Opportunity Research Project, there is a move under way to establish a Maternal and Child Health Information Service that will target women as one of its primary constituencies.

Despite these limited initiatives, and although numerous endeavors, such as oral history projects, archives, and information services, are keen to rectify the situation, there is still a paucity of documentation on women. Some women's organizations without actual resource centers have realized the importance of information they have collected and are attempting to make it more accessible. Rape Crisis in Cape Town has training manuals, pamphlets, booklets, and press clippings. The project is working on a simple indexing system and is shelving the resources in a communal space to encourage their use. CABW has collected training manuals, policy documents, legislation, pamphlets, and reports from various countries. It has set up a simple retrieval system and is encouraging the use of these resources.

CHANGE IN SOUTH AFRICA'S LIS SECTION

Library and Information Services (LIS)

The "alternative" and "establishment" library and information service streams are increasingly connecting to promote compatibility and cooperation. A Soweto librarian speaks of taking "the library out of the building and into the community." Interactive information work, which characterizes resource center methodology, is a fast-growing approach in the library and information service sphere generally. While resource centers may not structurally become the mainstream, their practices and work ethic are significantly influencing the style of information services in the LIS sector.

In the South African LIS sector, top positions are generally dominated by White men, despite the fact that the vast majority of LIS personnel are women, and there is polarization between what are traditionally regarded as "professional" and "paraprofessional" employees. These power relations are reproduced and entrenched in the establishment stream. The "alternative" stream challenges undemocratic practices both with respect to interaction with users and relations within the workplace.

The Translis Coalition (Transforming our library and information services) has brought together most (if not all) organizations and associations active in the LIS sector. In an era of negotiation and cooperation, it has actively attempted to engage practitioners in developing policy, to create a culture of democracy by providing channels for consultation with constituents.

The Centre for Education Policy Development (CEPD), which is developing education policy for the ANC, set up a LIS Task Team to develop a strategic plan for the LIS sector. CEPD set up a Gender Task Team to alert all teams to the importance of gender sensitivity in their reports. The LIS Task Team will work closely with TransLis, which has a mass base. This engagement will ensure that the collective voice of practitioners, the majority of whom are women, is heard and that their vehicle for expression, TransLis, is strengthened.

CONCLUSION

Resource centers have played a significant role in serving the information requirements of the democratic movement in South Africa. In the context of the transformation process under way in the country, resource centers have been urged to assess their role so that they can contribute more decisively to development. Given the increasing coalescence within the LIS sphere and the growing sectoral commitment to supporting the RDP, more space is being created for information services to consider proactive ways in which they can feed development.

Women, Libraries, and Information in Bangladesh

Nargis Jafar (Bangladesh)

INTRODUCTION

Bangladesh became a nation in December 1971, but it is an old country with a new name. In the Bangladeshi society, even though motherhood is glorified, the status of women is inferior to that of men. The majority of women live between two vastly different worlds—one determined by religious and cultural traditions that confine them within the home, the other shaped by increasing landlessness and poverty, which force them into wage employment for economic survival.

SOCIAL TRENDS

Although Bangladesh has elected a woman prime minister and the opposition leader is a woman, Bangladeshi women are, on every socioeconomic indicator, worse off than women in other South Asian countries. Nevertheless, significant changes have taken place, and women are gradually becoming more visible in various spheres of life. National and international policy changes and the process of social transition have contributed to move positively toward the achievement of goals over the past two decades. Norms that segregated and

Nargis Jafar was, at the time of the conference, Director of the Books Program of The Asia Foundation in Dhaka. She earned her library degree in New York and worked in libraries there and in Washington, D.C. She has also been in charge of the libraries of the Dhaka Business & Professional Women's Club, of which she is president, and other Bangladeshi libraries.

protected women have tended to break down as a consequence of the pattern of development. Today women have come out from behind the veil and have thrown away the chains of bondage. Women are no longer content with sole responsibility of looking after the family; now, work outside the family attracts them and offers a challenge to capable women.

The United Nations played a pioneering role in bringing women's issues to the forefront. Both the declaration of 1975 as International Women's Year and 1976–85 as the Decade for Women had tremendous impact on the worldwide concern for the cause of women. In pursuance of the Forward-Looking Strategies from Nairobi (1985), the government of Bangladesh formulated specific strategies for the advancement of women in various sectors. There is a Ministry of Women's Affairs, with a woman minister who has introduced many development projects for women. Libraries are under the Ministry of Cultural Affairs, also under a female minister.

LIBRARY INFORMATION SYSTEMS AND SERVICES

In Bangladesh, women writers, poets, and novelists are now publishing books; but hardly any books are available in women's studies. About 80 percent of the people live in rural areas, where libraries are nonexistent. Just as there is a need for libraries, so too is there a need for professional librarians. In the 1940s there were numerous public, college, and university libraries, but there were no library science courses until the 1950s; even now, only two universities have library science departments.

Because the profession is still new, it is not valued, and women have not been interested in becoming librarians. For more than fifteen years, I was the only woman librarian; by 1991 Bangladesh had produced only 741 professional librarians, of whom only 22 were women. But the situation is changing rapidly, and more and more women are joining this profession.

Despite these gains, library and information services have not yet reached the level of development required to support education, research, and industrial and socioeconomic development efforts in Bangladesh. A national library and information policy is necessary to coordinate the activities of library and information centers.

CHALLENGES

Among the many shortcomings are the absence of a national library and information policy, low professional status accorded to librarians and information scientists, and the lack of proper bibliographic control of national literature and of modern electronic and telecommunication facilities. Most district public libraries are run by nonprofessionals.

Proper education and training are essential for any program development. Provisions should be made in the development plan for advanced training of professional librarians and information specialists.

All libraries and information centers should have basic modern electronic and reprographic equipment. The planning, organizing, and implementing of a resource-sharing network are necessary in a developing economy like ours, since our resources are extremely limited. The successful operation of such a network will ensure convenient access to resources by users. By definition, resource sharing cannot be accomplished unilaterally, but rather requires the concerted effort of a number of libraries and entails changes in function and attitude on the part of users, librarians, and administrators.

Books about women are limited. Only one organization—Women for Women—is publishing books on women and also doing research on women of Bangladesh. It has published a *Bibliography on Bangladesh Women.* Dhaka University—the oldest and largest university in Bangladesh—has had courses in women's studies since 1985. Women For Women has a library that collects on women and admits only women; it is run by a professional woman librarian. So we hope for a bright future for women and information in Bangladesh.

Emerging Trends in Women's Studies Information and Documentation in India

An Overview

Anju Vyas (India)

INTRODUCTION: WOMEN'S STUDIES IN INDIA

Worldwide interest in the status of women prompted the Indian government to initiate a comprehensive review of the situation of women in India and to appoint a Committee on the Status of Women in India (CSWI) in 1971. In response to the committee's report, presented in 1975, and to the declaration by the United Nations of 1975–85 as the Decade for Women, the Indian government drew up a draft National Plan of Action for Women. The plan accords priority to purposive research in education, health, welfare, and employment.

Another landmark was recognition by the Indian Council of Social Science Research (ICSSR) of the status of women as a priority area for research. The ICSSR commissioned studies on various aspects of women's status and recognized the need to develop a long-term perspective for promotion of research on problems women experience in the context of social change. Its Advisory Committee on Women's Studies is comprised of leading social scientists.

Anju Vyas has been Librarian at the Centre for Women's Development Studies, New Delhi, since 1985. She holds master's and M.Lib.Sc. degrees from Banaras Hindu University, Varanasi, and a master's in Archives, Library & Information Science and Education from Loughborough University of Technology, U.K. She has also been Librarian at the Ministry of External Affairs and other libraries and has edited or compiled bibliographies in women's studies and other works. She is a member of the Indian Library Association and Indian Association of Women's Studies.

In India, interest in the status of women has resulted in the institutionalization of research; establishment of independent research centers; women's program units within the government system; and conferences, symposiums, workshops, and training programs. The first National Conference on Women's Studies, held in Bombay in 1981, voiced the need for a clearinghouse for research and other types of information, documentation, and bibliographic services to assist the promotion of women's studies in teaching institutions and the development of action by government and voluntary organizations.

INFORMATION ON WOMEN

Women's studies are multidisciplinary, drawing not only on the social sciences and humanities but also on law, management, science and technology, agricultural and allied sciences, and such interdisciplinary areas as environmental education, population development, and communications. The information is cross-cultural and interregional. The bulk of research is project specific and limited to specific sectors or issues. Often up-to-date, meaningful data are unavailable due to the limitations of data-collecting agencies. The information comes in a wide range of physical forms, much of it as grey literature, and little attempt has been made at bibliographic control and dissemination.

Producers

Information on women emanates from three major sources:

1. Governmental channels, which produce policy documents, reports, statistical surveys, and the like.
2. Institutional channels such as social science and development research institutes with a focus on women's issues, women's studies research centers and cells (sub-units of centers with a narrower scope), universities, donor and aid agencies, activist groups and forums, grass-roots organizations, and media groups. Their research reports, working papers, proceedings, and so on are rarely published, as the institutions generally lack resources and publishers doubt there is a market for these products.
3. Commercial channels now produce numerous titles and bibliographic control is relatively good.

Users

The other important link in this information chain is the user. The Regional Seminar on Development of a Women's Information Network for Asia and the Pacific (WINAP), held in Saitama, Japan, in 1986, identified four user groups: (1) government policymakers, program implementers, and evaluators; (2) the general public; (3) women at all levels, especially at the grass roots, and (4) donor agencies, both multilateral and bilateral. Several other categories could be added to this list from the Indian experience: nongovernment organizations (NGOs) and their regional counterparts, academic and other types of researchers, mass media personnel, and students. The information requirements of these different categories vary and need to be satisfied by making the information available in different formats and through a variety of channels.

WOMEN'S INFORMATION AND DOCUMENTATION CENTERS AND LIBRARY COLLECTIONS

There has been a mushrooming of women's information and documentation centers worldwide in the last two decades. In the Indian context, these centers may be broadly categorized as (1) library, information, and documentation centers of women's studies research centers and cells and women's organizations; (2) special collections in academic and research institutions; and (3) collections in national agencies and documentation centers.

Libraries and information centers are rarely established independently. Women's library collections came into existence primarily with the establishment of women's research centers during the 1980s. The Margaret Cousins Memorial Library of the All India Women's Conference at New Delhi was founded in 1981. Although the Research Centre for Women's Studies at SNDT (Shreemati Nathibai Damodar Thackersey) Women's University in Bombay came into being in 1974, its documentation center did not start functioning until 1982. The Institute of Social Studies Trust set up a small reading-room-cum-information-center in 1983. The Centre for Women's Development Studies (CWDS) was established in 1980; its library and documentation activities started in 1983. Later, with the program of the University Grants Commission to promote women's studies, more than thirty-one women's studies centers and twenty cells were established in universities between 1985 and 1993.

Most of the centers and cells have small libraries and documentation centers at various stages of development. All collect both published and unpublished material. Most centers keep news clippings on women's issues, and most make a conscious effort to collect literature in regional languages. Another recent trend is the emergence of women's libraries and documentation centers in large cities. Those in Hyderabad, Bangalore, Bombay, Pune, Mangalore, and Calcutta all aim to provide lending and reference facilities. These information centers face common constraints in terms of financial and human resources and space. The use of new technology is limited.

Collections in mainstream academic and research libraries differ from those in women's information centers in their focus on published material. Few collect unpublished material. Despite this, such libraries provide invaluable support to women's information and research.

National sectoral collections, such as the National Medical Library, and documentation centers have a broad scope and cater to the information requirements of a large community of researchers. Women's studies information may form a part of this wider spectrum. Because of the increase in the number of such centers during the last decade, there is an urgent need for a resource directory to facilitate access to them. A major effort in this direction was the Women and Development Studies Information Network, discussed below.

INFORMATION SERVICES

Bibliographic Sources and Services

Although the number of published bibliographies on Indian women is still limited, there has been a remarkable increase during the last decade in the number of institutional and individual efforts made in this direction. One example is Kalpana Dasgupta, *Women on the Indian Scene: An Annotated Bibliography* (New Delhi: Abhinav, 1976). There has also been a shift from general bibliographies to thematic and subject-specific ones. (For example, Suchitra Anant et al., *Women at Work in India: A Bibliography* [New Delhi: Sage, 1986] and Anju Vyas and Madhu Mudgal, *The Girl Child in India: A Bibliographic Compendium* [New Delhi: IBH, 1992]).

The scope and coverage of these bibliographies vary considerably in terms of types of material, languages, and period covered. Some bibliographies cover only material available in particular libraries. The majority emphasize published materials in English, but conscious efforts are now being made to include unpublished materials and those in regional languages. A three-part bibliography of resources on women by the Women and Development Studies Information Network (see below) is an example of this trend. Many women's studies documentation centers provide bibliographic services on demand, either free or for a nominal fee.

Although bibliographic sources and services have come a long way during the last decade, there is a need for more systematic effort in this area, for descriptive standards, and for computerized bibliographic databases.

Indexing and Abstracting Services

A few women's studies centers have made a beginning at indexing articles on women's issues. The CWDS library has published a *Documentation Bulletin* since 1985. What started as an in-house current-awareness service has been made available by subscription. This monthly bulletin indexes an average of 150–200 items from Indian and foreign women's studies journals and newsletters and from Indian newspapers.

In 1989 the AIACHE (All India Association for Christian Higher Education) Documentation Centre started a semiannual indexing service called "Documentation on Women's Concerns," and Jadavpur University Central Library launched a quarterly bulletin in September 1990 under the title *Women's Studies: A Current Awareness Bulletin*. Some centers keep thematic compilations of photocopied newspaper articles.

Currently no abstracting services on women's studies exist in India. It is necessary to initiate such a service.

Directory and Handbook Resources

Since 1975 a few directories have been released of women's organizations, training facilities and institutions, women's studies centers, and funding agencies for women. The number of such sources is quite limited, however, and often the coverage is not comprehensive. There is no mechanism for updating information on a regular basis.

There is an urgent need for directories on the local and national levels. This task should be given priority by women's studies resource centers in different parts of the country.

WOMEN'S INFORMATION NETWORKS

An informal network exists among women's groups and individuals because of their common interests. In recent years the need for a formal, organized structure has been realized at various levels, and some information networks on women and development have emerged. On the regional level, the Women's Information Network for Asia and the Pacific (WINAP) was initiated by the Economic and Social Commission for Asia and the Pacific (ESCAP) in response to numerous requests from members and associate members for an improved system of information on women in this large region.

The major objectives of WINAP are to collect, analyze, and disseminate views, ideas, and statistics related to women in development. Major activities consist of development of training programs for national women's information center staff, improvement of statistics and indicators on women, and provision of technical support and advisory services to upgrade national women's information mechanisms and strengthen the regional WINAP focal point at the Social Development Division of ESCAP.

Women and Development Studies Information Network

The Centre for Women's Development Studies took the lead to plan a Women and Development Studies Information Network along with like-minded institutions in India. The network aims to harness and pool existing information sources and disseminate them widely. The strength of this network is that it seeks to mobilize resources of the existing information infrastructure without creating new infrastructures, staff positions, or major investments in technology.

This open-ended, voluntary network of information professionals plans to bring out a resource guide on women and development in three parts: literature, institutional resources, and human resources. So far it has published three parts of a bibliography, *Resources on Women* (1988, 1990, 1991). In addition, the network proposes to undertake these activities in the near future:

1. Organize training programs in abstracting and indexing literature from various disciplines
2. Collect audiovisual documentation on women and development
3. Bring out a journal of abstracts on women and development

Workshops and Conferences

Workshops and conferences focus attention on women's information centers and promote networking among women's information professionals. In India, the first such workshop was organized by CWDS in collaboration with the Research Centre for Women's Studies of SNDT Women's University and held at Deolali in July 1988. During the three-day workshop information professionals from various parts of the country were exposed to the scope and types of information available in and required by this discipline and worked out the format for the "Resource Guide on Women and Development."

The National Conference on Women's Studies, held biennially, is the biggest such forum in India. As such, it should also provide a forum for regular sharing of ideas and views related to women's information.

A welcome trend in the 1990s has been inclusion and discussion of women's information in a broader context. At the Annual Meeting of Documentation Centres of NGOs, organized by the Centre for Education and Documentation (CED) and held in February 1992, for the first time a full session was devoted to "Documentation on Women's Issues." At the 58th General Conference of IFLA (International Federation of Library Associations), held at New Delhi in August 1992, the Women's Interest Group held its first session. In February 1994 SNDT Women's University organized a one-day "Workshop on Women and Development: Information Sources, Services and Systems" to provide an overview of sources of information, a forum for interaction with users, and a chance to share information on centers and systems that provide bibliographic services. There is a need for more such occasions to exchange views and information.

AGENDA FOR FUTURE DIRECTIONS

The following are major needs:

- Surveys at various levels on a regular basis to assess the information needs of different categories of users.
- Literature surveys to identify gaps in research and information and a mechanism to inform researchers of these gaps.
- More research and writings about women's information in India.
- Computerized bibliographic, directory, and statistical databases.
- Analysis and evaluation of existing reference sources—bibliographies, directories, and abstracting and indexing services—and efforts to prepare them in accordance with researchers' requirements.
- Repackaging of information in accordance with the information requirements of different user groups.
- A better flow of governmental, intergovernmental, institutional, and commercial publications at the international, regional, and national levels.
- More forums where on a regular basis information professionals can exchange views.
- More training programs at different levels.

Women's Libraries in India
Problems and Solutions

T. S. S. Lakshmi (India)

INTRODUCTION

Over the last decade and a half, a distinct body of scholarship on women has arisen in almost every academic field. Women's studies has not only developed tremendously in size and scope but also received considerable attention and acceptance from the establishment: colleges, universities, publishers, scholars, media, and even the state. The main impact of this research and writing about women has been the creation of new knowledge systems. But this virtual explosion of new scholarship has not found its way adequately into library and information sciences, particularly in India.

This article examines the nature of the impact that feminist scholarship has made on the information/classification systems in the Indian context. First, it describes some problems with the existing classification systems. Then it discusses the classification scheme designed for the Anveshi Research Center for Women's Studies in response to the inputs received from various activist groups and research scholars. We also discuss the difficulties Indian libraries have acquiring books and journals from abroad and note some attempts by Anveshi to reach out to women. Finally, we cite a few examples of alternative modes of information dissemination.

T. S. S. Lakshmi is librarian at the Anveshi Research Centre for Women's Studies at Osmania University in Hyderabad. She is a Gold Medalist from the Library and Information Sciences Department of Osmania University and a founding member of the women's magazine *Bhumika* and of Chelimi–Forum for Women, a nonprofit organization.

SOME PROBLEMS WITH EXISTING CLASSIFICATION SYSTEMS

Classification by Discipline, Not Subject

The Dewey Decimal System organizes basic classes by fields of study or traditional academic disciplines, rather than by subject. Thus, there usually is no one place for any one subject. This practice is not particularly suitable to specialized libraries. In Anveshi, for example, books on health are shelved in three different places: sociological studies of health are classified as part of the discipline Sociology; medical aspects as part of Medicine; and legal aspects as part of Law. Research scholars and activists who use the library do not find this system suitable; they would prefer to browse through the entire range of material available on health. It is left to the discretion, decision, and imagination of the librarian to place the entire collection of health under one broad category—perhaps Medicine or Sociology—and then to think of ways to make further divisions for social, medical, and legal aspects.

Lack of CIP Data

Most books published in India do not have Cataloging-in-Publication (CIP) data. Such cataloging copy would help librarians decide the appropriate subject headings and to a large extent, the classification number. As it is, librarians must use their own discretion in classifying most books.

Lack of Appropriate Categories in Standard Systems

Another problem faced by Indian librarians who use standard classification systems is that many issues have no place in the standard classification system. These include such sectoral, local, or national issues as reservations for *dalits* (the most oppressed class in the caste system), family violence across castes and communities, violence against women in rural and small towns in the name of suppressing "witchcraft," and issues raised by the women's movement all over the world, such as the invisibility of housework, sexual harassment, and wages for housework.

Most libraries and bookshops in India classify and keep books on women together under Women's Studies. A book on women and the law, for example, is kept in the women's studies section. Women's issues are thus in a sense "ghettoized," and all other issues become nonwomen's issues. But specialized women's studies libraries cannot classify and lump all their holdings under Women, as all are on women. Instead, books should be dispersed according to their subjects, while books on particular subjects, such as health or marriage, should be kept together. Books on marriage should be placed together regardless of whether they deal with the social aspects, customs, or legal aspects.

The standard indexing systems available do not address women's lives and experiences. At Anveshi we therefore decided to use *A Women's Thesaurus* to prepare indexes and to catalog the collection in our library. We have been able to use the thesaurus quite successfully, despite enormous problems in categorizing by subject, especially in the local and national context. We made some additions and extended the list of descriptors to include local and national issues, such as *stridhan* (bride price), caste politics, and custodial rape.

Another overall concern has been how to classify nonbook material: research reports, news clippings, surveys, monographs, magazine articles, and so on. Most such material is specific to the Indian context and therefore is not in the standard classification systems.

ANVESHI'S CLASSIFICATION SCHEME

An alternative system to classify nonbook material was needed. The new system had to incorporate the logic of the Dewey system (because we use it for books and readers are familiar with it), yet it had to be very user friendly. The system that was devised tries to reflect the complexities and subtleties of women's lives and work in our context. The headings in this alphanumeric system were made as straightforward as possible. The material to be classified was itself used as the basis for creating new sections and subsections. This system facilitates easy expansion.

At the broadest level, the classification index is divided into twenty-one main classes, further divided into sections and subsections. The twenty-one main classes are as follows:

A	Media/Arts
B	Philosophy
C	Psychology
D	Religion
E	Social Sciences
F	Politics and Civics
G	Economics
H	Work/Industry
I	Law
K	Education
L	Commerce, Communications, Transport
M	Customs/Etiquette
N	Geography
O	Science and Technology
P	Literature
Q	History

R   Health
S   Agriculture and Food
T   Ecology and Calamities
U   Personalities
V   Bibliography

Each class is divided into ten to fifteen sections numbered 000 through 150, although so far not all the numbers for the sections and subsections have been used. Each number consists of three digits; only the first and second digits are significant. The remaining digit is a zero. For example, A 000 is used for General works on Media/Art; A 010 for Portrayal of Women in the Media; A 100 for Fine Arts; A 150 for Architecture.

Each section is then divided into subsections, numbered 1 through 9. Here the significant number is the third digit of a three-digit number. For example, A 101 is used for Painting, A 102 for Drawing, and A 103 for Sculpture.

Each subsection can also be further divided, depending on the center's need for expansion, using lowercase letters. Thus A 010a can be used for the portrayal of rape in the media.

The following example summarizes and demonstrates this system:

R 000   Health
R 010   Alternative Medicine
R 060   Medical Ethics
R 080   Family Planning
R 081   Contraceptives
R 081a   Injectable Contraceptives
R 082   Sterilization
R 083   Abortion

The codes denote the following:

R   Alphabetic code for the subject: Health
080   One of the broad subsets of health: Family Planning
081   One of the methods of family planning: Contraceptives
081a   A subsection of Contraceptives: Injectable Contraceptives

Material on specific injectable contraceptives could easily be cataloged as R 081b for Net-oen and R 081d for Norplant.

PROBLEMS OF BOOK AND JOURNAL ACQUISITION

In India bookshops mark out the areas of interest of documentation centers and libraries and send books on approval. Thus the centers are apprised of recent

Indian publications. Books published outside India are also sent on approval, but very selectively. Various publishers and university presses send us their catalogs. But if we want specific books or the latest books published outside India, we face a difficult process. The banks need invoices before they can give us foreign currency; writing to the publishers for invoices and then approaching the banks for foreign currency take time, and by then the books may be dated.

Journals are becoming ever more crucial for carrying out contemporary research, as feminist scholars, like others, often first present research in article form. So subscribing to foreign periodicals is a must. But doing so is even more of a problem. It involves enormous costs for Third World libraries, especially the smaller ones. Most resource centers usually lack the funds to subscribe to a given journal for more than one year at a time. Indeed, an institutional subscription may cost as much as a middle-class Indian earns in a month. (Unfortunately, there are no differential institutional rates for libraries in developing nations.) Small libraries subscribe even to three or four journals only after a great deal of deliberation. What does sharing of information mean in such a context?

Due to such financial constraints, most libraries subscribe to journals only a year at a time. By the time all the paperwork relating to bank requirements is completed and the subscription order has been sent, two or more issues are out and are sent to us together in one lot. Often we receive an entire year's subscription in this way, and the renewal procedure has to start all over again.

At Anveshi we have temporarily resolved this problem by asking members who go abroad to buy books and subscribe to journals for us. A better solution would be to work out a centralized distribution network, especially for books and journals pertaining to women's studies. Once we identify some authorized distributors in India, we can make the payments in our own currency. Other solutions would be to bring pressure on periodicals publishers to have a differential rate for Third World institutions, or to set up a system for paying subscriptions in Indian rupees. We could then forward checks, in rupees, for subscriptions or renewals to the publisher.

SHARING INFORMATION: OUTREACH PROGRAMS

It is not enough to collect and store knowledge; it must also be shared. Only then can we reach out to women, many of whom work in isolated groups. Indian women's groups place great emphasis on decentralized functioning and so have created a movement that is at once multiclass, issue-oriented, and autonomous, with many ideologies and strategies. The vastness of the country, its social and regional variety, caste and class differences, and the perpetual urgency of immediate local issues usually result in the absence of frequent communication among women and between women's and other organizations. As a result a person new to a group or the movement has little awareness of the past or of the group's insights and problems. Only a few resource people have systematized information and created methods of communication. The paucity of these attempts results in a gap in the transfer of data, experiences, and strategies in the women's movement. Varied groups, including government functionaries at all levels, women's groups, and the community at large are now demanding information. Resource centers such as Anveshi have to cater to all these varied needs.

Most resource centers try to reach out to women by circulating newsletters, stenciled or cyclostyled papers, booklets, and magazines on women and gender. Newsletters and bulletins are among the best media for keeping women abreast of current developments. They not only communicate information but also promote networking among like-minded organizations and agencies.

Networking Strategies

In India most research is in the form of newspaper or journal articles, seminar papers, and so on. Seminar papers are rarely published. If libraries have difficulty acquiring books, getting articles is even harder. Unlike the situation in the West, the material is not computerized, and tracking down books and information is a problem.

Attempts are being made to pool and share information about resources, available skills and expertise, and experiences, by networking among women's groups and documentation centers. The Avinashlingam Institute for Home Science and Higher Education for Women in Coimbatore, South India, proposes to set up a regional network to facilitate women's development through educational institutions, voluntary organizations, and government agencies. This regional network is working toward the economic independence of women and helping them be socially assertive and politically aware.

The Women and Development Studies Information Network in India was started in 1988 by nearly thirty librarians who have pooled their skills and time to prepare bibliographies pertaining to women's issues. The goal is to link and coordinate many information networks. The network is a project of academic institutions, activist groups, and national institutions that collect information. One proposal is to compile a three-part resource guide on women and development: a catalog for women's studies, a directory of agencies actively involved with women's issues, and a directory of information on the expertise relating to women available in different parts of India.

Awareness Services

The success of an organization depends on how it gathers, preserves, and disseminates both its own and external knowledge. There is a need efficiently to identify, evaluate, and disseminate information derived from both internal and external sources.

Resource centers try to expand their collections to meet users' needs in particular, and the needs of the social and political context in general. Current awareness is one of the most valuable services an information center or library can provide. But both services and the contents and size of collections are affected by lack of resources: finances, personnel, storage space, and technology. Most centers in India suffer from these problems.

Anveshi posts information of forthcoming meetings, seminars, and conferences that are of interest to users. It produces indexing and documentation bulletins, which inform users of available literature on a regular basis.

Exhibitions relating to women's lives and work are used to raise awareness of women's issues. Anveshi also screens films on women's issues; screenings are followed by discussions, thus involving the women. An organization in Hyderabad has used street theater and feminist cultural evenings to disseminate information on women's issues.

Anveshi's library and documentation center are being used by research scholars, academicians, activists, journalists, and other women's organizations. Journalists come to Anveshi looking for information and statistics on women and for photographs. Women's organizations affiliated with the political parties and autonomous groups use Anveshi and its material for their training programs or their journals.

EMPOWERMENT OF WOMEN THROUGH INFORMATION DISSEMINATION

The implications of globalization of knowledge retrieval need to be studied. Whom is information for, and for whom is a library designed? In the present context of globalization, a major concern for us is the process of gathering information in the name of empowering the most disadvantaged women in the country, when in reality it does not happen. How can this codified information/ knowledge be taken to the women who need it the most? This is the priority for us now.

Knowledge means power. If the knowledge systems that are being constructed are not accessible to disadvantaged groups and communities, they stand to reinforce the status quo rather than promoting social change. The process of gathering information is therefore as important as the information itself. If the local people are involved in information gathering, collective consciousness can grow, as they will begin to recognize that it is *their* knowledge. Analysts who gather information by surveys may get complete information, but the danger exists that it will be manipulated to suit the interests of a small, elite group; the people who provide the information are not empowered, as they have only fragments of information. The local people should be asked to gather information, and research scholars and centers should assist them, as they have the methods for generalizing and conceptualizing the information base.

Alternative methods of dissemination are being used to empower women at the grass-roots level, women who do not normally use the formal modes of information retrieval or the libraries. The National Literacy Mission has taken up the program of adult education, which resulted in the recent antiarrack movement in Andhra Pradesh.

Antiarrack Movement

Over the last decade or so a series of struggles have been taking place in the Indian state of Andhra Pradesh (AP) against the government-regulated sale of arrack (an alcoholic beverage). Since about August 1992, the antiarrack movement has gathered rapid momentum in several districts of AP. No political group provided any ideological framework or strategic plan; rather, poor rural women were the primary instigators. A variety of experiences, events, discussions, and stories had a catalyzing role in strengthening and spreading antiarrack agitation. The strongest force was the Akshara Deepam program, or the National Literacy Mission, a government-initiated program to eradicate illiteracy, taken up in each district by voluntary organizations. Inspired by the lessons, charts, and discussion topics in the literacy primers, the women joined the antiarrack movement. Newspapers also contributed by reporting every arrack-related incident. Newspapers were circulated and read in a number of literacy centers. The movement spread to 800 villages in a matter of months, and more than 500 arrack shops were forcibly closed. As a result of the struggle, the AP government has instituted total prohibition of arrack in the state, and the movement has spread to two other states of South India: Karnataka and Kerala.

The Magazine Bhumika

Access to information, understanding, and knowledge of women's problems and issues help women to have more control over their lives. A group of women is bringing out a quarterly magazine in order to create awareness about women's issues. This magazine, called *Bhumika* ("role"), is being published in Telugu, a regional language spoken in Andhra Pradesh (AP) in South India, and also in some of the regional dialects of AP, so as to reach women in the rural areas. These women generally do not use the libraries, and reaching out to them is therefore of utmost importance.

The magazine has served as a platform for making public what may seem to be individual and private experiences. One main thrust of *Bhumika* has been to translate theoretical feminist research into understandable material by relating it to women's personal lives and experiences. The magazine tries to explain the women's movement to women unfamiliar with it; it features reports on the women's movement, stories and poems that depict women's lives and experiences, photofeatures exploring the dimensions of gender in the visual media, translations from other Indian literature and world literature, and a wealth of book reviews. It also provides a forum for women to voice their views on issues that directly affect their lives.

CONCLUSION

At Anveshi we are most concerned with the following issues:

- A classification system for women's studies libraries and documentation centers should take into consideration the various local issues and debates of different countries.
- Collection of information and documentation is not an end in itself, but information should be disseminated to empower women.
- Networking strategies should allow access to more information and avoid duplication of effort, but we need a network that is feasible given the realities of time and resources.
- We need an appropriate information system, one that is sufficiently flexible and accessible to suit the needs of the center, and a loose, informal network of women's information centers to access and disseminate information all over India.

The Life and Times of the Women's Studies Resource Centre

Alana Zerjal-Mellor (Australia)

INTRODUCTION

The 1970s were a time of political and economic growth in Australia. They were also a time of growth, strength, and assertiveness in the women's movement. Groups of women working in different areas of education questioned the functioning of schools and education. Women educators in tertiary (i.e., postsecondary) institutions began to develop and offer women's studies, and in secondary schools teachers questioned the curriculum and their work environment.

FORMATION OF THE WSRC

In South Australia a group of women—teachers, lecturers, and students—came together through their shared interest in women's issues and concern about the lack of information available to support research. In 1974 they submitted a proposal for a grant to establish a resource library with a focus on women and education. The group received a government grant in 1975, International Women's Year. The Women's Studies Resource Centre (WSRC) was founded in the back room of an education library in a teacher training college.

Alana Zerjal-Mellor grew up in Italy before migrating to Australia. Learning new languages led to an interest in information technology and distribution, and women's issues. She has worked in libraries in the Australian outback and in a women's library, and currently works in the library of the Languages and Multicultural Unit of the Department of Education.

Operating Principles

As a result of discussions on the function, focus, and management of the proposed resource center, the following principles were laid down:

- Employ teachers as coordinators
- Rotate paid positions on a two-year basis to give women an opportunity to develop their knowledge and bring their own perspectives to the WSRC
- Form a feminist management collective
- Focus on education
- Have a feminist perspective
- Be open and accessible to community users
- Remain independent but within the State Education Ministry

The State Minister of Education funded the center, and the State Education Ministry supplied teachers as coordinators. In recent years the ministry for tertiary technical education has provided the second coordinator.

Through the years the center has had many battles: to maintain funding, coordinators, and premises; to control the resource collection; and, in short, to remain in existence. Countless hours have been spent yearly in defending the center's existence.

The Center's Resources

The center grew out of the feminist movement of the seventies and the need for access to information that could be used to define women's lives, explore women's issues, and support campaigns for women's rights. The collection, as well as the work of the center, has always reflected this. While the collection is oriented to education, its focus is broad. In recent years, when information on feminism and feminist issues has been more readily available in general libraries, the WSRC remains one of the few libraries with a comprehensive collection on women.

Some resources are directly applicable to and for the education of girls. Others reflect the broad interests of women. All resources support women and women's issues. The collection ranges across topics as diverse as health, sports, women authors, politics, labor issues, and sexuality—in short, any topic of interest to women. The center also houses the Women's Archives, which are coordinated by a volunteer group.

As a feminist library the WSRC has actively developed a broad collection on lesbian issues. Not surprisingly, it is one of the few libraries in Australia with such a collection.

To ensure that the collection held current information, from the beginning journals were purchased. The center now has a comprehensive collection of journals on women's issues and, for some titles, holds the only copies of early volumes in Australia.

The WSRC has always considered part of its role to be to provide women with the opportunity to develop library and research skills in a supportive environment. The center is now computerizing and is expected to be fully automated by 1995. This will give women greater access to the collection and further opportunities to become familiar with information technology.

In 1993 the collection was entered on the Australian Bibliographic Network, which can be accessed worldwide through the Internet. The new women's electronic bulletin board, Feminist Byte, which will be on-line on Internet by the end of the year, is also located at the center.

WORK OF THE WSRC

The WSRC has many functions. It houses feminist educational resources, is a meeting place for feminists and women's groups, and is a center for information exchange.

The center is subject to influences from many groups. The Education Ministry funds and staffs the center and therefore has always sought to control it. The collective and coordinators bring their feminist perspective to the center's management. Volunteer workers and users influence the direction of the collection. The educational community wants resources on women.

Management

The center is managed by a collective and, day to day, by two coordinators supported by many volunteers. The collective was originally drawn from teachers, lecturers, and students, but over the years this group has broadened to include community individuals, health workers, and women from the tertiary sector. As part of its managerial role, the collective has responsibility for the selection of staff.

In accordance with WSRC policy, coordinators work at the center for two to three years before returning to the classroom. Each coordinator brings her own perspective and connections. This has resulted in an ever-growing network of users and supporters, which is valuable in maintaining a high profile for the center.

The coordinators also influence the direction of the collection. For example, some coordinators have focused on secondary education, and the resources reflect this focus; groups with similar interests then find the center particularly useful. This has meant a diverse collection of resources and a wide cross-section of library users. With coordinators who are responsive to user needs, users are more inclined to make suggestions about resources, and the collection continues to reflect their needs.

Volunteers have always played an integral role in the work of the center. They have taken on many repetitive tasks, such as processing and shelving materials; they are involved in cataloging, work to promote the center, and generally participate in all aspects of its life.

The WSRC as a Meeting Place

One consequence of the center's responsiveness is that it has become a focal point for action and activity. Many women who first visit the center to use its resources soon begin to use it as a meeting place. The staff of *Liberation*, the women's liberation newsletter for Adelaide, meets there regularly, as have a health group, a housing group, and various groups working on educational issues. Their meeting at the center leads to opportunities for interaction among different interest groups. Such networking has resulted in much information sharing. It has also meant that when issues require action there is an existing network that includes politicians, conservative and radical women's groups, and many others.

POLITICAL ISSUES

The WSRC was established by teachers and students who were active feminists to politicize the educational community of South Australia. The close association of education and feminism has always created tension in the work of the center, albeit a productive one. This tension has underpinned the management, the work, and the function of the center.

CONFLICTS   There have been conflicts between the broad women's movement with its diverse interests and the specific needs of feminist educators, students, and teachers. At times the center has been accused of not paying enough attention to the needs of certain women's groups, being driven too much by the Education Ministry's agendas, or even being overinfluenced by specific groups.

In defense of the collection, feminists and feminist teachers have often argued that too much is expected of this one center with its limited funding.

FEMINIST FOCUS AND "WOMEN ONLY" DEBATE   The management collective members have always maintained their focus on feminism. Regardless of other interests or changing views of education, there has been consistent support for the center as feminist and focused on women. This has not necessarily guaranteed peace and harmony, and there is always debate on what feminism means. One thing it does mean is that the collective has maintained a shared focus on women's issues and a strong commitment to the feminist principles of the WSRC.

Although the center is primarily an educational resource, it has depended for its survival on its integration in the women's movement. One issue under constant debate is whether the center should be a "women only" environment.

The coordinators have always been women. This is not the result of WSRC policy: when we seek feminist educators, the pool of people from which to choose consists largely of women. The center itself has always been open to both women and men and has been used by both, although, not surprisingly, the users are overwhelmingly women. It does seem that more women than men have an interest in women's education and women's issues.

RELATIONS WITH EDUCATION MINISTRY   Because the center is funded by the State Education Ministry, it must be responsive to the education community in the broadest sense. The issue is complicated by the fact that, although the center is funded and staffed by the Education Ministry, it is also an independent, incorporated body.

In the seventies, at the height of political liberalism in South Australia, a number of women's services were established on this semiautonomous basis. Others, such as the rape crisis center and women's health centers, began as semiautonomous bodies but have now become almost entirely subject to the direction of the Education Ministry. The WSRC is one of the few remaining semiautonomous organizations.

POLITICAL ATTACKS   Over the years the center has been attacked for

- Providing educational material on abortion issues
- Spending funds on women's resources
- Holding lesbian resources
- Being a feminist enclave

Survival has overwhelmingly been due to wide community support.

In the nineties the WSRC is facing renewed and more thoroughgoing attacks. The government agenda now is the economic rationalist one of "saving money." There is no discussion of the usefulness of the facility or of community support; it is now just a question of state money being used to support feminist goals.

The center began before there was a focus on the education of women and girls within the Education Ministry. The resources of the center were used to develop curriculum for girls and to support innovative educational practices. At the same time the Education Ministry developed supporting administrative structures. In the eighties issues relating to girls' education were mainstreamed, so that today there are again few policy structures focused on women and girls.

The support structures that contributed to the survival of the center are almost gone, and it again stands alone. The WSRC now looks for national and international support as well as continued support from its community to ensure that a valuable service and facility continues to develop on the basis of feminist principles.

Highlighting Women in Mainstream Information

A Danish Center on Women and Gender

Elisabeth Møller Jensen and Jytte Nielsen (Denmark)

INTRODUCTION

In the postindustrial service society of the nineties, much more information on women and women's issues is being produced than can be consumed. Information centers are flooded with information. Identifying the relevant information is becoming increasingly difficult. As a result, all types of organizations are hiring information officers in great numbers. Before focusing on the experiences of one information center, it is useful to look briefly at the history of women's information centers in Europe.

INFORMATION CENTERS IN EUROPE

There are women's information centers in all European Community (EC) countries except Ireland. They belong to the same three generations, or waves, as the feminist movement.

1. First-wave feminism: Fawcett Library in London (1926), Bibliothèque Marguerite Durand in Paris (1931), Internationaal Informatiecentrum en Archief voor de Vrouenbeweging in Amsterdam (1935)

Born in 1946, **Elisabeth Møller Jensen** is Director of KVINFO and Chief Editor of The Nordic Women's Literary History. She has a master's degree in Nordic Literature and Language from the University of Aarhus, Denmark. **Jytte Nielsen** was born in 1961, has a B.A. in Nordic Literature from the University of Copenhagen, Denmark, and is research librarian in KVINFO's library.

2. Second-wave feminism: Frauenforschungs-, Frauensbildungs-, und Frauensinformationszentrum (FFBIZ) in Berlin (1973), Biblioteca Donna-womanfemme in Rome (1978)
3. State feminism: the library at the General Secretariat for Equality in Athens (1984), the documentation center at the Women's Institute in Madrid (1984)

First Generation

The oldest extant library is the Fawcett Library in London. It was established by the Woman's Suffrage Committee in 1866 and was led for half a century by Millicent Garrett Fawcett, after whom the library is named. The members donated books, manuscripts, and other materials to the committee, and the library was formally established in 1926.

The Bibliothèque Marguerite Durand started as the private library of Durand, a French journalist and the publisher of the feminist magazine *La Fronte* (1897–1903). She donated her considerable collection of books and documents to the city council of Paris on the condition that the council run a public women's library. It opened in 1936.

The initiative for the founders of the International Information Center and Archives for the Women's Movement in Amsterdam was taken by a group of Dutch feminists worried about the decline of the women's movement after the battle for woman's suffrage had been won. Their slogan was "no documents, no history," and they established the center in 1935.

Later Generations

These pioneering libraries are publicly funded today, while many libraries in the second generation are still struggling for recognition and economic survival. They are often characterized by a more radical attitude, allowing only female users and collecting only feminist documents.

The third generation of information centers has from the beginning been publicly financed and run professionally. The fourth generation will undoubtedly be international centers. A comprehensive EC women's database was planned but still has not been realized. Smaller databases on special subjects—such as GRACE (feminist researchers and research centers) and IRIS (vocational training programs for women)—have been established.

HISTORY OF KVINFO

The history of KVINFO, the Danish Center for Information on Women and Gender Studies, goes back to 1964, when the Danish women's rights organization sponsored the establishment of a women's archives at the State Library in Aarhus. This event inspired a feminist employee at the Royal Library in Copenhagen to initiate a women's documentation service. KVINFO moved out of the

Royal Library in 1982 in order to reach a broader audience and to expand its cultural activities, which have been a part of the center's concept from the beginning. Four years later KVINFO became a self-governing institution financed by the Ministry of Culture. The governing body is composed of representatives of the women's movement, the women's studies centers, the Danish Research Council, the research libraries, and the staff.

The name KVINFO is an acronym for KVINder (women), INFOrmation, and FOrskning (research). As the name indicates, the center's primary objective is to disseminate the results of women's studies to the public.

ACTIVITIES OF KVINFO

KVINFO is fulfilling its objective through several activities: a public library, a journal called *Forum, Magazine for Gender and Culture*, and courses in women's studies. In addition, KVINFO is housing a major project, the Nordic Women's Literary History. It is being carried out by 100 Nordic feminist researchers and is to be published in five volumes from 1993 to 1996.

The Female Company (friends of KVINFO), founded in 1991, organizes cultural events, among them the celebration of International Women's Day, provocative exhibitions (such as posters by the feminist artists called Guerilla Girls), and panel discussions about various women's issues. In 1994 KVINFO began a project, financed by the government, to develop special arrangements for women tourists visiting Denmark.

Of all its activities and projects, the center of KVINFO is the library, with its large collection of books and its access to all kinds of information from throughout the world.

THE KVINFO LIBRARY

KVINFO's library is a public library. It is open four days a week, eight hours a day. The library collects and registers all Danish publications as well as important foreign publications in all subject areas. There are about 10,000 books; grey literature, including reports, brochures, and unpublished papers, numbers about 3,000 items. The library subscribes to 300 newsletters, women's magazines, and other periodicals from all over the world. The library also houses the Danish Women's Photo Archive, a file of photographs of women, in both the private and public sphere, from 1880 to 1940.

Forty percent of the collection is in Danish. Almost 65 percent of the foreign-language books are in English, and 25 percent are in other Scandinavian languages. The materials are available on open shelves, and library *users* can, if they want, pick up the literature on their own, just as they can use the on-line databases free of charge. The entire collection, except for the most recent issues of periodicals, can be borrowed for use outside the library.

User Profile

The typical user of the library is a woman (although there are male users, too) about thirty years old or younger who is about to graduate from high school or the university. Users also include researchers, teachers, social workers, and others interested in women's issues. The library also offers a telephone reference service that is used by journalists, politicians, teachers, and other persons in need of factual information.

RELATIONSHIP WITH THE NATIONAL LIBRARY SYSTEM

The KVINFO collection of books is classified and indexed according to Danish key words. The catalog is part of DANBIB (the computerized union catalog of holdings in Danish research libraries), which contains 3.5 million records from 250 Danish libraries, the British Library, and the Library of Congress. The catalog is also part of REX, the database of the Royal Library. In this way KVINFO's records have become visible and accessible in research and other major libraries throughout Denmark. At the same time, KVINFO has gained direct access to the holdings of all relevant Danish libraries and, more important, to a series of external databases.

Intensive use of the external databases (e.g. KVINNSAM, the Swedish women's database containing about 30,000 records) makes it unnecessary to index KVINFO's periodicals. By this means KVINFO is conserving resources and avoiding duplication.

KVINFO's integration into the national library network and its access to external databases worldwide have made it possible for the library to give users a better, more professional service and have made KVINFO more visible as a public library. Increased visibility means increased numbers of visitors and new user groups.

THE FUTURE OF KVINFO

This increase in the number of users is accompanied by a growing demand for factual information. KVINFO therefore plans to give factual information a higher priority in the future. It has begun building a databank on women experts in all areas, as well as developing smaller files, such as fact sheets on different topics and educational materials.

In 1997 KVINFO will move back to the Royal Library. It will be housed in a new extension. The new facilities will permit continued improvement of KVINFO as an information center with a high level of technology and easy access for many different user groups. While working in close cooperation with the national library sector, KVINFO will still remain a self-governing institution.

Getting It Together

Women's Information Services in the European Union

Marieke Kramer (Netherlands)

INTRODUCTION

The need to disseminate and exchange existing information on women and gender has been a major topic of interest during the last decade. One initiative taken was that of the Equal Opportunities Unit of the Commission of the European Communities (the administrative board of the European Union). The commission set up a Documentation Working Party with representatives of all the member states. Its goal was to devise ways in which to improve the international exchange of information.

To provide a solid basis for future arrangements by knowing the starting point, it was decided to carry out an inventory study. This study, "Resources for Providing Information and Documentation in the Field of Equal Treatment for Men and Women in the European Community," was carried out by Jytte Larsen (Denmark) and me from January to October 1991.

WOMEN'S INFORMATION IN THE MEMBER STATES

There are many documentation centers in the member states. The different types can be categorized according to the era in which they were established. Each generation has its own characteristics:

Until February 1995 **Marieke Kramer** was head of the Department of Consultancy and Research of the International Information Centre and Archives for the Women's Movement (IIAV), The Netherlands. She is now Project Leader for Databases and Networking, Databank of Expert Women, The Netherlands.

101

- Those that developed directly from the first wave of feminism (1930s) such as IIAV (Amsterdam), Fawcett Library (London), Bibliothèque Marguerite Durand (Paris). These are professional, publicly financed centers with large general collections.
- Those that came in the wake of the second feminist movement (1970s). These centers are often short of funding and must make do with volunteer workers. Subject specialization and a strong inclination for networking are other characteristics.
- Those set up within public bodies and organizations, such as national organizations for equality policy (1980s). These are planned from the beginning on a professional basis with paid staff and computerized information and documentation services, and they function as national centers.

There are some exceptions to the rule: centers that originated in the national libraries (e.g., KVINFO in Denmark; see the article by Jensen and Nielsen), centers connected to women's studies departments of universities, and some others.

Collections and Management

The scope of the collections of most centers can be defined as concerning women in general, although several specialized centers exist: for instance, on women in development in France and on the women's movement before World War II in Germany. No standardized system for subject classification is used, although many initiatives have been taken in this field. Bibliographic control is very high. In most states, one or several centers together cover all national publications. On the European level, there are some specialized information services, such as CREW (Centre for Research on Women) on women and employment and GRACE (not an acronym), a databank of women's studies research.

The level of professionalism is high. Even in centers that are staffed completely with volunteers, most staff members have degrees in library science. In most countries the centers have automated their catalogs, but all with different software. There are exceptions, though, such as France, where centers are not automated. The level of electronic exchange is rather low compared to, for instance, the United States, and there are few on-line databases.

There is a broad basis for cooperation and exchange, but there are some major obstacles. Language barriers make cooperation difficult, as does the lack of resources, among them sufficient financing, standardized indexing and classification systems, computerization in some member states, coordination in some member states, national bibliographies in many states, and national and international on-line retrieval systems.

EXISTING NETWORKING AND COOPERATION

There are networks, cooperation, and exchange, and the centers are aware of each other. Everything is informal, though. The following recommendations (from the Larsen/Kramer study referred to above) are proposed to make cooperation more formal and structural and to improve exchange among centers. The two most important steps, briefly summarized, are as follows:

- Establishment of a European Network of National Centers. Requests for information or for documents, books, and so on would be handled and disseminated by these national centers. Exchange would be facilitated by an electronic mailbox system. Interlibrary loan and other cooperative national networks are a prerequisite.
- Establishment of a European Database. This would be begun by the computerized centers; as many as 20,000 records a year might be added. Contents would be bibliographic descriptions of recent nonfiction material (books, grey literature, periodical articles, audiovisual material). The database should be accessible in English and French.

WHERE DO WE GO FROM HERE?

The situation in Europe has certainly improved, but more at the national than the international level. There are now many national networks; while the international situation has hardly changed, national networks provide a basis for an international one.

European Commission Efforts

After presentation of the report and recommendations of the inventory study in October 1991 and publication of the report by the commission in March 1992, the Documentation Working Party, now composed exclusively of representatives of (potential) national centers or focal points, met again to discuss the recommendations. One positive result so far is more knowledge and a greater awareness of collections and services in Europe. The report and the discussions of the results at several European meetings of women's libraries and documentation centers have been an incentive for further activities by colleagues in the member states.

A new idea, initiated by the commission, is being discussed within the working group: to disseminate material on equal opportunities from the commission to women in the member states. This complete change, from international exchange of publications to disseminating official publications, has not been welcomed by all members.

GRACE

The idea behind the GRACE databank on women's studies researchers (data include addresses, topics, publications, and so on) is that in each member state a focal point collects national data and sends them to Brussels, Belgium, where data will be merged. Each center will receive a copy of the total databank.

WIN (Women's Information Network)

Several Italian centers, with KVINFO and others as international partners, have applied for a grant from the European Commission to build an electronic network and develop an international indexing system. This project is coordinated by the Biblioteca del centro di documentazione delle donne in Bologna, Italy.

The International Newsletter on Women's Information Services

The internationalization of women's information, the need for international exchange of information on women's studies and the status of women, and the growing professionalization of women's resource centers have led to a growing need for information on the collections, developments in subject indexing, available retrieval systems, and so on of centers working in this field. Information on related centers is published in national newsletters and international bibliographies and is disseminated through press releases of individual centers and presentations at conferences. Yet until now these data have not been collected and published in one medium.

IIAV has undertaken the task of producing an international newsletter. To this end, IIAV could use its international inventory of women's information services: a regularly updated dataset based on information provided by the information services themselves. Although a printed newsletter requires much more work than does an electronic version, this format was chosen as the most suitable medium, since electronic bulletin boards and mailboxes are still not widely available to centers outside the United States. The IIAV has not yet decided whether to continue to publish the newsletter.

From Utopia to Reality

The Austrian Network of Women's Studies Information and Documentation Centers

Helga Hofmann-Weinberger and Christa Wille (Austria)

THE ORIGINS OF WOMEN'S STUDIES IN AUSTRIA

Notable Austrian Women

Austria, a small country in the heart of Europe, is the birthplace of Gerda Lerner, the well-known U.S. feminist scholar who greatly influenced us through such books as *The Creation of Patriarchy* and *The Creation of Feminist Consciousness*. Nazism forced Gerda Lerner to emigrate at the age of nineteen. For many emigrants and refugees arriving in the United States, the Statue of Liberty was the "symbolic gateway." It was Hertha Pauli, another Austrian woman who escaped from Nazi terrorism, who wrote the history of "Miss Liberty" for its 100th anniversary in 1986.

ARIADNE (not an acronym), the Austrian women's studies information and documentation center, is located in an institution with roots in the fourteenth century. Christine de Pizan, the famous French author born in that century, was the first woman known to have made a living as a professional

---

Helga Hofmann-Weinberger was born in 1949 and in 1968–69 worked as an au pair in Paris, where she was greatly influenced by the student movement. After studying French, German, and political science in Vienna and working as a research secretary and then as a teacher, she came to the Austrian National Library in 1987. In ARIADNE she has found a way to link her work with some of the political dreams of her early student period. Born in 1955, Christa Wille joined the Austrian National Library in 1973, working mainly in the cataloging department and the organization of reader instruction. Soon she felt a strong desire to speak for employees' interests, mainly women's specific concerns. Since the installation of ARIADNE at the library, she is in the lucky position of combining librarian's and feminist work.

writer. Her feminist utopia, *Le Livre de la Cité des Dames*, is one of the trea-
sures in our manuscript collection. It is a long journey from an imperial library
with its patriarchal structure, where women as readers and librarians were for
centuries invisible and ignored, to our modern institution, where library users
interested in women's studies find special service.

Social Developments

The foundation of ARIADNE is closely related to important events that led to
changed thinking in Austrian society with regard to women. The early twen-
tieth-century women's rights movement was destroyed by Nazism and World
War II. With some delay, the new women's liberation movement in Austria
came after those in Anglo-American, Scandinavian, and German countries.
Only at the beginning of the 1970s did some noteworthy actions by autonomous
and courageous women start to attract attention to feminist issues. For example,
there were provocative demonstrations against an inhuman abortion law, and, as
a symbol of oppressed women, Maria Mies, a well-known feminist, was driven
in a wooden cage down a crowded shopping lane in Vienna.

    Women's groups focusing on raising self-confidence were established and
the foundations laid for great changes and modernization in women's lives. Also
contributing to this political awakening was the fact that since 1971 the government has been Social Democrat. The establishment of a State Secretary for
Women's Affairs, which eventually became a ministry, was an important step
toward upgrading the value of women's interests on a general level. Johanna
Dohnal, the minister, is the most successful and longest-serving female member
of the government. Among the important results of her work are the achievement of equal rights for employed women and protection and social rights for
pregnant women and for mothers.

WOMEN'S STUDIES IN AUSTRIA

In the 1980s, feminist consciousness moved also into academic life. Women's
studies and feminist theory and their interdisciplinary character spread
throughout the universities. So far there has been only one official professorial
chair, at the University of Innsbruck, that is explicitly called a women's research
chair. But now three institutions in Austria coordinate and support women's
studies in participating universities and also off-campus autonomous feminist
research activities. These initiatives have resulted in an enormous production of
knowledge: articles, books, dissertations, periodicals, and so forth, but the institutionalized academic libraries could not satisfy the growing number of female
clients. With feminist scholars demanding better information services on
women's studies, something had to be done.

ARIADNE

That was when the idea of ARIADNE was born. From the beginning, we had three aims: to be a rich source of women-related knowledge; to be a "mediatress" between university research and independent activities; and to create networks. Although specialized women working in related information and documentation areas had some reservations, we were full of hope: we would divide our forces and tasks, avoid duplication, and avoid isolation by supporting one another.

As far as we know, the first initiative to deal theoretically with the issue of women-specific information and documentation in Austria was a feasibility study for such a specialized institution, prepared in 1986–1987 by Andrea Fennesz and Christa Wille on behalf of the Ministry of Science and Research. We analyzed the status quo in Austria and other European countries, such as Germany and the Netherlands, and worked out conditions and concepts for the future functioning of such a new institution in our country.

This study was followed by a stalemate for about five years. But then parallel activities appeared in different areas. In spring 1991, the ministries took interest in what they called the "wild-growing" feminist documentation scene. They gave approval to setting up a new information center within the Austrian National Library. In addition, we contacted a colleague working in the women's sector of a political institution, who proposed organizing a first meeting of all existing women's studies documentation centers—both autonomous and institutionalized—in Austria.

This historic meeting in the late summer of 1991 brought together, for the first time, all women working in the feminist information and documentation sector, a heterogenous group including women from the radical feminist, autonomous side; some from commercial or public documentation centers (where women-specific literature is only part of the collection); and those from the established scientific libraries who wanted to enlarge their holdings. Full of idealistic hopes and utopian ideas, we presented the concept of a centralized and common "Austria-Wide Women-Specific Database"—and provoked a big dispute! Many women did not agree to this project, and a seemingly endless discussion began about working conditions and psychological aspects of autonomous women and those in organizations. Some women were suspicious of any kind of centralization, fearful of being absorbed by large public organizations; others had reservations about women from the bureaucracy. As women with the rather secure background of a big institution—the National Library—we did not expect this full range of emotions; we were taken by surprise and felt rather helpless. But after two and a half days of discussions, we managed to minimize our prejudices and agree on three steps for carrying on with our exchange of ideas:

1. Formulate conditions and needs for cooperation in an Austria-wide network
2. Create an organizational framework for this cooperation
3. Prepare women-specific projects in the information and documentation fields

FRIDA

In the ensuing years this group met every two months. The organizational framework that had been created finally led to the founding of the Association for Women-Specific Information and Documentation in Austria; FRIDA is the acronym for the German title. FRIDA organized a workshop on a special topic every summer. At first, there were changing participants, and contentious discussions continued between the autonomous and the institutional segments of the group. But after three years, the process of knowing one another has led to a constructive kind of cooperation. Lively signs are two concrete projects: the elaboration of a feminist thesaurus for Austria and a special guide for biographical research.

THE ROLE OF ARIADNE WITHIN THE AUSTRIAN NATIONAL LIBRARY

In 1991, the Ministry of Science and Research asked the two authors to carry out the ideas we had proposed five years earlier. We started in March 1992, first incorporating ARIADNE into the library's rules of procedure and book processing. Our colleagues were kind, helpful, and ready to cooperate. We tried to include in our collection the recent developments of women's studies from the early 1990s and also considered what we had learned in the FRIDA meetings. We wanted ARIADNE to be based on three pillars:

* A women-specific database
* Information retrieval
* A network of Austrian and foreign centers

In order to cope with all these tasks, we had to increase the acquisition of women-specific and feminist literature and periodicals at the National Library. We informed our colleagues about the new collection topic within our well-established and rather traditional institution and started the ARIADNE Newsletter, an annotated acquisition list of women-related new publications that has become our "best seller." We wanted both female and male users to get the best, nonbureaucratic service. Our main tasks were collecting material, establishing a database, and informing users.

THE ARIADNE DATABASE

The source of material cataloged in the database is the holdings of the National Library. In our effort to close the major gaps we identified in women-specific literature, we are ordering new books and other material quite intensively. The documents selected are "Austriaca" (literature by Austrian authors or about Austria) and basic works on feminist theory, both European and other. We index articles from journals, anthologies, proceedings, and grey literature that we get mainly from Austrian women's studies scholars with whom we keep in close contact. We try to avoid duplication of work with others. In Austria, we coordinate with the FRIDA network; on the European level, with KVINNSAM in Sweden, the only, and very useful, women-specific database that can easily be accessed through the Internet. The Swedish database group has been indexing for ten years in a similar context (a university library) and now has more than 30,000 records. We use KVINNSAM, know the list of journals covered, and so can avoid duplication.

The cataloging and field structure are similar to those for any other database. We take care to ensure accurate, nonsexist subject indexing, which uses the new vocabulary of women's studies, different from official authority files. The Online Public Access Catalog (OPAC) will soon be located in the central catalog hall of our library and should enable readers to find what they need on their own.

To obtain a better structure for subject entries, we divide index terms into different types: topical headings, personal names, corporate names, title headings (literature, movies, etc.), geographical headings, and chronological subdivisions. We use authority files for personal, corporate, and geographical names and for title headings. For subject headings, we are looking forward to the standardized list of our feminist thesaurus project, called "thesaurA."

CONCLUSION

Some elements seem especially important to us:

- We were fortunate to be able to establish ARIADNE and the Austria-Wide network in parallel. The interaction between ARIADNE and FRIDA and the feedback of the group have been very stimulating.
- An important factor is the intertwining of ARIADNE with other networks: FRIDA, an active team of autonomous and institutional documentation centers; users and feminist scholars, who deliver and request materials on women's studies; female librarians in research libraries who are interested in women's studies and some of whom are organized in the Austrian Librarians' Association; and the three "Interuniversity Women's Studies Coordination Centers."

- On the basis of our experience at the National Library and with the core of autonomous and institutional women, we can offer these postulates: have patience and tenacity, for even centralized bureaucracies may eventually act; do not shy away from utopian proposals; stay in communication; develop structures and take responsibility; and not least, it should be fun to do feminist work and support consciousness-raising.

Feminist/Women's Archives and Libraries in Germany
Concepts, Equipment, and Networking

Helga Dickel (Germany)

INTRODUCTION

Figures about women's organizations in 1910 show that of 4,000 member organizations of the Association of German Women's Societies, about 400 had a library or a reading room. Most of these libraries were very small and were not the main focus of the organizations, and most closed in the 1920s. In most cases we do not know what happened to the books and other material after World War I or after 1933.

Some of the larger libraries and collections survived, in part, but the history of women's collections of the historical women's movement in Germany, especially of the radical feminists, ended with Nazism. New archives and libraries and some specific projects developed more recently, as a result of the women's movement that began in the 1970s, as did networking efforts among German-speaking women.

STILL-EXISTING COLLECTIONS FROM THE HISTORICAL WOMEN'S MOVEMENT

The Helene-Lange Archive

The most important and extensive collection of the historical women's movement in Germany that survives is the Helene-Lange Archive in Berlin, which

Born in 1957, **Helga Dickel** earned a degree in sociology from the University of Bielefeld (1980) and in 1982–85 was on the staff of the Research Group Women's Studies there. From 1986 to 1993 she was on the staff of a special project of the Feminist Archive and Documentation Center, developing the German Feminist Thesaurus. Currently she and Carolina Brauckmann are preparing a new project: the Women's Information Service in Germany.

111

belongs today to the Berlin League of Women 1945. Named after Helene Lange (1848–1930), the founder of the General German Women Teachers' Organization and of the Association of German Women's Organizations, an umbrella organization, this collection has been on loan to the State Archives of Berlin and open to the public since 1988. The collection was formed from the archives of the Association of German Women's Organizations and the General German Women Teachers' Organization. When the women's organizations were forced to dissolve in 1933, their libraries and archives were taken over by the Helene-Lange Foundation, founded in 1912 to fund young students. The archives of the General Society of German Women in Leipzig and privately owned material of women activists were added between 1933 and 1945.

The material was kept in a private apartment. One paid worker and numerous unpaid women volunteers continued to collect material until the war began. Topics included women's issues in Germany and abroad, biographical documents about women in the women's movement, the German movement against alcohol, education, and family and criminal law. Between 1935 and 1941 this group published a quarterly bibliographic newsletter about the legal position of women in Germany and Austria. Even though bombs damaged the flat, the women succeeded in preserving the collection until after the war.

In the spring of 1945 Agnes von Zahn-Harnack and the other surviving women of the women's movement founded the Berlin League of Women 1945, and the collection became the property of this new organization. During the 1960s and 1970s, members of the Berlin League still managed the collection, which was now of interest to researchers but in very poor condition. In the 1980s, with the help of various sponsors, documents were microfilmed, the books were restored, and a catalog was produced. Today the collection contains some 200,000 documents of the historical women's movement, 2,500 pamphlets and books, and news clippings from the 1920s and 1930s.

Archive of the Catholic Women's Association

This archive in Cologne contains papers dating back to 1903, when the Catholic Women's Association was founded. The 6,000 books, 450 periodicals, 1,000 photographs, and 240 running meters (263 yards) of filmed records survived World War II; more than half the materials date from before 1945. The archive contains an almost complete collection of the forty-three periodicals and journals of the historical women's movement.

Other Archives

Two libraries in Hamburg were built up by organizations founded at the end of the 1940s by women who had been members of women's organizations before

1933. The National Library of the German Women's Circle and the Hamburg Library of Women's Issues of the Association of Hamburg Women's Organizations were established in 1966–67 with members' donations, mainly books and pamphlets of the historical movement but also materials from the 1950s and 1960s. These libraries opened to the public in the mid-1980s.

Today the Library of Women's Issues, with 4,000 volumes and current material, is housed in the office of the Association of Women's Organizations. The National Library of the Women's Circle, with some 3,000 volumes, recently returned to Darmstadt, where it began.

COLLECTIONS OF THE NEW WOMEN'S MOVEMENT IN GERMANY

The importance of collecting books and papers of women and the women's movement was discussed in public again with the beginnings of the new women's movement. The members of the women's groups that founded these more recent archives and libraries were mostly students or academics; the projects were founded mainly outside universities, however. The first group to do this was Homosexual Action of West Berlin, which in 1973 began to collect materials pertaining to the lesbian movement; these are now part of the Lesbian Archive "Spinnboden" in Berlin. In 1975 a Berlin women's group began to build up an archives, which was taken over by the Women's Research, Education and Information Center (FFBIZ) when it was founded in 1978. In 1977 the Women's Archive at the University of Dortmund was opened, and in 1979 Image Change was founded by students of art and media sciences in Hamburg to advance women's film and art projects and to collect films and videos by and about women.

Since 1980 archives and libraries have emerged throughout Germany's bigger cities, especially those with universities. Thirty-one projects were started between 1980 and 1990; since then sixteen more have been started. Today there are more than fifty women's archives and libraries in Germany. Approximately half are concerned with the status of women and the new women's movement in general, some also with the regional history of women and women's struggle. The other half are more specialized, focusing on film and media, lesbian life and the lesbian movement, the historical women's movement, women and music, art and women artists, women's research and women's studies, internationalism, reproductive technologies, architecture and environmental planning, or religion and feminist theology.

In the former German Democratic Republic the first women's archives and libraries were set up in 1990, and soon ten had been formed. Before reunification women's and lesbian groups could meet only through the church. After reunification, these women were the first to set up women's projects. The first content of the archives was often the women's private collections.

Concepts and Practice

The archives and libraries are based on the following concepts:

- Archives are a prerequisite for exploring and establishing women's history; hence the importance of searching for and preserving the documents and books of the historical women's movement.
- The development of the new women's movement must be documented for researchers now and for posterity.
- Goals are to research the women's movement, to publish the results, to build public awareness and shape political ideas, and to support women's political struggle in general or in specific areas.
- Efforts must be made to document what women in all fields have produced. Each project translates these ideas into practice as it carries out its primary tasks.

In all the projects users are mostly female students. The second-largest group are journalists, politicians, and government officials. Those in the equal opportunities offices, for example, often need services such as bibliographies on special topics, copies of essays and newspaper articles, addresses, and so on. Only a few projects have the resources to offer such services.

A general problem is adequate financing. Almost all projects began without any funding except membership fees. Today only a few projects are regularly funded by either the state or the city; since reunification, funding for all social institutions and projects has been reduced.

New Technologies and Computerized Databases

Discussions about working with computers aroused great controversy. Most projects were vehemently against the installation of computers. The first computerized database, of the Feminist Archive in Cologne, led to intense discussions at meetings of women's archives and libraries. At the time new technology and the resulting working conditions of women were discussed intensely in the women's movement. Counterarguments of many project members were made about unhealthy working conditions and the possibility of controlling and building hierarchies.

Although some projects still oppose the introduction of computers, the need for them in archives and library work is now recognized. Women began to train themselves in computer skills and in special knowledge about documentation, information, and library science. Today databases are available in fewer than twenty projects, and there is only one database with entries on holdings in public state libraries (in the Saarland). Other databases on women and women's research do exist in Germany, however. One is part of a database on social sciences in the Information Center for Social Sciences in Bonn. Four others are the database of Important Women International (Hannover), of Women Writers in Germany since 1945 (Bremen), of Women in History (Munich), and of Women's Studies and English Literary Science and Writers (University of Cologne).

PROJECT DESCRIPTIONS

The following eight projects all exist outside universities and were chosen as examples of the different and specialized work of German feminist archives and libraries. The situation of women's collections at universities is hardly different from the general situation. They were often built up within or in connection with the centers of women's studies and research on women. The initiative usually came mostly from female students. The collections are an important supplement to the university libraries and contain mainly books, theses, and unpublished research papers on women. Only at the University of Bielefeld is there a special women's collection within the university library.

FFBIZ

The Women's Research, Education and Information Center (FFBIZ) was established in 1978, in what was then West Berlin. This autonomous feminist center broke down traditional divisions among research, education, and information; the division between theory and practice; and the hierarchy among women in the universities (secretaries and academics). Members of the association have done research on white-collar women workers in the Weimar Republic, on women's unpaid work and family policy, and on the history of women librarians. The center holds more than 7,000 books on all areas of women's lives. It is well known for documents and grey literature from the beginnings of the new women's movement, some published in a loose-leaf edition. A computer database has not yet been developed.

Archive of the Historical Women's Movement

This archive, the only one that collects all documents of all the wings of the historical women's movement in Germany, was founded in 1983 in Kassel as an autonomous feminist archives, library, and research center. Today it claims to have the world's largest collection of German-speaking literature about the history of the women's movement. The archive's main goal is to inform women and the general public about what women throughout history have done, fought, and won. Members are very active in giving presentations about the lives of feminists in the past; research results are published in the archive's own book series and its newsletter, *ARIADNE*. About two-thirds of the present library's 14,000 volumes are from the period 1800–1950. Only recently has computerization of the large collection of information begun, but it is now a priority.

Education Center and Archives for the History of Women

This center is an example of a regionally focused archives, specializing in the history of women's lives in the region around Tübingen, a rural area with few written materials about women's lives. The most important task of the archives thus is to obtain information in the form of oral-history interviews with old women as witnesses of the past. This work is based on the idea that finding correlations between women's lives in the past and today is necessary for developing future perspectives. The women organized "story cafés"—gatherings where elderly women talk about such topics as their lives during the Nazi era and during the war. The old women have also given the archives letters, diaries, and other papers.

Women's Education Center Denk(T)räume

Denk(T)räume is a play on words: *think* (denk), *dreams* (Träume), and *rooms* (Räume); this women's education center in Hamburg includes a library, a newspaper archive and video collection, and a women's café. The need for learning and training with other women led to the founding of the Education Center in 1983. The main focus of the project, which is partly funded by the city and so is one of the few projects with (four) paid workers, is on education and training: evening lectures, weekend workshops, film presentations, official educational holidays, long-running working groups, and language courses. The lending library contains about 8,000 volumes, divided about equally between nonfiction and fiction. A priority is to buy rare and expensive books, which women with little money are unable to buy. The collection also contains periodicals, documentary and feature films, and news clippings.

Women's Library and Documentation Center for Women's Research

This project in Saarbrücken, founded in 1989 and for the time being funded by the state, links research and the practical use of research results by women outside universities and research institutes. The main focus of the collection is women's research in social and natural sciences, feminist theory, the regional history of women and the women's movement, women's politics, and international women's fiction. The project has, from the beginning, worked with computers; its database contains about 10,000 indexed and abstracted titles, including all women's books in the public libraries in the Saarland. One of its planned projects is to scan the news clipping collection into the computer and index it.

Women's Media Tower

Formerly known as the Feminist Archive and Documentation Center in Cologne, this is the only project that has always had a strong financial basis; it has used automation from the start. The main focus is the new women's movement and, especially, the radicals of the historical movement. The main database contains 15,000 documents of feminist literature, indexed by the German Feminist Thesaurus (developed in the center itself), by personal names, and by organizational names; many of the documents also have short abstracts. Additional databases index the feminist journal *EMMA*, posters, and women's periodicals. The concept behind the documentation center is, besides the preservation of the material, the compilation of material regarding the actual situation of women; the relevant social forces, such as media, science, and government; gender ideology; and the feminist struggle against women's oppression. The archives will soon open its new home, a medieval tower on the Rhine. Hence the new name, Women's Media Tower (*FrauenMediaTurm*).

Women's Library MonaLiesA

The name is a pun, as "Lies" is part of some forms of the verb "to read." The history of this project highlights the strong commitment of women in East Germany after reunification in 1989. It is in many respects the history of one woman, Susanne Scharff, a German/English teacher in Leipzig.

After visiting friends in Vienna, where she was fascinated by the existing women's scene, she went to the House of Democracy, the home of the new Women's Initiative Leipzig and other political and social projects. There she found the first feminist books she had ever seen, which had been donated by women in West Germany to the emerging women's movement in the east. Although she was pregnant, every day after school she drove to the Women's Initiative and read and read. Excited and happy about the world of women she found, she began to collect more books and to look for money and for women to help her build up a women's library. She saved interesting books from libraries that were being closed; sometimes she even rescued books from garbage disposal sites.

After her daughter was born, she spent her maternity leave in the emergent women's library. When she had to decide whether to stay in the library or go back to teaching, she chose to stay in the library, which had become such a significant part of her life.

Today the library is the largest of the new women's libraries in East Germany, with more than 7,000 books and about 2,000 women's journals and magazine issues. The library holds weekly evening lectures about women's research and women's fiction. A special activity is the work with girls and boys. A section with nonsexist literature for children was built up, and there are monthly readings and talks. In 1993 about 15 percent of the library's 450 users were children.

Grey Area: Documentation Center of the Nongovernmental Women's Movement in the German Democratic Republic

Founded in 1992, the Documentation Center Grey Area collects material from and about women's activities in the former German Democratic Republic. A women's movement outside the governmental organizations did exist, but the situation was difficult for such groups. Women's and lesbian groups often got space and support from Christian institutions. Western feminist literature was difficult to get, except occasionally from Western Christian partner parishes. Women had discussions in seminars, at prayers, at universities, and at parents' evenings. Women academics tried to introduce feminist ideas into their seminars; especially at Christian education centers, feminist themes were accepted. The Grey Area collection contains letters, diaries, circulars, records of lectures and meetings, programs, invitations, and excerpts of Western feminist books. Further materials are photographs, posters, tape recordings, and amateur films from 1984–1990, which were shown in public in the former GDR only once. Much of the information about this time is available only through the reminiscences of the women. The main purpose of the archives is to provide material reflecting their own history for women in the former East Germany.

NETWORKING AMONG GERMAN-SPEAKING WOMEN'S ARCHIVES AND LIBRARIES

Networking began in 1983, with the first meeting of four projects. Meetings take place twice a year at different archives, with an average of twenty-five participating projects, including two or three from Austria and Switzerland. Regular meetings also occur independently in those two countries.

At first the meetings focused mainly on the financial situations of the archives and libraries and the kinds and subjects of their collections. More recently they have become an important arena for the exchange of information among specialists. Now topics may include strategies for funding and public relations work; discussions about various classification systems and the feminist use of subject headings; ways to document special developments and events, select news clippings, work with private collections, and develop computerized databases; and consideration of the use of terms and the role of a feminist thesaurus.

Practical discussions concern the exchange of duplicates and mutual support by means of solidarity statements to the press and to sponsors. There is still no exchange of computer data, however, except in the cooperation among three projects: the Video Collection (Hamburg), Women Artists' Archives (Nürnberg), and Lesbian Archives "Spinnboden" (Berlin).

So far, there are three joint projects: a loose-leaf edition of self-descriptions of nearly all women's archives and libraries in Germany, Austria, and Switzerland; a small newsletter disseminating information between meetings; and the development of a German feminist thesaura (using the female ending "a").

Germany does not have a central national governmental women's documentation center, as do some European countries. This is both a strength and a problem. On the one hand, it is advantageous that women can find women's collections in nearly all regions of Germany, and archives collect the material of the various regions. The specialized archives make sure that their collections are as complete as possible on their topics. On the other hand, the projects compete for government funding, and the funding is never adequate.

Another problem of the decentralized women's collections is that institutions such as the European Commission are accustomed to communicating with a single responsible organization. We hope that our umbrella association will be able to function as such a national institution. The umbrella association is called "i d a": inform, document, and archive.

Tasks that "i d a" should undertake include, for example, building up national contacts with general archives and libraries and their associations, and also international contacts (such as attending this conference!); beginning a public discussion among specialists on women's and feminist information policy; improving computer networking; offering training courses on indexing and database software; and organizing a conference on women's research and women's documentation work.

Overt and Covert Censorship in Building Women's Studies Collections in Ireland

Monica Cullinan and Ailbhe Smyth (Republic of Ireland)

INTRODUCTION

In a very real sense, contradiction and paradox are the major structuring forces of contemporary Ireland. To begin with, Ireland is not one state but two. Institutions, laws, and practices differ considerably in the two parts of the island; this paper focuses only on the southern part, the Republic of Ireland.

> *Irish society has changed more in the two decades leading up to the 1990s than in the whole of the previous one hundred years, going back to the Great Famine of the mid nineteenth century. An inward-looking, rural, deeply conservative, nearly 100 percent Roman Catholic and impoverished country has become urbanised, industrialised, and Europeanised. Its political and social institutions are challenged by the realities of today, and in many cases are proving unequal to the challenge. (Gemma Hussey,* Ireland Today, *1993, p.1)*

Ireland has a feminist president and a higher proportion of women in electoral politics (12 percent in Parliament) than, for example, the United Kingdom, France, or the United States. But divorce is still prohibited by the Constitution. Employment legislation now prohibits discrimination on the basis of sexual orientation, but information about abortion services available elsewhere (for

Monica Cullinan is Assistant Librarian at University College, Dublin, and has recently completed an M.A. in Women's Studies. **Ailbhe Smyth** is Director of the Women's Education, Research and Resource Centre at University College, Dublin. She has worked in feminist publishing and is a co-editor of *Women's Studies International Forum.*

example, in the United Kingdom) is still censored in principle, despite a constitutional amendment in 1992 formally acknowledging the right to obtain and disseminate such information. Nonetheless, Irish people—especially women—are choosing to go their own way in matters sexual, "moral," and social. Marriage separations are on the increase; growing numbers of married women are seeking to remain in or to reenter the labor force and are demanding education, training, and health and childcare services.

In short, Irish women who refuse the narrow roles allowed them by tradition, law, and practice face particular problems. Yet the obstacles placed in the way of women's freedom have only fueled the dynamics of feminist opposition and resistance.

IRISH WOMEN'S STUDIES

The growth of women's studies and feminist education since the early 1980s has been one of the most invigorating and encouraging developments in Irish feminism. Today about 200 women's adult and community-based education groups are involved in feminist educational projects, with many additional women-centered courses and programs. Formal women's studies programs now exist in six of the republic's seven universities (and in both universities in Northern Ireland), with plans for consolidation and future development well under way. In addition, feminist publishing has widened access to feminist thinking and creativity and helped in forging and strengthening channels of information and communication. The *Irish Journal of Feminist Studies*, edited by a group of women academics from the Republic and Northern Ireland, is scheduled to begin publication by Cork University Press in 1995. The journal will publish not only feminist research and reflection but also information about courses, research in progress, publications, networking, and other activities.

Information Resources for Women in Ireland

Despite the high levels of activity in women's studies over the past decade, there are no feminist libraries, archives, or women's documentation centers in Ireland. This is not because the materials do not exist. On the contrary, considerable historical and contemporary documentary materials, records, archives, and so on are held by institutions (such as the National Library, the National Archives, and the universities), by organizations (the Employment Equality Agency, the Council for the Status of Women, the trade unions), and of course by individuals. But these collections, archives, and miscellaneous holdings remain a largely unknown and inaccessible quantity; diffuse and disparate, they are an unusable and therefore unused resource for women.

Over the years, feminist scholars and activists have attempted to begin the work of identifying, collecting, classifying, and disseminating these crucial research and information resources. Despite much careful and hard work, however, none of these initiatives has led to the creation of a library or documentation center.

DUBLIN WOMEN'S CENTRE (1982–86)   Those aiming to create a feminist library and resource center floundered when the center ran into serious funding problems, exacerbated by organizational (and some ideological) difficulties. The painstakingly acquired and partly cataloged materials have now been dispersed.

EMPLOYMENT EQUALITY AGENCY   This state-funded statutory body has a relatively large collection of books, journals, and documents about women's employment. Some years ago, the agency commissioned a researcher to compile a bibliography on training and labor market issues relating to women, but funds ran out before the project could be completed.

COUNCIL FOR THE STATUS OF WOMEN   This umbrella organization for more than 100 women's groups in Ireland receives a small annual grant from the state. The council is having increasing difficulty providing basic information services for its affiliate groups. Established in the 1970s, the council now has considerable if heterogeneous information files on women's groups and activities in Ireland and elsewhere and also receives or exchanges information and publications with a number of other groups both nationally and abroad. It has not been able to realize its aim of creating a women's information center, despite its already substantial contemporary archives.

UNIVERSITY-BASED WOMEN'S STUDIES CENTERS   A database on rural women in Ireland and the United Kingdom has been built by the Women's Studies Centre at University College Galway and compiled by Ann Finn and Catherine Forde as *Rural Women: An Annotated Bibliography* (1993). The Women's Education, Research and Resource Centre (WERRC) at University College Dublin has a small collection of books and documentation on women. WERRC also produces short bibliographies on a wide range of topics, responds as possible to research and information queries from Ireland and abroad, and facilitates consultation of its resources on request.

ACADEMIC LIBRARIES   These libraries have a considerable number of books and other documentation on women. Since these holdings are integrated in the general collections, however, they are difficult to identify, even though most catalogs are now computerized. Because bibliographic control of literature on women does not exist in Ireland, it is impossible to estimate the number of documents published annually.

Effects of Censorship

The absence of funding for the development of women's information resources, precisely echoing the absence of financial support for feminist research and scholarship, is an indirect form of censorship beyond the confines of statute law. Laws are superfluous when ideology and tradition have the same result. The absence of policy means an absence of funding and support and is thus a powerful instrument in maintaining the status quo.

Censorship has long played a prominent role in Ireland. For example, the Censorship of Films Act (1923) provides for the censoring of films that "would be subversive to public morality"; films representing divorce, marital infidelity, and extramarital relationships were indeed censored. The Censorship of Publications Act (1929) permitted the banning of books on three main grounds: indecency or obscenity, a focus on crime, and advocating "the unnatural prevention of conception or the procurement of abortion or miscarriage." Thus books, magazines, and papers containing almost any reference to sexual activity— heterosexual as well as homosexual—were censored in whatever context they appeared: literary, scientific, technical, and so on. A medical or sociological treatise on sexual behavior or sexual dysfunction was therefore as likely to be censored as a pornographic magazine or a novel about a sexual relationship. The negative impact of such repressive censorship on Irish writers, and on Irish society and culture as a whole, is incalculable. It was a rare publisher who would court commercial disaster by braving the Censorship Board. The most destructive effect was the self-censorship thus induced in generation after generation of Irish writers and thinkers.

The Censorship of Publications Act was "liberalized" in 1946 and again in 1967, when a twelve-year limit was placed on the length of time for which a book could be banned. In fact, no literary works by Irish writers have been censored since 1988.

In one area in particular, however, censorship has continued unabated. The Health (Family Planning) Act, 1979, removed the prohibition against books "advocating the unnatural prevention of conception" but retained the ban against information about abortion. Over the years, large numbers of women's health books have been banned, including books by Marie Stopes and family planning guides issued by the British Medical Association. In 1992 the revised edition of *Our Bodies, Ourselves* was (temporarily) removed from the shelves of Dublin's public libraries.

The consequences for women of this censorship are intricate. For one thing, the reduction of "women" to, in effect, nonspeaking and nonwriting (or reading) objects does not recognize them as complex social and sexual persons. In addition, the extreme difficulty for us Irish women in obtaining information about issues that materially affect our lives and life choices is a source of ongoing hardship for many thousands of Irish women.

THE LIBRARY AT UNIVERSITY COLLEGE DUBLIN

University College Dublin (UCD), the largest university in Ireland, offers courses at undergraduate and postgraduate levels in nine faculties to 15,000 students. The library's collection process is driven by the teaching and research interests of the academic staff. The purchase of any item can be justified simply by stating that it is on a reading list. In the early 1980s, the gaps in the library's collection became apparent. Why were so few women writers and so few nonmainstream publications in the library? Many interesting subject areas were not on the curriculum, yet students asked for material in those areas. One of the authors of this article (Cullinan) attempted to fill those gaps on her own. Such efforts were rebuffed, and she brought the matter to her trade union. Eventually the library set up a "book selection committee," and subject librarians had thenceforth to send all orders to their department heads for approval. Such paternalistic attitudes resemble those that underpinned state censorship for so long.

CONCLUSION

In a general sense, the election of Mary Robinson as president in 1990, together with the coming of age of what one might call the "U2" generation in Ireland, signify the emergence of a more tolerant climate. More specifically, the establishment of a women's studies program has been most useful. The students need books, and one has to try to obtain the items on their reading lists. Equally, a change in personnel is often significant; minor restructuring brought us a more sympathetic sub-librarian.

In addition, a more general and looser funding structure, or coding system, was established in the library as a direct result of government policy. In the late 1980s the government wished to cut its public payroll, and many library staff members left. But recent increases in funds due to increased numbers of students have led to purchases needed for women's studies or other subjects.

Of course, all these obstacles and impediments may themselves simply be part of the development process. Development will no doubt be more modest, given our relative poverty in Ireland and in UCD, but even in the short time since women's studies has been established at UCD, the situation has improved, and the collection grows.

Between Memory and Invention

Toward a National Women's Library in Italy

Annamaria Tagliavini (Italy)

ASSOCIAZIONE ORLANDO

In 1979 the Associazione Orlando, a group of women active both in the women's movement and in academic research, decided to build a Women's Documentation Center and Library in Bologna. This initiative was designed from the start to combine research with practical activities in the context of an institution run by women for women, for making women protagonists. The administration of the center was entirely independent of all parties and institutions, while the financial base was provided by a contract with the municipal government. At that time many other places of this kind were already flourishing in Italy.

The Bologna center is unique in that from the beginning efforts were dedicated to two particular elements:

- We wanted to establish a publicly supported institution. This requires an ongoing relationship with local governments for financial support.
- On a theoretical level we stress the importance of understanding the individual woman's relationship with the society of women, an original and key idea in the Italian feminist panorama.

With a degree in Philosophy, **Annamaria Tagliavini** has been active in the Italian women's movement since the 1970s and is the Director of the Women Documentation Center and Library in Bologna.

127

Moreover, the cycles of activism that in Italy characterize the history of women's mobilization convinced the Associazione Orlando to seize the opportunity to create an institution dedicated to the memory and transmission of women's traditions of political and cultural activism to new generations of young women.

Since 1979 women's centers have played a unique role in women's politics throughout Italy, dedicating themselves to a variety of areas of action, such as self help, information gathering, consciousness raising, and the like. Unfortunately, not many centers survived. This was due to the great difficulty they had in forming a satisfactory and theoretically acceptable relationship with such formal institutions as the state, political parties, or trade unions. However, while many women's initiatives of the 1970s and 1980s disappeared, feminist philosophers, historians, and scientists continued to carry on their work within the context of their academic disciplines, both inside and outside the university.

REASONS FOR A NATIONAL LIBRARY

In this context, the Women's Documentation Center and Library in Bologna has established itself and is now trying to reach a more ambitious level: to become the first national women's library in Italy and a key cultural institution in the European context. There are several reasons for this goal.

First, although not a single women's studies department has been created in any university in Italy, gender studies have grown in many disciplines and subjects without formal support from the university. The lack of institutional academic support has forged close links between women's research and the politics pursued by women's groups. A national library promises to become a meeting point for researchers of all disciplines throughout the country. It will also provide an effective instrument of support for research conducted independently by women. The location of the library is ideal for several reasons: Bologna is geographically central to Italy as a whole, it has the largest number of women's groups in proportion to the total population of the city, and it has a long-standing tradition of women's participation in public life.

Second, Italy lacks institutions concerned specifically with the preservation of women's history. In other countries, such as the United States, Great Britain, the Netherlands, and France, libraries and archives have been constructed solely to collect and investigate the roots of the first stages of the long and difficult path to women's liberation. In Italy we now face the task of reconstructing what was not preserved and collected in the past. The main objectives of the library are the preservation of history and the implementation of new research.

THE PRESENT STATE OF THE LIBRARY

The library contains 15,000 books and 250 periodicals covering a wide range of languages and subjects. Given that the concern with the earliest years of women's emancipation struggle is a relatively recent phenomenon, materials on this period are seriously lacking. Under the circumstances, collecting on the history of the Italian suffrage movement in the nineteenth century is now being carried out with special attention to the collection of books available only in antiquarian book shops.

The library does possess a strong collection on the history of Italian feminism of the 1970s, comprised mainly of published materials and unpublished archives focusing on activities at a regional level. It is hoped that a multimedia archives system with hundreds of videotaped interviews that survey the full range of women's experience will be created in the near future.

The feminine inner world of childhood imagination, fantasy, and the subconscious is being investigated through a special collection named Sofia's Library. This collection is dedicated to literature for young girls. But Sofia's Library also serves a group of researchers active in both the center and the Education Department of Bologna University. A contract has been signed with the university making the library a training center for students in the field of education.

The library is already equipped to support research on topics new to Italy, such as multiculturalism from a gender perspective. In November 1992, at an international conference organized by our center, American researchers such as Trinh T. Minh-Ha and Kirstie McClure presented their work on "Theories in American feminism."

Another well-represented field is the wide range of subjects concerned with the politics of peace from a gendered point of view. Work has been done in recent years with Israeli, Palestinian, and Bosnian women. The center is planning an international meeting on "Crimes against women."

THINGS TO COME

How can the continuation of this important activity be ensured? How do we achieve permanent support, not only from the local but also the national government? Moreover, how do we get an increasing number of women throughout the country to join and contribute to our enterprise?

An institution of this kind requires a new model of leadership. A single women's association cannot handle the enormous amount of work involved. Our aim is to transform the Associazione Orlando into a private foundation, with its own financial resources. We hope to convince women in positions of authority in different areas—management, arts, professions, research, publishing—to invest energy, money, and resources in the project.

New Quarters

Mayor Walter Vitali of Bologna has granted the Associazione Orlando a building to which it will move in the next two years: the sixteenth-century convent of Santa Cristina in the heart of the old city. This building needs restoration. It is hoped to arrange a joint venture between the public and private sectors to gain financial support for the restoration. It is our intention to launch a campaign whereby women will pledge to fund part of the expenses.

Services by and for Women

This huge building will contain not only the library and documentation center, but also many other services and activities run by women. Plans include a restaurant/coffee shop, a *hammam* (Turkish bath) for Muslim women, a gym for self-defense training, a guest house for foreign visitors attending conferences and seminars, a bookshop, and a school for professional training.

Rather than reinforce the ethnic separation of minority women in Italian society, this center will bring together women of many different cultural backgrounds and experiences in a gendered autonomous space, in which we hope to provide the means by which women may be empowered.

Professional Training

The center has received European Community (EC) funding, directed to professional training. In 1994 the center offered a course for "librarians specialized in gender documentation." The course provided 800 hours of study in women's history and research balanced with technical training in library science, archives, and communication sciences applied to libraries and documentation.

A Telecommunication System

EC funds are not directed only to training programs. Using EC funds, the center has applied for an important developing telecommunication system. The project, named WIN (Women Information Network), aims to develop a friendly interface system for multimedia information from European women's documentation centers based on a client/server model. The goal is to set up a new network by means of existing international networks (Internet, Janet, and so on).

This network will be used by women's libraries and centers at both a national and international level for the implementation of advanced bibliographic services. It will enable centers to carry on extensive research on the handling and use of multimedia documents and information services, such as the production of special bibliographies, newsletters, listservs, document delivery, automatic access to nonbook materials, and interlibrary loans. The network will use public domain software and will not modify the management of existing centers. It will also provide a ready-use service for a vast audience with the capability of integrating available European sources of information on women. Networks and information are, in fact, the future of our work.

The Archives Acquisitions Policy of the IIAV, 1935–1994

Annette Mevis (Netherlands)

INTRODUCTION

Collecting archives differs from collecting books or periodicals, if only because there is always just one copy of an archive. This aspect makes the question of acquisitions policy all the more pertinent: How does one get the archives one would like to have, and what is the best place for a particular archive? Some feminist and women's archives are national; they collect archives only from persons and organizations of their own country or state. The scope of others is international. It would be interesting to compare the acquisition policies of a number of women's archives, to exchange experiences and information, and to discuss the similarities and differences in each other's collecting strategies. Other issues to discuss are where to store the archives of international organizations and conferences and what criteria to use in making those decisions.

But first, it is important to be clear about the definition of an archive. An archive is the whole of the records received or created by an organization, a person, or a group of persons. So, in contrast to a book or a newspaper, an archive is always unique. The word *archives* is also used for the building in which archives are stored. Confusingly, some organizations are called *archives* even though they collect only books and other published material.

Annette Mevis has studied history and is archivist of the IIAV.

131

INTERNATIONAL INFORMATION CENTER AND ARCHIVES
FOR THE WOMEN'S MOVEMENT

The Early Years

The International Archives for the Women's Movement in Amsterdam, the IAV, was founded in 1935 by three Dutch feminists: Johanna Naber, Rosa Manus, and Willemijn Posthumus-van der Goot. Their goal was to promote the knowledge and scientific study of the women's movement in the broadest sense. All three founders wanted to establish a center to collect and preserve the cultural heritage of women, including adequate documentation of the past. The founders believed that the feminist past could hold valuable lessons for the future. They also wanted to publish books about the past and present of the international women's movement. The motto preceding the preface in the first *Yearbook* was "Science is not the discovery of facts. It is the reasoning about facts" (from the sociologist Lester F. Ward). The strong international aspect of the women's movement from its start in the nineteenth century is the reason the IAV, from its beginning, has aimed at collecting material from all countries; hence its name, International Archives.

The beginning years of the IAV were prosperous. Rosa Manus donated the papers of Aletta Jacobs, the long-time leader of the Dutch suffrage movement, who was the first Dutch woman to enroll in a university and the first woman medical doctor in the Netherlands. Rosa Manus was the first president of the IAV, and one of her tasks was to gather archives; because of her national and international connections she obtained important material. The other members of the board were active as well. They wrote to numerous important feminists in the Netherlands and abroad and sent an announcement of the IAV's founding to national and international women's periodicals. A pamphlet in German, English, and French contained a clear call for sending material to the IAV. When the board members attended meetings abroad, they always brought forward the interest of the Archives.

Of the ninety donations the IAV received in the first year, one-third came from abroad. The IAV librarian visited her colleagues at the Women's Service Library (now the Fawcett) in London to study their systematic catalog. There were also contacts with the Bibliothèque Marguerite Durand in Paris, and with both institutions there was an agreement to exchange duplicates. The IAV had an International Advisory Council, and visitors came to Amsterdam from abroad.

World War II and the Early Postwar Years

By 1940 around 4,000 books had been collected, as well as several archives, many pictures, and periodicals. But this flourishing beginning of the IAV came to an abrupt end on July 2, 1940. Less than two months after the Germans occupied the Netherlands, Germans knocked on the door of the IAV, told the two women who were present to leave, and sealed the door. The Germans took the complete contents of the IAV to Germany: all the books and archives, as well as the curtains and furniture. Rosa Manus had just brought in all the valuable papers she had collected during more than thirty years in the women's and peace movements. Charlotte Matthes, IAV treasurer, immediately protested the confiscation but to no avail. She did not even receive a written confirmation of it. The Germans closed the IAV because it was an international organization; because its name began with an A, it was one of the first on their list. The explanation for removing everything to Germany was: "Die Deutsche Frauen haben es sich gewünscht" ("The German women wanted it for themselves.").

After the war, extensive efforts were made to trace and retrieve the stolen property. All possible contacts with women and women's organizations in Germany and Eastern Europe were used. The Dutch state archivist was a member of the committee for the recovery of goods from Germany. Thanks to him, the IAV received, on the day of its reopening in 1947, one-tenth of its material. By then, only one of the three founders was still alive. Naber had died in 1941 at eighty-two; Rosa Manus, in 1943 in the women's concentration camp Ravensbrück. Posthumus-van der Goot, together with other women, started again.

For many years, the American feminist Carrie Chapman Catt had been a close friend of Manus. After hearing of the death of Manus and the theft of the IAV possessions, she sent a small collection to Amsterdam. It contained part of their correspondence from the 1930s and Catt's seventieth birthday album, consisting of pages sent in by women from all over the world.

The first decades after the war were a quiet period. Only a few archives were donated, primarily by Dutch women's organizations and women who were or had been active in the women's movement. These archives were put away in book cases. There was no written acquisitions policy, in part because, although the IAV had always had a fully qualified librarian, it had no trained archivist until 1977, and then for only four hours a week. She started to catalog the archives, and she started to inventory the archives of the National Exhibition of Women's Labour, held in 1898.

THE PRESENT IIAV

The decade 1970–80 was the beginning of a flourishing period for the IAV. The range of ideas of the so-called second feminist wave was expressed in magazines, programs of action, pamphlets, posters, essays, memoranda, and books. The need for more information about women and their role in society became visible in the growing number of visitors. The Dutch government provided financial aid, so more books could be bought and more staff paid. The archives situation improved after 1982, when the IAV was able to hire a full-time archivist. She made the archives of the National Bureau of Women's Labour and of the Dutch Association of Women's Interests accessible. She also helped visitors do research in the archives. There still was no active acquisitions policy, but a change occurred in the unwritten policy.

Previously, the IAV had acquired only papers of well-known women, but in 1982 it decided to collect documents of "unknown" or "anonymous" women. The IAV was responding to developments in the discipline of women's history, which brought with it a need for historical sources about women in the private sphere. A huge campaign provided a basis for the 150 collections now in the IIAV, some consisting of a few leaflets, another of 700 notebooks written by one woman, recording the blending of her real and fantasy lives during a period of forty-five years.

In 1988 the IAV, the IDC (Information and Documentation Center for the women's movement), and the feminist journal *Lover* merged. As a result, the archives became an independent department, with eighty-four hours a week in staff time. We have become more active in collecting archives and have formulated an acquisitions policy. In 1991 we published the *Survey of the Archives in the IIAV,* which gives detailed descriptions of the IIAV's archives and manuscript collections.

Thus the lack of both trained archivists and of a policy was overcome in 1988. The problems of lack of space and poor storage conditions remained until the beginning of 1994.

In January 1994 the IIAV moved to its present location at the Obiplein, a beautiful restored Catholic church. The circumstances are finally optimal to work professionally. There is space enough to store the archives, the temperature and humidity levels are kept constant, and we have a beautiful reading room for visitors. The IIAV is the repository for the records of about 200 organizations and 100 individuals, altogether some 1,700 linear feet. Most of these archives and manuscript collections are from Dutch women and women's organizations.

Our acquisitions policy is generally as follows:

- Archives from national women's organizations, companies, and action groups (we refer local organizations and branches to municipal archives)
- Archives from women who are or have been active in important issues for women
- Archives of international congresses on women's subjects

We hope to build up a well-balanced collection, representing all subjects and all trends.

A general factor in the decision whether to accept an archive is its research value. Another limitation is that we collect only 60 meters—200 feet—a year,

FEMINISTA ELÓHARCZOSOK

Mrs CARRIE CHAPMANN-CATT

From a 1906 album given by Hungarian suffragists to Aletta Jacobs (left) and Carrie Chapman Catt. Original in Moscow; microfilm at IIAV.

Photo: Myriam Everard.

because storage space and staff time to make the archives accessible are still limited.

Recovery of Documents

All postwar efforts to trace the documents that had been stolen during the war failed. In 1966, a librarian in the Czechoslovakian town of Hradec Králové discovered four books stamped IAV. He sent them back to Amsterdam. Nothing further was heard until January 1992, when a small announcement by Dutch historian Marc Jansen appeared in a Dutch newspaper. He had visited the so-called Special Archive in Moscow, where he discovered archives from Dutch organizations and people. This Special Archive had been established in March 1946 to house foreign archival materials brought to Moscow by Soviet authorities at the end of World War II. It also held foreign archives taken by the Nazis to various storage points in Eastern Europe. Until the end of 1991, hardly anyone knew about the existence of this Special Archive.

The day after the newspaper announcement, I called Marc Jansen in Moscow. He told me that among the collections he had seen were twenty-five boxes of the archives of the IAV. This news seemed like a miracle to us.

At first it looked as if all the Dutch archives would be returned soon. The Dutch state archivist and his colleague in Moscow signed an agreement. But month after month went by and nothing happened. In February 1994, Mineke Bosch and Myriam Everard, researchers in women's history, decided not to wait any longer. They went to Moscow to see the archives of the IAV. They had enough time to go through all the boxes and saw many interesting papers, including an album from 1906 given to Aletta Jacobs by Hungarian suffragists.

They drew two—maybe temporary—conclusions. First, to judge from the minutes and correspondence, the prewar IAV was an incredibly lively and energetic institution. Second, Mineke Bosch was confirmed in the opinion she had already expressed in *Politics and Friendship* that the IAV was founded by Rosa Manus "for the purpose of putting Aletta Jacobs' legacy to a worthy cause."

The Dutch state archivist and the Department of Foreign Affairs continue their attempts to bring the collections back to the Netherlands. The IIAV itself is negotiating for a microfilm of the material. We are hopeful that this will succeed soon. (As a postscript, as this book went to press, the IIAV had received the microfilms, a total of 33,663 frames.)

Information Services for and about Black and Migrant Women

Tanhya Mendeszoon (Netherlands)

INTRODUCTION

The Project Information Services for and about Black and Migrant Women is a project of the International Information Centre and Archives for the Women's Movement (IIAV) in the Netherlands. The IIAV is the central information service in the Netherlands on the position of women and women's studies. Its main activities are organized around two services:

- Information services
- Consultancy and research

BLACK AND MIGRANT WOMEN IN THE NETHERLANDS

What is meant by the terms *Black* and *migrant*? *Black* is a political word that in the Netherlands is used for women from the former Dutch colonies: Surinam, the Dutch Antilles, Indonesia, and the Moluccas. *Migrant* is used for people coming from Greece, Yugoslavia, Spain, Turkey, and Morocco.

The Black and migrant women's movement has long stressed that the position of these women is fundamentally different from that of White women. This difference in position has led to the development of a Black and migrant women's movement and Black women's studies.

Tanhya Mendeszoon works at the International Information Centre and Archives for the Women's Movement (IIAV) in Amsterdam.

Black and migrant women in the Netherlands have much in common: their socioeconomic position in the Netherlands, their non-Dutch history, and social obstacles and discrimination. They also have to struggle against sexism and racism, as well as the disadvantages and problems they experience as women. This series of problems sets their struggle apart from that of White women.

At the same time, there are many differences between Black and migrant women in the Netherlands: their history and background, their way of life, and their numbers. The differences are the basis of other differences, including religion, culture, and ethnic group. Thus, although Black and migrant women in the Netherlands have much in common, they nonetheless differ in many ways.

Flamboyant

A special center, called Flamboyant, was founded in 1985 to support the emancipation of Black and migrant women in the Netherlands. The women of Flamboyant recognized that information is an important factor in the emancipation process and that to investigate the position of Black and migrant women and their problems, it is necessary to have access to relevant information—not only on the present situation but also on the history of Black and migrant women.

Feeling that their information needs were not being met by existing information and documentation centers, the women of Flamboyant started their own library and documentation center. Their main goal was to collect information not only *about* Black and migrant women but also *from* them.

One project, bibliographical research on the sources available in Dutch libraries, resulted in a four-part bibliography on Black women. Problems encountered during this research included the diversity of terms used as subject headings and the difference between Black and Third World women.

The researchers concluded that, although there was information on Black women in Dutch libraries, it was neither visible nor accessible, because of the way the subjects and publications were classified. They found the information only by browsing and by using specific terms. They also found that the subjects documented were mainly health care, racism, jobs, and welfare. In short, the information in White women's libraries was insufficiently accessible and was documented from White perspectives. Besides, different status/position leads, among other things, to different information needs.

Unfortunately, Flamboyant, including its library project, closed down about four years ago.

PROJECT INFORMATION SERVICES

The results of Flamboyant's research and the fact that the center closed led the IIAV, in October 1992, to start the Project Information Services for and about

Black and Migrant Women, especially those engaged in scientific research and study, politics and administration, education and training, and campaigns, congresses, and other activities. The overall goal of the project is to improve information services for and about Black and migrant women—by IIAV itself and other Dutch women's libraries.

In close cooperation with the target group, a program has been under way for about three years. This program is directed at IIAV's collection-building policy, its indexing system, its publications, its consultancy activities, and so on. Financed by a special grant from the Ministry of Social Affairs and Employment, this program is carried out by two project assistants: a documentalist for the projects related to information services and a specialist in the field of Black and migrant women in the Netherlands.

Collection Building

One of the program's collection-building efforts focuses on four activities:

- Surveying relevant international databases and sources
- Searching for "grey" material (also called ephemera)
- Surveying for Blacks' and migrants' magazines in Dutch libraries
- Acquiring archives

The goal of these activities is to adjust the collection-building criteria to the information needs of Black and migrant women with regard to books, grey literature, periodicals, and archives. The focus is on current material. Priority will be given to grey literature.

More generally, these activities occur in two phases: evaluating present IIAV policy, and making suggestions for improvement. An evaluation of the present collection-building policy showed that the way it is formulated should lead to the availability of adequate material on Black and migrant women.

To verify this availability, I did a search to find out what the IIAV has on Black and migrant women. I based my search on the bibliography of Black women and a new literature guide on Black and migrant women—books that had already been compiled from searches in other Dutch libraries, in accordance with the program's collection-building efforts. By using them as reference material, I had a good view of what was available in other Dutch libraries. And if they were available in other libraries, why not at the IIAV?

I started by identifying which of the publications listed in these two books were available in the IIAV library. On the basis of that information, I analyzed the reasons some materials were not available. The preliminary conclusion is that the present policy does not cover some of the subjects, languages, periodicals, and countries of origin. In addition, some compilations that were in the IIAV library were not cataloged individually: a book with various subjects and authors was cataloged only by the general title, not by the individual titles and authors. This was one reason some Black authors were not in the catalog.

SURVEY OF FOREIGN DATABASES AND SOURCES   This part of the project is aimed at gathering information about relevant sources and databases in foreign libraries. I started by making a list of foreign libraries and writing them to get an insight into relevant sources and databases for collection building. Other reasons were to broaden our supply channels and to learn which systems, methods, and techniques of indexing or classifying are being used with regard to information on Black and migrant women.

SEARCH FOR GREY MATERIAL   Through the network of Black and migrant women that we have established, we want to get an insight on their grey publications and to acquire relevant publications so as to improve the IIAV collection in this area.

SURVEY OF BLACK/MIGRANT MAGAZINES IN DUTCH LIBRARIES   A search will be made in selected general Dutch libraries of the magazines that can be relevant to Black and migrant women, even if they are not women's magazines.

ACQUIRING ARCHIVES   We have started with a mailing to Black and migrant women's organizations to make them aware of the possibility of preserving their archives at the IIAV.

Indexing/Classifying

The main goal of the Information Services project is to make literature about Black and migrant women more visible in the IIAV catalog. The point of view of Black and migrant women is therefore very important.

This phase consists of adjusting the criteria for indexing and classifying magazine articles and, most important, adjusting our Dutch women's thesaurus. Through research and by developing adequate terms, we want to make the Dutch women's thesaurus useful for Black and migrant women's information as well.

Other activities, such as networking, public relations, and improving the expertise of IIAV personnel, are meant mainly to support the information service project.

Creating an Information Network for Women in Russia

Zoya Khotkina (Russia)

INTRODUCTION

The independent women's movement does not have a long history in Russia. Its beginnings are connected to *perestroika* (economic restructuring), part of Mikhail Gorbachev's three-part plan for creating a new, democratic Soviet Union.

Until 1990, only one official women's organization existed in the former Soviet Union, the Soviet Women's Committee (SWC). Its purpose was propaganda on the so-called benefits of socialism for women, not truthful information about the actual situation of women throughout the country. Speaking as a monopoly and substituting propaganda for information was typical not only of the SWC, but also of other social organizations under the totalitarian regime.

Beginning in 1990, women all over the country created and developed grass-roots women's organizations. Unfortunately, these organizations were largely unaware of each other, and hardly anyone knew about them. This is why information became one of the most important issues of the women's movement in Russia. The most important goals for the women's movement today are not merely an exchange of information within the movement but social visibility for women's problems.

The first step in this direction was establishment of the Women's Information Network (WINET), which was founded during the First Independent

Zoya Khotkina is senior researcher at the Moscow Center for Gender Studies, Institute for Socio-Economic Population Studies, Russian Academy of Sciences. She has a Ph.D. in economics and is founding Director of the first Russian women's archives; besides technical articles, she has published *How to Organize Your Home Business*.

141

Women's Forum in 1991. Since 1992 WINET has developed a database that now contains information about more than 1,500 women's organizations, initiatives, events, seminars, and women leaders.

The next step in creating an information network for women in Russia was the establishment in Moscow in 1993 of the Women's Information Project ADL (archive, database, library). ADL plays an important role in the development of information about and for women and in the establishment of new information technology as a basic tool of the contemporary Russian women's movement.

WOMEN'S INFORMATION PROJECT ADL

Women's Information Project ADL is a nongovernmental, nonprofit organization; it was founded in 1993 with a special three-year grant from the German women's organization Frau-Anstiftung upon the request of the Moscow Center for Gender Studies. The main goals of ADL are as follows:

- Organization of effective information for the women's movement and women's/gender studies in Russia
- Collection, storage, preservation, and cataloging of books, periodicals, and other materials and publications in the field of women's/gender studies
- Creation of a database containing information on women, women's organizations, and initiatives as well as on meetings and events related to the women's movement
- Inclusion of women's organizations and research centers in international and Russian networks
- Planning and implementation of seminars, courses, lectures, and training sessions for women and women's organizations

ADL funds are open to all women and men, participants in the women's movement in Russia and abroad, researchers and students working in the field of women's/gender issues, the mass media, and representatives of the state management bodies.

Within the framework of ADL are three projects: Women's Archive in Moscow (WAM), a database, and a library.

Women's Archive in Moscow

The first specialized archives on women in Russia is the Women's Archive in Moscow (WAM), founded in 1993. Its main goal is to document the history of the women's movement, creating documentary portraits of our contemporaries and reconstructing the history in which women will occupy a deserved place.

WAM's mission is aimed at collecting, storing, and cataloging as much material as possible depicting women's life, events, and activities and making this information accessible to everyone who is concerned about the women's movement. Its principles include openness for all women and men without exception, the inadmissibility of using any criteria when selecting donors of materials, and an orientation to writing biographies of our women contemporaries and depicting the history of the modern women's movement in Russia.

WAM has formed six record groups, eight collections, and an archive of photographs, and has made audio- and videocassettes. At present more than 2,000 documents, 72 audiocassettes, 4 videocassettes, and more than 150 photographs depicting the women's movement in both past and present Russia are stored in the archives. Beginning in 1993 the materials of all seminars, training sessions, conferences, and meetings organized on the basis of ADL, the Independent Women's Forum, and the Moscow Center for Gender Studies were being collected and processed for the archives.

In its literature, WAM solicits donations of personal letters, diaries, articles, photos, poems, stories and memoirs on audio- or videotape; of organizational records; and of regional women's periodicals, news clippings, and the like. WAM promises to acknowledge donations by a special stamp with the donor's name. It accepts exchange copies or photocopies of publications, buys them when necessary, and seeks information on forthcoming and on old books.

Database

The database CET (Zhiset) contains data on participants in the women's movement, organizations, and events, such as forums, conferences, seminars, initiatives, and so on. The system is simple and convenient to use. It is easy to display and print out information about leaders of women's organizations, participants in the events, themes, and so on.

Women's Information Project Library

The mission of the library is to accumulate knowledge through which women can become free, strong, and sure of themselves. The library collects literature based on feminist thought, which analyzes cultural stereotypes in different spheres of activity. The collection includes books on philosophy, history, culture, and religion, as well as fiction in which women and men are represented in unstereotypical ways. Literature on the women's movement and feminism is available in both Russian and English.

The library subscribes to Russian periodicals, especially those published by and for women. Special emphasis is on "informal" publications from women's NGOs, such titles as *Women Plus* (Moscow), *Women's Theme* (Kuzbass), and *Business Women Plus* (Yakutsk). It is beginning to collect books

related to problems of reproduction and women's health, and it includes literature on the problems of lesbians and other sexual minorities.

OTHER INDEPENDENT WOMEN'S ORGANIZATIONS

Women's Information Project ADL uses, processes, and further increases the
resources and materials of the Moscow Center for Gender Studies, Independent
Women's Forum, Women's Information Network (WINET), and other independent women's organizations in Russia. What follows is a brief description of
some of these organizations, which have played and continue to play an important role in the formation and development of an information network for
women in Russia.

Moscow Center for Gender Studies

The Moscow Center for Gender Studies (MCGS) appeared on the academic
scene when social transformation began to gather momentum and the symbolic
character of gender equality under socialism became evident. MCGS was
founded in April 1990 as a unit of the Institute for Socioeconomic Population
Studies of the U.S.S.R. Academy of Sciences. The first such institution in the
Soviet Union and in Russia, it is still one of a few. Its staff consists of fifteen
full-time and three part-time researchers. All except one hold Ph.D. degrees in
economics, history, psychology, or sociology and are experienced in fieldwork,
training, and communication.

Independent Women's Forum

Given the crisis in the state and in social politics, the independent women's movement has become an important factor in creating a democratic society. The Independent Women's Forum, the organization trying to solve this problem, was
founded in March 1991 when a group of women met in Dubna (a city near
Moscow) and called for action to be taken against all kinds of discrimination
against women in what was then the Soviet Union. This conference worked under
the slogan "Democracy without women is not democracy."

Women's Innovation Center East-West

The Women's Innovation Center East-West, a joint Russian-German project, is
working to introduce telecommunications technology into the women's movement. This center holds courses to teach women electronic technology and how
to work with on-line facilities. It has installed computer modems in five regional
women's centers, in Murmansk, Perm, Naberezhnie Chelny, and Ufa, as well as
in Moscow, and held a seminar to teach on-line functions to women from these

regional centers. This will enable the centers to hold an on-line teleconference on feminism and gender.

A NEW BEGINNING FOR RUSSIAN WOMEN

In a country where official ideologies perceived "the women's question" as having been solved, the empirical database on women has been extremely poor and in most cases falsified. The situation has worsened. A standard of statistical indicators for monitoring the situation in gender relations has been substantially reduced in recent years. The mission of the Russian independent women's movement is to start building a new information environment on women.

MCGS initiated the rise of new concepts and new realities for the women's movement. It gave birth to the idea of an Independent Women's Forum; within the framework of this forum, the Women's Information Network arose. Now this very network is playing a critical role in the development of the women's movement. A new information sphere has been formed that unites all the country's women's organizations and initiatives. This became possible thanks to the free exchange and circulation of information, which opened the door wide to the future for the women's movement in Russia. The next step will be the setting up of regional information centers in different towns of Russia and ensuring them electronic resources for information delivery. This process has begun.

The Francesca Bonnemaison Public Library

Anna Cabó (Spain)

In St. Anna's Parish in Barcelona in 1909 a women's group wanted to create a library for its own use. One member, Francesca Bonnemaison, had long intended to found a social service for young women, and she suggested forming a library for working women. The other women as well as the priest of St. Anna's accepted the idea. The intention of the library was to promote culture for and among women, and especially to improve the level of education of working women in order to help them obtain better jobs.

FRANCESCA BONNEMAISON

Francesca Bonnemaison was born in Barcelona in 1872, the only daughter of a bourgeois Catalán merchant family. As the wife of Narcis Verdaguer i Callis, a lawyer, intellectual, leading Catalán nationalist, poet, and magazine editor, Bonnemaison could only be a housewife and charity worker. But she had ideas about the role of women, which she disseminated in the Institut de Cultura i Biblioteca Popular de la Dona (Cultural Institute and Public Library for Women), founded a year after the library. Bonnemaison believed that the three essentials in a woman's life are an active *religion* (with emphasis on meditation and the study of Christian doctrine), cultivation of her *intelligence*, and *family*. The best thing

Anna Cabó qualified in librarianship at the University of Barcelona. She has worked for twelve years in public libraries services in Barcelona, eight of them at the Francesca Bonnemaison Public Library.

147

for a woman was to be a wife, mother, daughter, and housewife. Religion and education would make women better wives and mothers.

THE FOUNDING OF THE LIBRARY

The library began with a donation of 100 books and 500 pesetas by the priest of St. Anna's. Bonnemaison and her colleagues contributed books or money and asked friends and other like-minded people for help. The library first opened its doors in March 1909, proclaiming "Free entry for all women." It opened on Sundays and holidays to make use easier for working women. Donations continued over the years, and the library twice moved to larger quarters.

Organization

The Cultural Institute and Public Library for Women had a board of directors with Bonnemaison as president. The school had numerous subject sections, among them Religion, Education, Work, and Library. Each section was directed by a committee and a president; the only contact among sections was through President Bonnemaison.

The institute was supported by donations and student fees. There were common and "protector" members; the latter paid ten times the dues of the former. All members could use the library's bibliographic and lending services, but common members could use the loan service only on Sundays and holidays, while "protectors" could use it every day. Those who were not students of the institute could use the library but not borrow books. This is reflected in the organization of the library, which had two parts: Biblioteca Circulant (Lending Library): literature and nonfiction books for home use; and Biblioteca Pública (Public Library), also called "Study Library" or "Pedagogic Library." This was a reference library with more specialized books than those of the Lending Library.

History

This was the organization of the library and the institute until the Civil War broke out in 1936. (Because of her political ideas, Francesca Bonnemaison was forced into exile and the institute closed. She returned to Barcelona in 1947, two years before her death.) For a short time in 1937 the library came under the control of the Public Library Network of the State Government of Catalonia, and was renamed the "Professional Library for Women." When the Civil War ended in 1939, the library was absorbed by the Public Library Network of the Provincial Government of Barcelona, under whose control it remains today. It was named "Biblioteca de la Mujer" (Women's Library), now in Spanish rather than Catalán, due to Francisco Franco's repression of minority languages.

In 1942 the school building was occupied by a school for women but with Spanish culture and Falange ideology, almost fascism, called Sección Femenina de Falange Española (Women's Section of the Spanish Falange). The library, however, now independent of the school, had reopened in September 1940 after the obligatory "cleansing" carried out in all libraries when Franco's dictatorship began: removing all books in Catalán or about the movement for Catalán autonomy or ideologies opposed to Franco's ideas. Some libraries' books were destroyed, but the Bonnemaison books were kept in a depository until the 1980s, when they were reincorporated into the library. Until 1963, the library was public but mainly for women; after 1963 it accepted everybody, without sex discrimination.

Library Resources

A library index published in 1909 shows that it had 676 volumes, 51 percent of them novels. The first idea was to create a literary library, but this priority changed with time. Books about religion made up 22 percent, reflecting the fact that the library was created in a Catholic parish. Social sciences (6 percent) included feminism and work, but also housekeeping and education for women and children. The library provided books necessary for the institute's students, who studied languages (Catalán, Spanish, French, English, and German), shorthand, geography, physical education, needlework, dressmaking, history, economics, cooking, and other subjects.

The periodicals collection was, along with reference, the most widely consulted section. It included newspapers and magazines from different countries: magazines about fashion (from France, Spain, Great Britain, and the U.S.A.), feminism, religion, cooking, geography, literature, and so on.

Library resources were sustained by donations of books or money, many due to Bonnemaison's connections among the bourgeoisie, intellectuals, and publishers. Requests for purchases came from teachers, librarians, members of the Committee of the Library Section, and readers, for whom there was a "Request book" in the library. The committee strictly determined the suitability of each purchase and each donation. Between 1922 and 1935, the library added 12,712 volumes (978 a year): 57 percent donated, 42.4 percent purchased, and 0.6 percent through exchange. During Franco's time, the library barely grew. At the end of 1936 there were 23,226 volumes, and at the end of 1975, 32,752, an increase of only 244 volumes a year.

Control of Reading

Beginning in 1922, the committee had an increasing preoccupation with the amount of fiction that students and other users read and hence introduced strict selection criteria for novels. It also removed some titles that had been on the shelves but were now considered to have "little literary value or a dubious moral message." As a result of this preoccupation, in 1925 the "Lectures dirigides" (guided readings) were begun. Groups of readers were organized, each with a list of books in accordance with reading level and age. In a given period, readers would read the books on the list, fill out a questionnaire for each book, and list the titles in order of preference. At the end of the time, each group met with a committee member and everyone voiced an opinion about the readings. Later, the library rewarded participants by presenting each with a book.

FRANCESCA BONNEMAISON PUBLIC LIBRARY

Since the re-establishment of democracy in 1975, the Provincial Government of Barcelona has been modernizing the Public Library Network. In 1976 the library was renamed for its founder. With modern resources characteristic of a public library in a large city, it serves a wide variety of people, from children and students to housewives and retired people. It has 44,000 volumes and more than 275 periodical titles. Because of its history, the library has some special holdings not common in a public library. The following five areas are prominent and popular at this library:

FASHION AND NEEDLEWORK   Both old and new books, and magazines from 1860 onward are used by fashion students and designers, and people in charge of costumes in theater or cinema.

COOKING   Books in several languages about gastronomy from different cultures, Spanish magazines, and some unpublished manuscripts are used by students of cooking and nutrition, and lovers of fine food.

WOMEN   This large section on education, feminism, morality, housekeeping, and other subjects contains books, magazines, and documents from various countries, especially in Europe. It serves researchers on women and everyday life from 1850 onward, and also on the women's movement in Catalonia, 1900–36.

NOVELS   Researchers of women or of fiction find numerous novels in Catalán, Spanish, French, English, and German, including novels for teenagers and many popular novels with little literary value.

ARCHIVE OF THE CULTURAL INSTITUTE AND WOMEN'S LIBRARY   The library has most of the archive; the rest is in the Arxiu Historic de la Ciutat de Barcelona. We add any new publications about the Cultural Institute. Historians of women and education in Catalonia between 1909 and 1936 use this section.

The Women's History Collections

A Documentation Center Integrated into a University Library

Helena Wedborn (Sweden)

INTRODUCTION

The first generation of European women's archives and libraries was founded during the struggle for suffrage by members of the women's rights movement in the first part of this century. The second generation came into being well after World War II, when women's studies were emerging at European universities, although the term *women's studies* was not generally accepted in the Nordic countries until much later.

Within this tradition, a distinct Scandinavian model emerged. Although founded in collaboration with important academic libraries, the Nordic women's documentation units were at the same time created as a deliberate protest against these libraries: in opposition to mainstream acquisition policies, which tended to be extremely male-centered, as well as in opposition to the gender-blind classification systems that made information on women invisible.

Helena Wedborn has studied at universities in Scotland and France and in Sweden at Stockholm and Gothenburg, where she graduated in 1972. She studied library and information science in Oslo, Norway, and worked there as a librarian before joining Gothenburg University Library, where she has been Director of the Women's History Collections since 1988. In 1987 she was Visiting Librarian at Stanford University. As of 1995, she is in Linköping, at the Centre for Women's Studies and the University Library. Her publications in English include a quarterly bibliography, *New Literature on Women*, issued at Gothenburg, which she edited 1988–94; and "Nordic Women's Studies Centres," in *Nora: Nordic Journal of Women's Studies* 1 (1993): 2, pp. 125–130.

THE WOMEN'S HISTORY COLLECTIONS

The Beginnings

In Sweden, a women's archives was founded as a private initiative in 1958. The aim was threefold: to collect manuscripts and archives documenting the Swedish women's movement; to support scholarship on women by publishing research reports and dissertations on women's history for a wider market; to collect and catalog literature on women and to index it in such a way as to make gender aspects manifest. The work of the founders of this women's archives was truly pioneering, as in 1958 the idea of "supporting scholarship on women" was unheard of, with no such phenomenon existing officially in academe at the time.

A decade later, after some effective lobbying in the Swedish Parliament by members of the then powerful women's liberation movement, this private archives was declared to constitute the beginnings of Sweden's National Documentation Centre on Literature on Women. Its collections were transferred to the Gothenburg University Library, where two of the founders were employed, and where the archives consequently became state property. The government granted the money to employ a curator of the Women's History Collections (WHC), as it was then named. The center was—and is—organized as an integral part of the university library, and its operations are funded by both the University of Gothenburg and the Ministry of Education in Stockholm. Currently the staff numbers 3.5 full-time employees.

As the name indicates, during the first period in the life of the center the overall subject was history. The subject area of the WHC has gradually widened, and for many years it has been a documentation center for multidisciplinary women's studies. We have kept the original name for the sake of tradition, although today it is a bit misleading.

Present Activities

Present activities show how integration into a parent institution functions in everyday work. The purpose of the WHC is to facilitate study and research into the terms and conditions governing women's lives historically and in contemporary times.

Looking back at the original goals of the founders, we no longer support scholarship on women by publishing research reports or dissertations; nowadays publishing houses know that there is money to be made on textbooks in women's studies, and numerous gender-related books come onto the market every month. So we concentrate our resources on the two remaining original goals: compiling bibliographies and collecting manuscripts and archives on and of the women's movement.

The Archives

The most important files in our collections date from the early part of this century—from the time of the struggle for suffrage and other civil rights. The documents include manuscripts of Swedish suffragists and archives of pioneering associations of professional women. Not all the documents reflect feminist attitudes; many interesting files mirror women's activities in such nonmilitant areas as charity organizations, literary study circles, or art clubs. The manuscripts show that the Swedish women's movement has a long tradition of international cooperation, most notably with the Women's International League for Peace and Freedom (WILPF). Also worth mentioning are international contacts with members of the Society of Friends.

New Literature on Women

A current bibliography has been published regularly since the WHC began in the late 1950s. *New Literature on Women: A Bibliography*, in Swedish and English, is published four times a year and has approximately 1,000 references in each issue. This bibliography can be found on the shelves of many general and women's research institutions and libraries in Scandinavia and elsewhere, even in the United States.

The KVINNSAM Database

During the last decade, 35,000 references have been accumulated in a separate on-line database called KVINNSAM, from the Swedish name of the Women's History Collections (KVINNohistoriska SAMlingarna). The database is updated quarterly. KVINNSAM is available to the public via LIBRIS (LIBRary Information System of Sweden), the Swedish national union catalog for research libraries, and is accessible at no extra charge. All items cataloged, including manuscripts and archives, are available on interlibrary loan from Gothenburg University Library.

Each of the 35,000 items in the database has three specific qualities. First, all are gender-related; second, no indexing is done from commercial catalogs, MARC, or BNB (British National Bibliography) records (i.e., every item is actually examined by the indexer); third, all items can be obtained on interlibrary loan from a single library, at Gothenburg University.

INDEXING

Scope

The quality of the database, of the current bibliography, and of the card catalog (now frozen) depends on the quality of the previous indexing. What literature is indexed, and how is it done? In our case, the area of interest is cross-disciplinary, but the acquisitions in the humanities and the social sciences of the Gothenburg University Library constitute the basis of the indexing at the WHC.

All documents acquired by the central library are studied with a view to highlighting texts relevant to women. All the books in women's studies are of course included, as well as articles from a large number of women's studies journals. But—and here is one essential characteristic—"all documents" also means that many books that might not immediately appear to be relevant are examined, and if one or several chapters are found to be of interest to women's research, they are examined and indexed separately. For example, *Portraits in Steel*, a book published in 1993, does not at first sight seem to be of interest to gender studies, but on examination, we found a chapter called "Women in Big Steel," which contains interviews with female industrial workers in male-dominated occupations.

All new periodicals, however irrelevant they might at first seem, are searched for gender-related articles. This means that many issues of (to take just one example) the journal *Written Communication* may be examined in vain, until one suddenly stumbles across a relevant article, "Technical Writing for Women of the English Renaissance," published in issue 2 of 1993.

Keywords

The texts are indexed according to both English and Swedish keywords. The keywords are set in a list established over many years and expanded when required. The gender aspect is implicit; the keyword *journalists* implies female journalists, *Middle Ages* refers to women's lives in medieval times, *urban planning* implies a women's perspective or perhaps the absence of it, and so on. A document may be cataloged with the aid of an unlimited number of keywords, but only the five most central ones are included in the printed bibliography.

It is worth noting that, although in the rest of Europe big thesaurus projects have been initiated to cover all aspects of gender studies, we find that a simple alphabetical list of keywords is satisfactory. We share this belief with other centers in the North; this may be one characteristic of the Scandinavian model.

Languages and Types of Documents

The dominant language is English, which accounts for 63 percent of all references; the rest is in Scandinavian and other Western European languages. Of course, the dominance of the English language makes for a general accessibility that is essential to the international interest in *New Literature on Women* and the KVINNSAM database. Of the references, 63 percent apply to journal articles, 17 percent to entire works (monographs, reports, brochures), and roughly the same proportion to chapters in books.

INTEGRATION OR INDEPENDENCE?

The issue here is to assess the phenomenon of integration in a university library in contrast with the fundamentally opposite way of doing things: namely, the establishment of a separate and independent institution.

Premises

The Women's History Collections constitutes a library within a library. We are physically located inside the central library at the University of Gothenburg, with a separate reading room, including a reference and bibliography collection, on-line and card catalogs, open stacks for books and journals, news clippings, and so forth.

Many of our users are critical of the fact that our reading room is not in a separate building; they feel disturbed by the presence of people not concerned with gender studies. The advantage as far as integration of space goes is that the central library has decidedly more generous opening hours than would be possible with any other arrangement. The facilities are available to all, even at hours when no one from the staff of the WHC is on duty. Integration also works to our benefit in that every university library reference librarian is able to assist our users—with searches in the KVINNSAM database, for example.

Holdings

All the indexed documents are acquired and cataloged by the central library. A small part of the holdings is shelved in open stacks at the WHC. The entire holdings of the central library, which collects in the arts, humanities, and social sciences, constitute the basis for our bibliographical endeavors. As described above, we practice a method of indexing in depth, whereby a great number of scholarly periodicals and books in a variety of academic disciplines are searched for relevant articles or chapters. Had the WHC been a separate institution, it is unlikely that there would have been the same potential for working with such a wide variety of disciplines and documents. Then again, if the WHC had been on its own, there would have been a total concentration on research on women, and there would not have been male-centered acquisitions or gender-blind classification and shelving to waste our time.

Information-Retrieval Guidance

In a documentation center, the user has the right to expect not only information on collections available at the center but also skilled help to retrieve relevant material wherever it is to be found. Advanced information retrieval demands, apart from professional personnel, expensive and sometimes rare bibliographic tools. It is more realistic to look for all this in a documentation unit integrated into a larger research library than in one that relies entirely on its own resources.

A subject such as women's studies, comparatively new on the academic scene and of a distinctly interdisciplinary nature, cannot be self-reliant in terms of information retrieval. There simply are no special abstracting services that cover such an interdiscipinary array of fields potentially relevant to gender studies. And no on-line database reaches as far into the past as is necessary to trace the hidden history of women. All advanced research on women must therefore go beyond the subject's own bibliographical facilities and use information-retrieval tools from other disciplines. This is yet another reason why it may be wise to integrate a women's documentation center into a large research library.

The "Double Strategy"

The network of feminist scholars in the Scandinavian countries has adopted the policy of the "double strategy." This means *both* integration and independence. Gender studies must be integrated into all academic disciplines, must be a natural perspective of every subject field. But gender or women's studies must also be established as a discipline in its own right, with specific curricula, teaching positions, research grants, and an academic career path of its own.

Documentation in women's studies should also work along the lines of the double strategy. It must be an independent, specific subject for information retrieval, with its own thesauri or lists of keywords, and specific databases, bibliographies, directories, and electronic conferences. In its effort to identify information on women in history and gender-related literature wherever it is to be found, women's studies must also benefit from the entire field of information and documentation in other disciplines.

CONCLUSION

An independent women's studies documentation center, furnished with old and new literature, with all relevant reference and bibliographic tools and the latest information technology, and managed by special librarians and documentalists, is a dream come true in only a few places around the world. In most instances, women's studies libraries have meager funding and are forced to economize. I believe that a good way of making the most of existing resources is to integrate a women's documentation center into a large, modern research library, utilizing its expertise, literature holdings, information technology, interlibrary loan facilities, and general service to the public. In times of budget reductions, a small documentation center is less exposed to funding cuts if it does not rely only on its own collections and staff.

On the negative side, with an integrated documentation unit you cannot have premises admitting women only, you cannot collect women-specific types of documents exclusively, and you will have to tolerate gender-blind subject headings and classifications. The primary reason not to establish an independent center is financial. You get longer opening hours, more professional librarians, more information technology, and more literature for the same amount of money, and thus you can use your resources better for research on women. A second reason is that integration means easy access for many user groups that would not otherwise come to the women's studies unit.

Although speaking for integration, I wish to underline that a documentation center should proudly maintain the character of a special department with specific knowledge of and service to women's studies. As such, it is a most valuable component of its parent institution, which in turn will benefit from its expertise and public recognition.

Bridging the Gap Between Women's Studies and Grass-Roots Feminism

Jenny Collieson and Beth Follini (United Kingdom)

INTRODUCTION

The Women's Research and Resource Centre (WRRC)—as the Feminist Library was originally called—opened near the University of London in 1975. Initially the center's purposes were to maintain a register of current research on women, provide a support and contact network for women engaged in research, and disseminate the results of research through seminars, publications, and a quarterly newsletter. The group also published a directory of women's studies courses throughout the country in 1981. The final stated aim of the WRRC was the establishment of a library to collect the increasing quantities of printed material emanating from the women's liberation movement, most of which was in either periodical or ephemeral form and was not being collected by other libraries. Within a year, however, in answer to the demands of those doing feminist research, this subsidiary aim had become the main focus of the center's work. Researchers realized that the collection and development of resource materials were critical for the future of women's studies.

Jenny Collieson has been a member of the Feminist Library management collective since 1988, when she qualified as a librarian. She currently holds the post of Assistant Librarian for Health Studies and Social Work at the University of North London. **Beth Follini** has been a Feminist Library collective member for the past three years. She is active in feminist, lesbian, gay, and socialist politics and has recently completed an M.A. in Women's Studies at the University of Kent.

159

SERVICES

Today the Feminist Library (FL) is open three days a week and provides more than 10,000 books (most of which are available for loan); 1,500 journal titles, pamphlets, and research papers that may be consulted on site; and an information service handling approximately 100 inquiries a week from all over the United Kingdom. In addition, the library offers training for volunteers and work experience in a range of office and library skills, educational courses run in conjunction with London University, a weekly feminist discussion group, readings, publishing events, and a quarterly newsletter that is sent to 1,000 individuals and women's groups worldwide.

FL is the largest contemporary feminist resource and information center in Great Britain. Its collections complement those held by the country's two other major libraries devoted to women and gender, the Fawcett Library in London and the Equal Opportunities Commission Library in Manchester. Its collections also compare favorably with similar women's collections in other European cities. For the past six years, however, the Feminist Library has survived without public funding and has been maintained entirely by volunteers.

PROBLEMS WITH FUNDING

Funding difficulties are especially acute for a library with a strong feminist profile and a commitment to remaining independent. FL shares common features with many other feminist voluntary organizations in Great Britain, both in ethos and structure and in the problems of raising the funds necessary to safeguard its continued existence. Becoming a registered charity, which the library achieved in 1979, does bring financial benefits, although there can be disadvantages in the political sphere, in that the archives of charities are required to be strictly educational and not aligned with any political campaigns or movements. Charitable income too is essentially limited, especially for organizations like the library that suffer from a lack of fund-raising expertise and must compete with larger charities with a wider scope.

In the 1980s, FL benefited from the financial support of the Greater London Council (GLC), which in 1984 gave grants to London-based women's organizations totaling £8 million. However, the abolition of the GLC in 1986 left the library and other women's organizations extremely vulnerable. The general public suspicion of feminism and ignorance of the valuable work many women's organizations undertake have been exacerbated by hostile media and perpetuated by the conservative backlash in national politics, which does not appear to be diminishing. FL has spent much of the past twenty years existing at the subsistence level, dependent on membership subscriptions, donations, and the occasional one-time grant. It is currently maintained on an annual income of £7,000 to cover the production of the newsletter and all running costs.

In practical terms, lack of funding affects FL in three main areas: accommodations, staffing, and collection development.

Accommodations

FL is now in its fifth home since 1975 and was threatened with loss of its present quarters in 1993, when its lease expired and the nominal rent was raised to current market value. However, a grant from Southwark Council (Southwark being the borough in which the library is located) enabled the library to cover the rent increase and negotiate a new lease.

Staffing

Since the loss of funding in 1988, FL has been dependent on the energy and commitment of its volunteer work force, most of whom are either employed full time or studying. At present it has a pool of about forty volunteers recruited through women's centers, advertisements, volunteer bureaus, and word of mouth. This obviously affects the range of services the library can offer and also determines whether it is able to maintain its advertised hours of operation. Dependence on volunteer labor is obviously unsatisfactory insofar as the provision of a service is concerned, but there are positive aspects in that many volunteers feel empowered by their involvement in running FL, and for several who were unemployed FL volunteer work led to paid employment.

In "What Is Feminist Library Policy?" a 1992 study of FL's organizational structure (and an M.A. thesis at Sheffield University), Hilary Sayers commented that "the informal, nonhierarchical structure and atmosphere of the Feminist Library was seen as very important and welcomed by all volunteers . . . . It is seen as essential to the Library's purpose and to running the Library in the interests of women."

Collection Development

Since its inception FL has demonstrated considerable and sustained growth, but the collection has a very different character from that first envisaged by the founders of the WRRC. At that time the emphasis was on collecting research papers, newsletters, and ephemera. Although these remain important, the books now form the most substantial part of the collection. The nonfiction stock, which focuses mainly on European and American feminism from 1968 on, has expanded in recent years to include much more material on women's lives worldwide and is complemented by a large fiction section of works by women writers. This reflects FL's shift toward meeting the demands of a wider readership and away from a narrow academic focus.

With the exception of some money allocated for book purchase in the mid-1980s, the bulk of the collection has been acquired through donation: review copies from publishers and material given by private individuals. FL has been fortunate in benefiting from the support of most of the United Kingdom's mainstream publishers with women's studies lists and, of course, the smaller feminist presses. Continued publication of the quarterly newsletter is of special importance in this respect, both as a means of publicizing new books through reviews and as a publication in its own right that is exchanged for other journals to which the library cannot afford to subscribe.

Obviously, dependence on donations creates difficulties in developing a coherent collections policy. At present the main criteria for requesting and accepting materials are that they concern some aspect of contemporary feminism worldwide and reflect the library's equal opportunities policy of promoting materials on traditionally marginalized women.

Possible Solution

One possible solution to the problem of operating in an atmosphere of perpetual insecurity might be to become part of a larger institution. FL's collections are obviously attractive to academic institutions that offer courses in women's studies. Since its funding was withdrawn it has received several offers from universities and colleges interested in housing its material. Despite the prospect of more secure accommodation, paid staff, more resources for collection development, and greater prestige, the library's management collective has always been very reluctant to pursue this option, seeing it as only a last resort if FL were in danger of being dispersed. The collective is committed to the library as a feminist organization with an agenda that goes beyond the provision of a library and information service. It seems unlikely that FL could retain its particular structure and ethos if it were to become part of a much larger academic library.

One principal objective of FL over the past decade has been to make it accessible to women from traditionally marginalized groups: women of color, Irish women, Jewish women, lesbians, older women, and women with disabilities. Merger with a larger institution would undoubtedly limit access both in principle and in practice and would likely result in the library's becoming inaccessible to many of its current users.

FEMINIST PERSPECTIVE

Over the past decade FL has developed a more explicitly political profile. In its first annual report, published in 1976, the WRRC's management collective stated that its political commitment to the women's liberation movement did not extend beyond "the expansion of education, information and research into areas which although of importance to women have often been ignored by traditional education." At that time the center was open to all those interested in using its facilities, although membership in the collective was limited to women. As with the early British women's liberation movement, most members were socialist, university-educated, middle-class women, and the center's initial development reflected their concerns, which were essentially academic.

Women-Only Policy

In 1983 WRRC adopted a new name—the Feminist Library and Information Centre—which, it was felt, better reflected its functions and services. The name change also signaled a desire to become more explicitly feminist in profile, boosted by the support and recognition of the GLC Women's Committee. In 1991 the management collective, in consultation with the membership, decided to make the library a women-only space. Although in the past few men had used the library, the adoption of a women-only policy was a political step that placed the library firmly in a radical context and indicates that its frame of reference is feminism rather than librarianship.

Classification Scheme

Such an identification ensures that FL policies and practice differ markedly from those of mainstream libraries. One example of this orientation is the Feminist Library classification scheme, which takes women as the primary point of reference and reflects a feminist viewpoint. The next major tasks facing the library—should funding become available—are revision of the classification scheme and computerization of the catalog, since it is evident that much of the library's stock is currently vastly underexploited.

Management Collective

This commitment to accessibility also underlies FL's organizational and management structure. The library is administered by a voluntary collective that is open to all women willing to commit themselves to attending fortnightly meetings and to taking some responsibility for library business. The role of the collective has necessarily changed since 1988, when paid workers had to be let go, and it is now forced to spend most of its time on routine library business, which leaves little time for formal policy making.

USER SURVEYS

A recent survey by Helen Jones (for her M.A. thesis for Sheffield University, "The Feminist Library: A User Survey," 1992) revealed that the women using the library's services consider it to be a unique resource holding a concentration of feminist material not easily available elsewhere. The majority of those interviewed preferred FL because of its holdings and the fact that it is a women-only resource organized from a women-centered perspective.

Most users were strongly in favor of FL's women-only access policy because it facilitates a comfortable environment in which to study, network, and socialize. The policy aroused much debate among members, however, reflecting the different ideological viewpoints within feminism and contrasting views of FL's essential role. Some feel that it is important for men's education that they have access to the materials. For others, this raises the question of male access to sensitive materials, including contact numbers for groups and individuals on the noticeboards. Some volunteers, although personally supportive of the policy, see adherence to it as placing the library perpetually on the margins and alienating potential funders. While this has to be acknowledged, it is evident that for most users, having a women-only space at a time when such spaces are under increasing threat gives it a special atmosphere that is much appreciated.

OUTREACH AND NETWORKING

Many FL volunteers are active in a wide range of feminist activities, groups, and campaigns; they bring their knowledge and experience into the library while simultaneously publicizing the library and its work to women who may not know of it. This is important because of the danger that always exists when women's studies become institutionalized and academic feminism becomes distanced from grass-roots movements. The library has an active presence in the community, marching with its own banner at Gay Pride events, supporting other feminist groups and campaigns, attending conferences, and hosting book promotion events and its own weekly discussion group.

The collective intends to reach out in two specific ways: (1) to continue to broaden the membership base so that it reflects the diversity of women in the community, and (2) to build stronger links with other women's libraries and information providers both nationally and internationally. At present FL is part of an informal network of resources for women that includes the Fawcett and Equal Opportunities Commission libraries, and smaller organizations such as the Women's International Resource Centre, the Feminist Archive, and the Lesbian Archive. The majority of these centers also exist on shoestring budgets, making resource sharing and cooperative schemes difficult to organize. The links established so far are based on referral of users and personal contacts. There is a real need to develop more formal links among mainstream and alternative women's studies libraries, ideally under an umbrella organization that could serve as a focal point for all those working in the field.

CIDHAL's Documentation Center

Helping to Build Feminism in Mexico

Rocío Suárez-López and Leopoldina Rendón Pineda (Mexico)

INTRODUCTION

CIDHAL (Communication, Exchange, and Human Development in Latin America) Women's Center in Cuernavaca, Mexico, began its work in 1969. We are the oldest women's organization in the country. We began by setting up a documentation center to translate and disseminate information about women's issues and to organize seminars and conferences on feminist themes. Our overall aim has always been to contribute to the growth and development in all spheres of women's lives: from personal and family to social and political. We work from a feminist perspective, taking gender, class, and ethnicity into account.

CIDHAL'S ACTIVITIES

In 1977 we began to work directly with women in poor rural and urban communities, trying to respond to the women's basic needs and demands. Along with

Feminist sociologist **Rocío Suárez-López** has for the last ten years represented CIDHAL to the mass media, defining the problems of Mexican women and proposed feminist solutions. She is a member of CIDHAL's board of directors, has lectured on women's issues, and has published newspaper articles on women's issues and an essay about women's NGOs in Mexico. **Leopoldina Rendón Pineda** is Technical Coordinator at the CIDHAL Documentation Center. For twenty-three years, she has managed and counseled libraries at Mexico's main academic institutions and recently has focused on organizing and automating women's documentation centers in Mexico and Central America. She has published articles on electronic networking, documentation centers for women, and the use of documentary information in scientific research.

other organizations, we were involved in women's consciousness raising and in leadership development among women's grass-roots organizations. Since 1979, our activities have developed in three main areas. First, we provide medical services for women and infants, as well as workshops on women's health issues. Second, we have continued to develop our information and documentation center. Third, we have a program of education and organization for women, giving priority to training and supporting the autonomous organization of women in the workplace and other social settings that reflect women's interests. We challenge public policies that affect women's lives and provide information to influence policy.

CIDHAL's Mission

We have recently redefined our mission as follows:

> We are a multidisciplinary group of women who form a feminist institution, a part of the civil society with a pluralistic, democratic, and autonomous nature with a long history. Our utopian ideal is to achieve the full and harmonious realization of women, that we may become the protagonist of our own life. We thus offer comprehensive health services, documentary information dissemination, and education for women in general and specifically for underpriviledged women from urban and rural settings. In addition, we coordinate with other groups, we propose public policies that may eliminate gender, class, and ethnic inequalities, and we work toward the achievement of the full development of human beings in harmony with the cosmos. We consider ourselves to be agents who promote and encourage change and not actors who only give support or act as intermediaries.

We focus our work on four specific issues affecting women: the feminization of rural poverty; ecological damage; women's health, particularly reproductive health; and communication and information. Each of these issues has been made into an operative program. Each program provides services, training, network organization or participation, and research and dissemination of information.

The Documentation Center

Originally the primary purpose of our documentation center was to fill the existing gap in documented information about the condition of Latin American women. From the start in 1977, we have kept in mind the importance of

- Maintaining documentation with easy access for the public
- Providing basic orientation about areas of interest to the public
- Developing book and document bibliographies in Spanish
- Increasing materials for the files
- Translating basic materials
- Promoting the services of the documentation center

Since 1979, the documentation center has focused on organizing materials, as well as on increasing acquisitions. This work was originally done without qualified librarians.

The documentation center has continued with its work and publications, despite financial problems and lack of resources and staff. In 1990, the center received funding from the Ford Foundation for computer equipment, which we have used to automate the collection. Today we have two reference databases: one for periodicals and the other for books, memoirs, theses, papers, and audiovisual material. Our data bank has about 5,000 references, mainly on violence against women, abortion, prostitution, population, and reproductive health.

Establishing a network of documentation centers is of the highest priority, and we have had several meetings in Mexico and Central America with this goal in mind.

The development of CIDHAL has been financially supported by European and Canadian NGOs and ecumenical communities such as Novib in Holland, Bread for the World, Peace and Development, and Solidarity, as well as such North American foundations as Ford and MacArthur. Today there are two problems with this source of support: one is the recession, and the other is a change in the priorities of the foundations, which are now funding projects in Africa and Eastern Europe rather than Latin America. These changes are drastically reducing contributions and are endangering the continuation of the programs we have developed.

Together we need to find new ways to continue building and strengthening feminism at the global level.

Getting the Word Out
Disseminating Information on, by, and for Women in Peru

Mariella Sala (Peru)

INTRODUCTION

The work of the Centro de la Mujer Peruana Flora Tristán from its inception in 1983 has been to create a means of communicating ideas, debates, and proposals of the feminist movement through the mass media. The intent has been to communicate with women directly. Diverse media and strategies have been used to achieve this goal, including radio and television interviews, a magazine, and brochures.

CHANGING ATTITUDES AND LAWS THROUGH INFORMATION

Since 1983, public attitudes toward violence against women have changed. Together, the Centro Flora Tristán (CFT) and the feminist movement have made visible problems that previously no one seemed to see: exploitation of domestic workers, sexual harassment in the work place, domestic violence, and rape. There are now laws in Peru against domestic violence, and rape is considered a crime.

Mariella Sala is in charge of the publishing fund at the Centro Flora Tristán de la Mujer Peruana (Peruvian Women's Center) in Lima. She is also president of the Feminist Radio Consortium, a member of the board of directors of the World Organization for Rights, Literature and Development, and a correspondent for *Fempress*.

169

WAYS OF DISSEMINATING INFORMATION

The provision of information to the public was instrumental in bringing about these changes.

THE MAGAZINE *VIVA*   In 1984 CFT decided to publish a magazine about the feminist movement in Peru and the activities of women. Nineteen issues of *Viva* appeared before publication ceased in 1991. They included information on feminist campaigns and debates in Peru and elsewhere during that period.

RADIO PROGRAM   In October 1988 the radio program "Cortocircuito" was born. Just as *Viva* was the first feminist magazine published in Peru, "Cortocircuito" was the first feminist radio program, the first to talk to women as individuals, not merely as wives or mothers.

LIBRARY   CFT has also been building a library to gather information and provide it to the mainstream media. At first the library was used primarily by those in CFT as a practical tool for feminist training in women's grass-roots organization in poor urban neighborhoods. Its main purposes were the collection and preservation of information and documents.

In 1984, the library opened to the public; as the first feminist library in Peru, it was named for the Peruvian feminist and writer Magda Portál.

By 1994 the library had 5,000 books in three languages: Spanish, English, and French. The books cover many topics related to women and come from the literature of social science. An ancillary collection not specifically about women provides background reference material for studies on women. The library is now computerized and is trying to connect with women's information networks throughout Latin America and the rest of the world.

Four hundred readers a month visit the library, 90 percent from universities. Many students research theses on social problems from a gendered perspective. Other users are journalists investigating stories on women's issues.

The library serves as a place of connection for women wanting to know more about feminist activities. This function, along with providing information to journalists, fills a fundamental role in the orientation and education of people about gender issues.

PUBLISHING FUND   CFT is now focusing its efforts on the establishment of a publishing fund. The objectives are to publish women's writing and to centralize women's publications, so as to foster, rescue, and distribute writing on and by women.

The publishing fund is developing the following activities: (1) publishing scholarly research in women's history, violence against women, and other areas; (2) publishing records of CFT's work in the community; (3) publishing the work of women who lack financial support; (4) conducting a short story contest and printing winning entries in an anthology; (5) preparing dossiers on special topics for journalists; and (6) publishing "Nuestra Historia" ("Our History"), a series of brief biographies about important women in feminist history, to be distributed in the schools.

In 1993, books published by CFT were introduced to the mainstream market. They are now available in bookstores throughout Peru.

FEMINIST BROADCASTING NETWORK CFT has affiliated with four feminist institutions in Peru to begin a feminist broadcasting network that will have its own radio station. Its purpose is to provide women with information in a way that will help them feel connected to the great political issues of our time.

PART III

Information for Information Workers

Mariétou Diongue Diop (left) training newly literate women who will manage the Caytu village library in Senegal.

Like the term *information, information worker* is a useful bit of shorthand, encompassing librarians, archivists, statisticians, automation experts, oral historians, and all others who do information work.

Jacquelyn Marie's article raises many basic questions that anyone thinking of starting a women's library needs to consider, while Hur-Li Lee investigates issues that arise when libraries collect in an interdisciplinary field. Questions she raises are echoed in Marilyn Grotzky's experiences with library instruction in the same interdisciplinary field: women's studies.

The next two articles concern archives. One reports on a very practical matter: a preservation survey at The Fawcett Library. The other is more theoretical, considering the implications of women's papers being more or less hidden in traditional repositories. Several articles in Part II (e.g., Dickel and Mevis) also discuss women's archival collections.

Marieke Kramer explains a somewhat controversial women's thesaurus developed in the Netherlands. At least one article in Part II, that by T. S. S. Lakshmi, includes a description of a locally developed classification scheme that may be applicable in other libraries. Luciana Tufani's article briefly discusses descriptive terminology in the context of a developing information network linking women's libraries in Italy and elsewhere.

This brings us to two further articles on automation, specifically on the use of the Internet for women's studies information and as an organizing tool for activist organizations.

Setting Up a Women's Studies Library

Jacquelyn Marie (U.S.A.)

In this era of growing interest in and enthusiasm about women's issues, women's studies are of primary importance in higher education. Women's studies scholars often lobby for the development of a center to disseminate information on women's studies courses or to encourage professors to teach such courses. The fledgling center often needs a board or committee to discuss the options: perhaps it will be a women's center at a university that will also be open to community women and their needs as well as to scholars; perhaps it will be a center affiliated with a women's studies or gender studies program and open only to scholars.

Soon after such a center (whether academic or community or both) opens, people start bringing in books and materials from their personal libraries; faculty bring in papers, reports, and journal articles; others bring in bibliographies; and fliers and announcements of events of interest to women appear in the mail. Unfortunately, the center is often unprepared for this influx of materials. It may have been set up with no intention of having a library, or perhaps there is already an excellent library on the campus. Then again, a gender or women's studies center may wish to have a library attached to it, or perhaps

With a B.A. and an M.L.S. from the University of California at Berkeley, **Jacquelyn Marie** was Librarian of the Women's Center Library there, 1976–82. She is currently Reference and Women's Studies Librarian at the University of California at Santa Cruz. Her published writings include "The Gender Studies of Prague," in *Women Library Workers Journal* 16:4 (Winter 93/94); "Gloria Anzaldua," in *Gay and Lesbian Literature* (1993); and "Resources on Women of Color," in *Across Cultures: The Spectrum of Women's Lives* (1990).

there is a need for a reading room with a bulletin board. Thought should be given to a policy for such a library.

QUESTIONS TO CONSIDER

These are some questions to be asked:

- Should there be a library?
- Who will use this library?
- Will people be able to check out the materials or just use them in the library? Will there be copying facilities?
- What types of materials should be collected? Books? Journals (popular, women-related, academic)? Newsletters? Student papers? Bibliographies? Ephemeral materials, such as articles, letters, leaflets from organizations or demonstrations? Audiotapes or videotapes? Films?
- Will periodical indexes be available, such as *Women's Studies Abstracts* or *Studies on Women Abstracts*? Will these indexes be in paper or on computer?
- Should there be funding for materials, and where should such funding come from?
- How should the materials be arranged? Should the books be cataloged? By author, title, subject? Will a numbering scheme be used? Will a subject classification scheme be used? Will it be the Library of Congress classification, another library classification system, or one made up for this particular collection? Will there be handwritten or typed cards, or will there be a computerized catalog?
- How long will materials be kept? Where will older materials be housed? Will there be any attempt to preserve materials?
- Who will be present to help users? Will a librarian be hired? With library training?
- Who will do the collecting? The classifying? The weeding?
- Who will make the decisions about this library, its focus, its parameters?

These questions may seem overwhelming, but they need to be thought out, hopefully before a single book is put on the shelf or a single article is filed away.

Criteria for Inclusion

Innumerable books have been published in practically every country and in many languages on women's issues and the women's movement; these topics have also generated many pamphlets, oral history tapes, videos, films, and articles in alternative magazines as well as academic journals. There are also unpublished reports, bibliographies, and guides. Materials on women's issues are proliferating.

The rule seems to be that when a women's center has empty shelves, they will be filled almost immediately. Women are generous in donating books and other materials. Sometimes these materials are not relevant for the center and must be rejected. This is when the center's criteria for inclusion will come in handy. Women's studies are interdisciplinary and cover many fields of knowledge. It will be impossible to collect in all areas, so a focus on particular areas of special interest to the people using the library will be beneficial. Duplication of materials in other nearby libraries may not be necessary. Ephemeral materials, such as newsletters and fliers, are useful and are not usually collected in university libraries. They should be weeded regularly, however, unless this will be a historical collection and these materials will be preserved.

Classification of Materials

Classification of materials makes them easily accessible to users. The language of women's studies changes as new topics arise, new terms are invented, or old terms are changed to reflect a new awareness of cultural, racial, and sexual differences. For example, in the United States the terms used by and for a person of African heritage residing in the United States have changed from Negro to Afro-American to Black to African American. The words used to define a subject and under which to organize library materials should not be offensive to anyone. They should be words that come to mind readily when a user researches a topic.

Traditional subject headings are often inappropriate for women's collections. Therefore, after close consultation with librarians, scholars, and women in community women's organizations, the National Council for Research on Women (NCRW) in the United States developed a list of terms in English used for various women's issues, published as *A Women's Thesaurus* (Mary Ellen Capek, editor; New York: Harper & Row, 1987). As stated in the foreword to this excellent book, "*A Women's Thesaurus* sets national standards for terms to use in writing, cataloging, and research and is an up-to-date reference guide for non-sexist use of language." This thesaurus can serve as a start to developing subject headings for files and even for books. Then the needs of the particular library and its clientele should be analyzed and other headings developed to fit those needs. A broad heading, such as "health," probably needs to be broken down into narrower headings, such as abortion, birth control, nutrition, and pregnancy, but probably not into even narrower headings, such as ectopic pregnancy, types of birth control, and so on. The main priority for subject headings or any kind of classification system is their ease of use; they should enable users to find materials as quickly as possible and staff to file or shelve them in a timely manner.

INTERNATIONAL WOMEN'S ISSUES

All libraries in women's centers, whether affiliated with a community or women's organization or a university program, should be aware of and perhaps be collecting in international women's issues. Many resources are available. The various agencies of the United Nations, the Commission of the European Communities, and other women's agencies around the world produce pamphlets, bibliographies, newsletters, and other materials. The most useful directory is *Encyclopedia of Women's Associations Worldwide* (Detroit: Gale, 1993), which lists the principal official and unofficial organizations for each country. Many of these organizations publish materials in a variety of languages.

Interdisciplinarity, Women's Studies, and Library Collection Development

Hur-Li Lee (U.S.A.)

INTRODUCTION

It is some twenty years since the first women's studies courses appeared in college curricula. From the beginning, women's studies has been interdisciplinary. Feminist scholars became acutely aware not only of their second-class status in the academy, but also that women as subjects were either ignored or treated unfairly in virtually every academic discipline. Feminists began to work together to develop new courses on women's issues and to conduct research on women from a new perspective. They brought with them specialization in a variety of fields, such as psychology, sociology, and history. Women's studies was thus not only a response to the political movement demanding equality for women but also a challenge to the established academic disciplines.

Women's studies librarians at Rutgers University, a complex, multi-campus public university, have raised at least four issues growing out of this interdisciplinary scholarship: boundaries of women's studies, bureaucratic library structure, bibliographic control, and library training.

Hur-Li Lee is a Ph.D. candidate in the School of Communication, Information, and Library Studies at Rutgers University in New Jersey. She has an M.L.S. from Rutgers and has also taught there. Her B.A. is from National Taiwan University, and she has worked in publishing and in academic libraries.

ISSUES IN COLLECTION DEVELOPMENT

Defining the Boundaries of Women's Studies

Women's studies started out in the United States as a few courses, designed by a few professors. They disagreed, however, on how to incorporate the element of women. Some feminists insisted on creating a new field, asserting that an autonomous department could offer the women's studies faculty strengthened positions, visibility, and academic freedom. Unlike these _separatists_, the _mainstreamers_ advocated integrating information about women, and their concerns, values, and viewpoints, into every discipline to achieve a more balanced liberal education.

This debate between separatists and mainstreamers persists and has serious implications for managing library resources. The first question is who is responsible for selecting women's studies materials in a university library. If the institution chooses the separatist model, should this task be one librarian's sole duty or should it be only part of her responsibilities? If the mainstreaming model is chosen, how can we be sure that materials selected will adequately reflect women's concerns and values, or that they will be selected at all?

The development of women's studies at Rutgers University illustrates this debate. An English professor offered the first women's studies course there in 1969. A few more courses were soon added. In 1974 women's studies programs were established at two of the undergraduate colleges, including Douglass, the women's college. A centralized women's studies program was founded as part of the 1982 university reorganization. From the beginning, women's studies has been regarded as an independent entity.

There is no evidence that, from 1969 to about 1974, any librarian was consulted about this new program; this is typical of what happens at universities. The first "Book selection policy for women's studies" was formulated by a reference librarian at the Douglass College Library in 1975. From 1975 to 1990, many versions of a collection-development policy were written, and even more proposals for establishing a women's research center. The librarians who wrote these policy statements and proposals—none of whom was officially designated as the women's studies librarian—did this work because of their own beliefs and interests. In the mid-1980s, the bibliographer for professional schools was given the responsibility for coordinating universitywide selections for women's studies. That continued until the first women's studies librarian was hired in 1990. The library system moved in the same direction as the faculty, but much more slowly.

The problem of the definition of women's studies is magnified in the argument over the location of its collections, which has led to the proposals to establish a women's research center or a women's archives in the Douglass College Library mentioned above. But the question of how to separate materials for women's studies from materials for other disciplines remains. The high cost of many research materials inhibits the library from buying duplicate copies, but many materials may be used by scholars in other fields. For example, Dee Garrison's *Apostles of Culture: The Public Librarian and American Society, 1876–1920* (1981) contains a long section on the feminization of public librarianship. If only one copy can be bought, to which collection does it belong: women's studies, history, or library studies? Where do we draw the line to separate materials that are seen as useful only to women's studies scholars and students? Is it possible or practical to draw such a line? How useful would this limited collection be once the line is drawn?

The first women's studies librarian was hired at the Douglass Library in 1990, but the dispute on defining the women's studies collection has not been satisfactorily resolved. The temporary definition says that women's studies is whatever falls within class HQ in the Library of Congress classification scheme. Thus, the women's studies librarian is responsible only for selecting new books about women and feminism classed in HQ, and those books will be housed in the Douglass Library. On the one hand, a separate women's library offers a focal point in the university for women's studies, helps form a nationally (even internationally) known entity (with the women's college and other women's institutes at Rutgers), and facilitates fund-raising activities to enrich the collections. On the other hand, this HQ arrangement leads to inconvenience and awkwardness. For one thing, many feminist works and books about women are classified outside HQ. It is troublesome for feminist researchers to have to go back and forth between libraries on two campuses in order to find material of relevance.

Bureaucratic Structures

Most U.S. universities are highly bureaucratic. Academic disciplines are usually represented by departments, with funds allocated along departmental lines. The university library is organized in a similar fashion, with responsibilities divided to serve individual departments or divisions. Each collection development librarian is assigned selection responsibility for one or perhaps several related fields and has the authority to spend the funds allocated to those areas. When a new program or department is approved, one librarian will be assigned to collect materials for it, often taking on this new topic or area as an extra responsibility. A new librarian will be hired only if the program is high on the university's priority list.

Public universities have limited funds, and all departments and programs contend for resources from the same pool of funds. New programs are likely to generate controversy because they tend to take money and other resources from existing programs. So the eleven proposals for a women's library, a women's research center, or a women's archives at Rutgers have been rejected; insufficient resources and the field's interdisciplinary nature were usually given as the reasons.

In *Building Library Collections* (1981), H. F. Cline and L. T. Sinnott found that under bureaucratic organization, many materials for an interdisciplinary field were not bought when the budget was cut and no particular librarian had the primary responsibility for that field. Librarians in related fields all expected the others to spend the money. At Rutgers, collecting of primary information resources and foreign materials suffered. Many women's grass-roots political organizations and groups have kept records or printed brochures, newspapers, or newsletters; these are invaluable sources for studying the individual groups and the movement as a whole. Unfortunately, these published and unpublished materials, along with foreign materials, lack effective distribution networks. With tight budgets and staffing, many librarians simply ignore them, for it is too time-consuming to pursue these materials and for most this interdisciplinary field is only a secondary responsibility.

There is also a fear of being ghettoized through the separatist model of women's studies. Some librarians maintained that making the Douglass Library the women's library will hinder feminism since that library provides little research support. Most research materials needed for interdisciplinary work in women's studies are not available there, and its staff has the training and knowledge to serve undergraduate students, but not necessarily those doing advanced research.

Bibliographic Control

When women's studies emerged in the United States, existing bibliographic tools were not effective in helping locate information about women. Tools used in individual disciplines were inadequate for interdisciplinary work. As interest in women's studies accelerated, course syllabi were collected, women-centered bibliographies and biographical dictionaries were published, such pioneering women's studies periodicals as *Signs* reviewed books, and specialized indexing and abstracting services were created. Some publishers saw the demand and began republishing and repackaging old materials on women. Although acquiring publications in women's studies has become easier, it is still difficult to collect primary sources and foreign materials.

A number of Rutgers librarians are committed to building a sound women's studies collection. They managed to acquire most of the books and serials published in English in the 1970s and the first half of the 1980s, even though few reference tools existed to help them locate materials. To help patrons find information, these librarians produced in-house finding aids.

Training of Librarians

At Rutgers, as at many other U.S. universities, most bibliographers or collection-development librarians have some advanced degrees in their respective areas. More and more have doctorates. Throughout the years, however, none of the librarians who have selected materials or coordinated selection for women's studies have had formal training in the field. But what knowledge and qualifications should a women's studies librarian have? Does he or she need to be trained in women's studies to understand how feminist scholars and students learn and study and in order to choose high-quality materials? As an interdisciplinary field, women's studies is based on a variety of concepts, theories, approaches, and terminologies. How can one librarian know them all? If this is not necessary, how can one person make sound decisions about materials produced under a wide range of disciplines?

Some librarians argue that having an advanced subject degree, preferably a doctorate, will make the librarian equal to and therefore respected by the teaching faculty. Rutgers librarians gained faculty status in the early 1970s and have assumed primary responsibility for building library collections. Librarians still complain, however, about unequal treatment by the administration and teaching faculty. It will be interesting to see how the women's studies faculty perceives librarians, what relationship they have with them, and what qualifications they think a women's studies librarian should have.

RESOLUTION OF ISSUES
Library Organization

The bureaucratic organization of most libraries is so inflexible that new, interdisciplinary fields cannot easily be accommodated in existing systems. Much energy is wasted in fighting the system and competing for resources. Knowledge itself continually evolves and does not necessarily conform to the structures we impose. According to a UNESCO study (1983), interdisciplinarity has a long history in Europe and is becoming more and more common. New fields emerge on the academic scene periodically and carry with them perspectives from more than one discipline. Existing bureaucratic arrangements become less and less useful and more and more cumbersome in managing library resources. We must reconsider and redesign library organizations to adapt to current needs and to incorporate feminist approaches to organizational structures; see, for instance Kathy Ferguson's *The Feminist Case against Bureaucracy* (1984).

Tools for Bibliographic Control

As mentioned, feminist scholars and librarians have made enormous efforts to create more reference tools and to correct biases against women in existing tools. These achievements deserve high praise and this work should continue. But a drastic change is needed in classification and subject indexing. Both the Dewey and Library of Congress (LC) classification schemes, the two systems used most commonly in the United States, arrange subjects by discipline. These structures were basically determined in the late nineteenth and early twentieth centuries and are male-biased, Europe-centered, and hierarchical. Disciplines and fields of study that emerged later are awkwardly squeezed in. For example, in the LC system, Computer Science is a subclass under Mathematics, and Women's Studies, under Family, Marriage, Woman. In addition, women as subjects have been researched from a number of perspectives in a number of disciplines. A biography of a feminist philosopher, for instance, is classified in Philosophy. Books about women or feminism are found in almost every class. This scattering of material generates difficulties for feminist research. Subject-indexing systems are much worse, full of sexist terms and usages. Together, classification and subject indexing form a difficult barrier to information access in women's studies. To change this will require further investigation.

A Feminist Model of Collection Development

Feminist theory not only questions the concepts and theories of traditional scholarship but also challenges its research methodologies. For example, positivists ignore the context of phenomena and insist on studying rigidly defined variables in a well-controlled environment. Feminists are correct in criticizing such a context-free and unnatural model. It is my belief that collections are built as the result of social interaction over time. The historical, social, and organizational contexts within which a collection is built have tremendous impact on it. The individual elements of collection development should be examined within these contexts. To date, however, the study of collection development has been fragmented, teaching librarians about the tools for finding materials, the strategy to calculate funding formulas, and the procedure to write up a collection-development policy statement, rather than the *process* of collection development and the way all the factors interact in that process. In my opinion, this is why we are still trapped in the old, androcentric model of collection development.

Finding and Using Information

Scholars and students in an interdisciplinary field not only borrow perspectives, theories, and research methods from related fields but also create a new body of knowledge, theories, and research methods. In her dissertation (Rutgers, 1980), Elizabeth Futas proved that women's studies researchers cite information from a number of fields. Few studies, however, have investigated the nature of such information exchanges. In what manner do feminists borrow and use information from a particular discipline? Through what channels do they retrieve the relevant information? How do they cope with the terminologies of diverse disciplines? And what roles do the library and other information agencies play in their information seeking? If we can answer these questions better, we as information professionals will be able to improve services to meet users' needs. We can also then improve subject access mechanisms.

CONCLUSION

This is a first step toward understanding interdisciplinary collection development in the United States. The situation at Rutgers, a multicampus public university, amplifies the issues in interdisciplinary collection development, which in turn helps us see the problems clearly.

Library Instruction and Women's Studies

Marilyn Grotzky (U.S.A.)

INTRODUCTION

Auraria Library in Denver, Colorado, is an academic library serving a full range of students and providing information for a full range of disciplines. Its faculty and staff have produced resources and instructional materials that may help others provide instruction for library users interested in women's studies and women's issues.

In library instruction sessions for women's studies, one of the most frequently asked questions is, Why are women's studies materials so hard to find? Why is there no "one best place" for these sources?

Women's studies books were once placed in the women's studies section, thus reaching only, or at least mostly, feminists. Now, books about women and woman-related issues are usually found in related subject areas: women mathematicians in the math section, women in India with books on Indian history, and so forth. In one way, this is very useful. Anyone might find a woman-related book in her or his field and become interested. On the other hand, a researcher looking for a woman-related book will not accidentally discover many of the newest books while she is browsing the women's studies section. Although books about women are now increasingly where they belong—everywhere—it is no longer relatively easy to find a specific woman-related book.

Marilyn Grotzky is Assistant to the Head of Library Instruction at Auraria Library (University of Colorado at Denver). She also teaches Freshman Research Writing at Metropolitan State College, Denver.

187

At our library, finding information about women in the on-line catalog (called CARL, for Colorado Alliance of Research Libraries) is not as easy as it should be. The word *women*, for example, a "monster word" in the catalog, appears more than 15,562 times; the computer will not accept it as a first word in a search. Nor will the computer respond to other words that frequently relate to women: *social, science, United States*, and *history* may not be used as the first word. Computer-friendly words, such as *feminist*, often don't bring up the books feminists want, because *women* has been preferred for book titles as a less threatening word; other useful terms, such as *feminist social criticism* and *feminist literary criticism*, do not spring to the mind of the beginning researcher.

THE PURPOSES OF LIBRARY INSTRUCTION

To help women's studies majors find words or phrases that might lead them to useful information, the Ten Ways list was developed. This list provides suggestions for ways to use information that students already have or can easily find in order to locate more information. The Handbook, LUGs, and RSGs described below are available through ERIC—ED342 410—as part of the Auraria Library Instruction Program. (ERIC [Education Resources Information Center] is a U.S. information clearinghouse for education. Those unable to find the ERIC microfiches in their countries may write to the author at Auraria Library, Lawrence at 11th Street, Denver, CO 80204.) Except for the *Auraria Library Handbook*, these materials are not copyrighted, and no permission for use is necessary. They can be used as a springboard for finding materials in other libraries.

The Ten Ways sheet was developed for course-related library instruction. We have developed other materials as well, as part of our overall instruction program. The purposes of library instruction are to help patrons access information in library collections and to help library staff by making patrons more knowledgeable and independent. (See pp. 189–190).

The need for, and efficacy of, library instruction has been called into question in some circles. As a teacher, I see that it makes my students' research ability grow. But students, teachers, and others who support the idea of instruction do not usually have to pay for it, while libraries do, so we must consider means that are as cost and personnel effective as possible, ways that provide benefits and avoid drawbacks.

One piece of advice: begin with a small program. It is easy and pleasant to be able to add access assistance, and a successful small program may lead to funding for expansion. It is much more difficult to pull back from a program that patrons have come to rely on, and moving away from a popular program may lead to reduced funding.

A second useful concept is to use print resources.

WOMEN'S STUDIES—TEN WAYS TO LOOK FOR A SUBJECT

1). Find a recent WS text (most cover a wide range of topics) -- use the bibliography for the section most relevant to you. Bibliographies are sometimes found at the end of the book, sometimes at the end of a chapter or section of the book. *Thinking Women* [their text: *Thinking Women: Woman's Studies* by Jodie Wetzel et al.] is an obvious choice here; another of my favorite multi-topic books is Marilyn French's *Beyond Power.* Check CARL to see if this or any nearby library owns the books that seem most relevant.

2). Find a general book on your subject (*A History of Their Own* by Anderson and Zinsner for European history, for example) and choose the bibliography for the section that interests you. By the way, writing citations for a bibliography is the best way to learn to read citations. Learn enough about the forms that you can tell an article from a book and a chapter from an article. Need help? The library has several style handbooks, including MLA, APA, Chicago, and Turabian.

3). Find an anthology or a book of readings (look for something that lists an editor) on your subject. The authors of the individual articles may have written books and often have written other articles. Check CARL library catalogs for books and UnCover and Expanded Academic Index for articles.

Look through the list of articles fore key words or phrases that might work on CARL.

Literary anthologies such as the *Norton Anthology of Literature by Women* or the *Longman's Anthology of World Literature by Women* allow you to discover dozens of women writers you may not have known about. For more information about writers, see the *Dictionary of Literary Biography* and *Contemporary Authors.* An index to both is located near *Contemporary Authors.*

To find information about notable women, try the *Biography and Genealogy Master Index*, located on the shelves nearest the Ref Desk. This will lead you to other collected biographies.

4). Make a habit of checking the bibliography of every book or article you look at that has been of use to you or might be. You will often find bibliographies in unexpected places, partly because finding material relating to women has not been easy, and good material is often valued and shared.

5). Many books published by academic presses and small presses seem to disappear from the market quickly. Browse women's studies sections of bookstores frequently. Keep notecards to record citations for books that look interesting. Many will be available in academic libraries and through interlibrary loan long after they are out of print. Never forget the value of photocopiers.

6). If you are browsing the shelves of a library for books that relate to women's issues, note key words or phrases that appear often (I find "rewriting," "gender" or "gendering" or "engendering," or "their own" or sometimes "her own" appear often in women-identified history and lit criticism.)

7). Check the reverse side of the title page of books that are on-target for your subject. Increasingly you will find Library of Congress cataloging information printed there. Toward the end of the material will be a series of numbered headings (*feminist literary criticism* or *social reformers women biography*, etc.) Use the most relevant of these terms in CARL to bring up books on the same subject.

8). Information about women is everywhere. The women's studies section of libraries and bookstores is growing less important as information about women moves to subject areas, and information is less easy to find. Do not count on any one area to be the only place to check. In literature, for example, criticism may appear with books by a particular woman, for a particular time period (modernists, for example), or with a particular genre (mystery writers).

9). Key words in CARL will not bring up only information about your subject and from your point of view. WOMEN and THERAPY will give you books about different kinds of therapy, written in different years and with different viewpoints. Feminists do not all hold one point of view (thank heavens), and books written by women are not necessarily women-centered. READ WITH CARE AND EVALUATE CAREFULLY.

10*.When you use an older bibliography, as in *Beyond Power*, pay particular attention to the "Other Entries" listed on CARL. You can use Express Search to lead you to newer related books. Remember that CARL sorts by date.

PRINT RESOURCES

PRINTED WALKING TOUR WITH MAP   For patrons unfamiliar with a library, this can be a time-saving and extremely useful aid. We also have an audio tour, but many students prefer this shorter, go-at-your-own speed and skip-what-you-don't-need version. Teachers like it because they can use it for quiz information. It helps with requests for group tours, which can disrupt a busy library. We now reserve group tours for adult basic education, reading, and study skills programs.

Because women's studies materials are integrated into the collection in most academic and public libraries, it is especially important that women's studies students know their way around the library. Teachers might be encouraged to take copies and change them to suit their disciplines; if departments hand out their own tours, the library saves money.

RESEARCH STRATEGY GUIDES (RSG)   We based this series of thirty-six single-sheet guides on our general instruction format: look at reference materials for background, books for in-depth information, periodicals for recent (or historical) information, and reference materials for statistics and single facts. We followed the basic breakdown of the Library of Congress classification system and considered the subject areas of most interest to our introductory-level students. Women's libraries might consider basing a series on most frequently asked questions or most frequently researched subjects. These guides were produced quickly, all in the same format; because they were written by library experts, little extra time had to be spent in preparation.

LIBRARY USE GUIDES   These guides, created by librarian subject experts, are more detailed than the RSGs. Some subjects have both types of guides, some one or the other. We create LUGs for areas in great demand or in which there is limited expertise among reference personnel; in other words, these are almost as much for our convenience as patrons'. The LUGs were created over a period of years, out of perceived need or special interest. Librarians generally choose their own topics, and their own schedules. A set might be created quickly if materials from other libraries can be used as a basis. The LUGs were originally printed on full-sized sheets; we have recently gone to half-size as an economy measure.

POINT OF USE GUIDES   These inexpensive and time-saving materials give a brief explanation of how to use a resource. We laminate one two-sided sheet of instructions for CD-ROM stations and one single page of instructions for index use, then tape them to the index tables next to the appropriate index. A sample Point of Use Guide, written by Diane Turner, is provided on p. 193.

The Auraria Library Handbook has met a very favorable reaction. Friends of Auraria Library, an organization that contributes to and supports the library, gives a copy to every student or patron who wishes one. We have had several outside requests to use our ideas; many campus teachers use it as a supplementary text.

These are some ways that print material can save librarian time. Once students become accustomed to checking for relevant print materials, they become less dependent on library personnel. Often a combination of personal help and a LUG works best; we may demonstrate how to find a periodical article, then offer a LUG that repeats the same information in more detail or suggest two sources and offer a LUG on the subject.

NONPRINT SOURCES

Print sources do not substitute for contact with library personnel. In fact, once patrons know the help that is available, they take more advantage of it. All print sources do is allow librarians and staff to distribute time more effectively. A written guide can explain something as clearly as, and in more detail than, a staff member usually has the time to do. If a student needs in-depth assistance, a librarian whose time is not taken up with answering routine questions may be free to help.

LIBRARIANS AND STAFF AT SERVICE DESKS   Desk service remains the service we would probably eliminate last. Our library uses experienced staff members, as well as librarians, at the reference desk. Staff members maintain circulation, interlibrary loan, periodicals, and reserve/media desks.

COURSE-RELATED INSTRUCTION   These classes, mostly upper division and graduate level, are presented almost exclusively by librarians, who decide whether to give instruction and determine the content of sessions.

DEMONSTRATIONS   Demonstrations of the use of the CARL on-line catalog were originally given by librarians but are now the responsibility of a team of volunteers (librarians and other staff) from all departments of the library. Many staff members consider this a welcome break in routine.

AUDIO TOUR   This forty-five-minute tour is accompanied by a packet of LUGs and a library map. A script is available for teachers who want to preview the tour or write exercises to go with it, or for foreign students who want to see and hear the words simultaneously.

WOMEN STUDIES ABSTRACTS

Published quarterly since 1972, the abstracts are taken from a wide range of periodicals (including some foreign-language journals) and also some books and pamphlets. There are quarterly subject indexes which are arranged alphabetically but it's faster to use the annual cumulative author or subject indexes to aid in finding material on your subject.

1) Think of several words or phrases to describe your topic, then look them up in the index section.
2) Note any "see" or "see also" headings and check for articles under these as well.
3) When you find your topic in the index, write down the citation number and then look for that number in the abstracts section of the volume. Numbers followed by an A lead to abstracts (summaries) as well as citations.
4) To see if we have the periodical, go to the CARL terminal and get into the Auraria library database. BROWSE <B> by TITLE <T> and type in the name of the journal or magazine. This will tell you the call number and holdings (what years of the journal the library owns and the format of these journals - i.e. current, bound, microfilm or microfiche).

example from annual index section (note underline)	feminist science, 771A, 946A feminist sociology, 660 feminist studies, <u>656A</u> see also gender studies, women studies

==

example from
abstracts
section
(using citation
underlined above)

656A.Coyner, Sandra. **Feminist bywords-Women's studies.** NWSA JOURNAL 3:349-54 Au 91.
The words "women's studies" rarely specify' an identity. When part of one's self-description, they designate a position in a program. The term is thus mostly a location-institutional, political, and sometimes physical. Discussed are the word "studies" (used for interdisciplinary programs), other manifestions of feminism on campus, political agendas, and alternative names used, e.g., "feminist studies" and "gender studies." However, these names more clearly identify our position toward male dominance than they acknowledge the diversity among women. Over the years we are learning, painfully and with discouraging slowness, how to actualize the intention of women's studies being about and for all women. What would happen if we renamed our discipline "womanist studies?" Would the name be appropriated by white women or would white women try to take it as a hope for diversity rather than the mark of achieving diversity? "Would our discipline vibrate in shades of purple, and dance, and love, and sing? Would we define ourselves right out of the old questions of politics and correctness? Wouldn't it be worth a try?" S. WHALEY

When you find an article which looks relevant, write down the citation, which includes <u>title</u>, <u>author</u>, <u>periodical/magazine</u>, <u>book or pamphlet</u>, <u>volume and issue number</u>, <u>page numbers</u>, and <u>date</u>.

5) If you have any questions or problems in your information search, please ask at the Reference Desk for assistance. We are here to help you!

rev 8/84

SUMMARY

To begin and build an instruction program, we believe that the following are useful:

1. Start with a small program, then build on success.
2. Use print sources whenever they can help save librarian/staff time. Give recognition for this work too.
3. Consider librarian/staff strengths, talents, and interests. No one can do what he or she likes best all the time, but allowing each person to use strengths often creates a more efficient and effective program.
4. Give everyone space to be productive, but guard against overwork and burnout. If your staff is burning out, change the program.

Developing and Preserving a Feminist Collection for Posterity

Anna Greening and Veronica Davis Perkins (United Kingdom)

INTRODUCTION

At the beginning of the twentieth century, the emblem of the National Union of Women's Suffrage Societies (NUWSS) was an oak tree with a strong trunk and many branches. This symbol forms the frontispiece of the "Bound Suffrage Pamphlets" in The Fawcett Library, named for NUWSS President Millicent Garrett Fawcett. This item and others like it prompted the library to begin a conservation survey. As used here, *preservation* is the prevention of damage to holdings, *conservation* is the repair of damage, and *restoration*—rare in libraries—is the rebuilding of damaged items.

THE FAWCETT LIBRARY

In 1926, when the library was formally established by the London and National Society for Women's Service (formerly Suffrage), the society looked back on a sixty-year campaign to enfranchise women and its involvement with women's employment. The Fawcett Library is the only British library to offer comprehensive coverage of this period up to the present time from the woman's point

---

Anna Greening is part-time Archivist at The Fawcett Library and has a postgraduate Diploma of Archive Administration from the University of Wales. **Veronica Davis Perkins** is a former picture librarian and works part-time as The Fawcett Library's Visual Materials Librarian and concurrently as Pictures Editor in a publishing house.

of view, in its book collection and in periodicals, pamphlets, press cuttings, archives, photographs, banners, and other objects.

Background to the Conservation Survey

Although The Fawcett Library is not large, holding about 26,000 books and more than 30,000 pamphlets, it is complex, because different kinds of collections have been donated to the library at various times. Some have been kept as separate entities; others have been subsumed into various categories.

Over the last few years, it has become obvious that rare and old material has suffered from heavy use. At the same time, scarce resources meant the gradual loss of an integrated overview of library holdings and their condition. The authors recently undertook a conservation survey to determine the comparative size of various possible conservation and preservation projects.

The survey encompassed every aspect of library administration that might help reduce wear and tear on holdings. The final report included ideas on documentation (including catalogs and other finding aids), accessions and collection-development policies, use of space, reader flow, controlled access to the stacks, computers, staffing, provision of surrogate records, and environmental controls.

THE CONSERVATION SURVEY

Aims of the Survey

Aims of the survey were to give a picture of the physical state of the library and its holdings, identifying individual items and groups of holdings in need of treatment; to provide both qualitative and quantitative descriptions of collections, backed up with observed and recorded data; and to provide a sound basis for the future development of the library and policy planning. To conduct the study, we had to find out what and how much we had, and where it was; the result was a color-coded location plan. The next stage was to survey groups of holdings. What was the intellectual content of the group? Was it classified or cataloged? If so, what about indexes? Individual items were sampled and their appearance and condition described, as were the type and condition of their boxes or enclosures and the ways to access that particular material. A standard vocabulary was used on a basic form so that data could later be analyzed in detail.

Survey Findings

The survey showed the same problems arising again and again: the challenges of age and historical significance of holdings, combined with lack of resources. We soon developed a range of necessary action or preservation/conservation options on a five-point scale:

1. **No action necessary:** items in very good condition and well documented.
2. **Preservation necessary,** such as mounting or wrapping cuttings, arranging and classifying material, enclosing and boxing, and removing fragile material from open access. These simple but often labor-intensive housekeeping tasks might be undertaken by staff or volunteers.
3. **Simple conservation tasks** to be undertaken by a professional conservator, or by library staff trained by a conservator, such as taking out rusty staples and restitching pamphlets, or cleaning dirty documents.
4. **More complex conservation tasks** to be done by a professional conservator, such as photograph cleaning and stabilization, album disbinding, cleaning and repair, or making repairs to a single artifact.
5. **Very expensive repair** to complex items or series of items, or a large project, such as microfilming a category of holdings, that implies buying in services over months or years.

It should be possible to identify ways in which work in the last two categories might be prevented many years ahead of time, on the premise that prevention is cheaper than cure. If simple but perhaps tedious tasks are done (by volunteers, if necessary) when material comes into the library, the life of the documents would be significantly prolonged. It became apparent during the survey, for example, that some pamphlets were showing signs of deterioration after only ten years, and much of the material in really poor condition dated from the 1970s.

Issues Raised by the Survey

Each category of holding presented slightly different problems, many typifying issues arising from the conflict between access and preservation.

VOLUMES   The material in the main book sequence was generally perceived as low priority in terms of conservation status because it is well documented, in good condition, cataloged on LIBERTAS (the university cataloging system), and its use is controlled. But the special collections of old and rare books, with their vulnerable physical condition, their provenance, and their subject matter, are major categories within the survey and within the library.

PERIODICALS   Dating from 1858 to the present, the periodicals reflect the wide range of interests and concerns of women across nationalities, classes, and age groups. They are on open access, shelved alphabetically. Some have been bound into volumes; others are stored in boxes. Outsize titles are on lower shelves; conserved, rebound volumes are available to readers on request.

Only current titles are cataloged on LIBERTAS. Most older titles are cataloged on a card index, sometimes cross-referenced by subject.

The condition of the periodicals as a whole was difficult to quantify. Storage needs to be rationalized. Some boxes were half empty; others were overcrowded and of different sizes and varying quality. In general *any* wrapping—even a manila envelope—was better than nothing.

Microfilming is one way of preserving vulnerable material and making it accessible, but staff, helped by volunteers, can do such basic work as rewrapping, boxing, and copying well-used material onto archival copying paper.

PAMPHLETS AND EPHEMERA   In The Fawcett Library, a piece of ephemera consists of one to eight pages, a pamphlet of nine to fifty pages. Anything larger is regarded as a book. Pamphlets are boxed together and shelved in the main book sequence, with open access. Boxes may not provide adequate protection. Older material—some from more than a century ago—rubs against modern spiral-bound items. The sequence of individual pamphlets may be destroyed by browsers. The pamphlets are heavily used, and the ideal solution—wrapping and reboxing them and taking them off open access—is impractical because of staffing constraints.

Ephemera are arranged in alphabetical order by provenance and subject and stored in document boxes. Although the material is in good condition now, it does need preserving by, say, wrapping items with similar provenance together within the boxes.

Some pamphlets have been bound together in volumes, a once-popular preservation measure that would not be used today. The volume of suffrage pamphlets, for example, has brown and brittle pages, the weak, acidic newsprint having given way at the folds. There is evidence of acid migration, acidic paper having damaged and discolored its more robust neighbors. The Fawcett Library's solution has been to photocopy such volumes onto acid-free paper, slip the photocopies into polyester envelopes in a ring binder, and offer readers this surrogate record. One shortcoming of surrogate records is the loss of color.

PRESS CUTTINGS   Press cuttings have been taken very seriously in The Fawcett Library; the Conservation Survey identified about fifteen series, the longest and largest running from about 1920 to 1967 and classified according to the Universal Decimal Classification system. This series is heavily used and is being microfilmed. The survey team found that enclosing cuttings before boxing them is a more effective preservation measure than just putting them loose into boxes. Best of all would be to glue them to good-quality paper with nonacidic glue and then enclose them in envelopes or folders. The work is labor-intensive but can be done by volunteers. At The Fawcett, one volunteer collects recent cuttings from three major newspapers and indexes them on a quarterly basis; another volunteer cuts, sticks, and files the biographical series.

ARCHIVES The archives are perhaps the most significant category of library holdings—the raw material of history. Access to archival material at The Fawcett is as strictly controlled as staffing constraints allow. Finding aids need to be helpful. Records of usage kept since 1988, when compiling statistics began, enable the identification of readers using any particular box. Readers are asked to sign a pledge to treat the records with respect, not to eat or drink in the library, and to use only pencils.

Although the Conservation Survey showed some correlation between the physical condition of archival items and the amount of use they had received, the relationship did not seem to be quite that simple; more analysis of use and condition is necessary.

VISUAL MATERIALS Most visual materials are costly to preserve, difficult to store, and even more difficult to access. A collection should be assessed carefully, considering what is there, how it should be listed and indexed, what storage equipment there is, who will be using the material and how, whether funding for preservation is available, whether the collection can be used as a fund-raising tool, and whether it is to grow. Donors should be asked for all available information, including the identity of the copyright holder.

A management plan should incorporate basic good housekeeping. Due to the unstable chemicals used in their production, photographs are a volatile medium. Problems include curling due to rolling large photographs, image browning due to humidity, silvering or mirroring due to oxidization, loss of image caused by atmospheric contamination, acidic mounting materials, unsealed wood frames, and reflective glass, which traps dirt and exacerbates fluctuating temperatures. Photographs should be copied if possible. The originals can then be stored in silversafe or melinex (mylar) while copyprints are used for research, exhibition, and reproduction. If possible, photographs should be removed from such contaminators as acidic mounts and wrappers, and stored away from light in a cool (15 to 25 degrees centigrade, or 60 to 75 degrees Fahrenheit), not-too-dry atmosphere (ideally 30 to 50 percent relative humidity). Staff should wear cotton gloves when handling prints, use only a soft pencil for annotation, and avoid labels. If possible, the image should be documented on the wrapper rather than on the reverse of the print.

ARTIFACTS AND TEXTILES Objects and artifacts can create storage problems. The Fawcett Library has a collection of suffrage badges, textiles, and such miscellaneous items as a WSPU porcelain tea set and a silver trowel, which may not fit into an archives box. Storage of the decorative suffrage banners in the Fawcett collection creates problems. The banners have been photographed and the transparencies are used for research.

CONCLUSION

Preservation and conservation work hand in hand. Documents are at risk both from the atmosphere and from handling. Much significant material is produced on cheap, acidic paper, not designed to survive for long. Much important material is slowly degrading on library shelves.

The survey of Fawcett Library materials shows that any enclosure is better than none. An enclosure protects and also dignifies material in the eyes of readers, encouraging them to treat it with respect. Identification and classification numbers may be written on enclosures rather than on fragile documents.

If archival-quality stationery and envelopes are too expensive, photocopy paper and ordinary manila folders may be used. Their acidity should be checked, however. It is pointless to try to protect fragile or vulnerable materials with newsprint, for example, as it will cause dreadful damage over the years. Similarly, caution should be used when buying boxes. Some older boxes in The Fawcett Library are very acidic and may have contributed to paper embrittlement.

Low-acid or acid-free boxes protect contents from dust, dirt, air pollution, and even from flood. Boxes should never be filled absolutely full; paper compacts itself during storage and swells in use.

Battered books can be supported by half-wrappers tied around the volumes. Corners of wrappers and labels should never be acute. Items should never be lifted by the tape holding them together and should never be folded, as paper will tear at the folds.

Finally, press cuttings can form significant collections, especially if access to computerized editions of newspapers is limited. When mounting cuttings, leave a margin of at least five centimeters around the edges to prevent damage from air pollution reaching the cutting. Wrap or box them. Classify and index them. Be rigorous about marking provenance on each clipping. Such a large, contextualized and rigorously contemporary with the events being described resource requires little outlay except patience and a pair of scissors.

Evaluation of Sources in Women's History

Sara Janner (Switzerland)

INTRODUCTION

What standards of evaluation must we introduce in order to sort, arrange, and inventory sources on women and women's organizations in general archives? This question faces me daily in my work as an archivist and historian. It is a basic question, relevant beyond the strict limits of my personal field of research: the women of the upper classes in nineteenth-century Basel, Switzerland.

COLLECTION OF SOURCES IN SWITZERLAND

Although the steps being taken in Switzerland to collect sources for the history of women and women's organizations are still insufficient—financial and human resources are lacking, and so, too, is the necessary sense of awareness among historians—nonetheless all major Swiss archives concerned with developments in research on recent history understand the importance of this issue. Two factors are responsible. One is the pioneering work of Marta Gosteli in founding and managing a private archival repository for the history of the Swiss women's movement. The second is the first generation of female historians, who have established the scholarly disciplines of women's and gender history in Swiss universities.

Historian **Sara Janner** was born in Basel in 1961 and has studied there and in Florence, Italy. (This article was translated into English by S. N. Tranter.)

However, collection and securing of source material for the history of women and the women's movement in specialized and public archives are, in my opinion, insufficient to solve the problem of adequate documentation of women's history. Anyone intending to study women's and gender history is forced back on collections in archives that took on their present form in the nineteenth century. Even today cataloging and description of archival material are based on a male perception of documentary material, reflecting a male perception of public life and a male historiography. As a result, large quantities of source material for the history of women are buried in Swiss public archives; the principles of selection used in cataloging and description do not take account of such material. Because of inadequate cataloging, this material remains unnoticed by historians, even by those concerned with the history of women and of gender. Making these sources of women's history available for historical research should be a high priority of historians and archivists.

DESCRIPTION OF SOURCES

The inadequacy of description of sources for women's history is often lamented, but the theoretical, strictly archival issues underlying these everyday problems of historical research are rarely examined. This grave defect makes it impossible for today's scholarship to deal critically with surviving sources for women's history and bars access to a further substantial source area: the context in which sources are discovered. Reconstructing the history of the origins and transmission of archival collections provides valuable information for historiography and archival studies.

As both a historian and an archivist, I view the structure and selection of material within any specific archive as an expression of a period-related concept of history that is characteristic of the social group that established and built up that archives. But I am also concerned with applying the results of historical research on women and women's organizations to the selection of criteria for arrangement and description in archives, and with scrutinizing prevailing archival methods to see whether they provide appropriate access to sources for women's history.

This dual approach raises three main questions:

- How can sources for women's history best be described and cataloged?
- Are present techniques of description and cataloging adequate, or must new techniques be developed?
- How did the present situation in existing archives develop, and what historical and methodological conclusions may be drawn from this development?

A practical example from my own work demonstrates this dual approach and allows us to examine these three questions in more detail.

Hidden Collections

A few months ago, I found, entered in the card index of an archives, eighty letters from a clergyman's wife. She wrote them between 1830 and 1833, while she was living with her husband in a rural village. As the wife of a representative of urban authority, she experienced the full force of a revolution in which the rural areas subject to the city of Basel declared themselves independent of the city, and which led to her family's being expelled from the village. The young, recently married woman described these events for her mother in Basel.

These letters form part of the personal papers of the writer's mother, but had at an unspecified date been removed from her papers, and are preserved apart from their original provenance as a separate collection. I do not know how or why this happened. The families of both the mother's husband and the daughter's husband have archives in the Cantonal Record Office in Basel. Sources in which women comment on their own situation and on public events are considered rare. Yet these letters are not entered under the name of the writer or the recipient in the latest edition of the national inventory of private papers, nor under the name of either husband, even though the private repository where I found the letters is among the libraries and archives cataloged in this national inventory.

When I investigated why these letters do not appear, I learned that, in the system of cataloging in use in Basel, collections consisting entirely of letters do not count as private papers and are therefore not included. The small size of the collection was another factor, so that both quantity and type of material led to its exclusion. These criteria, objective and unbiased at first glance, need further critical examination in view of the historical conditions concerning the preservation of women's private papers in Basel.

Women's private papers in family archives, if inventoried at all, are usually subsumed under the papers of a male relative. Women have to be assigned to a man, even in the domain of the archives, and do not appear as independent individuals. In the case of the private archives of the Basel merchant-aristocracy, maintained by the families themselves, we can interpret this as a reflection of the perception of women in the social class and period concerned. What is somewhat astonishing, however, is that even the finding aids provided by the state archives adopt the male-oriented cataloging system of the private archives, making no attempt to balance out this defect by providing a suitable index to family archives among their own overall finding aids. Archivists overlook the fact that there are collections of women's papers whose existence can easily be proved historically but that were apparently dispersed and either destroyed or assigned to other collections, thus ending up as so-called fragmentary or remainder collections. In the case of our eighty letters, one can assume that they were once part of a man's collection.

Nineteenth and Twentieth Century Women's Papers

Seen historically, therefore, women were not in a position to amass private papers in modern terms—at least not before the turn of the century, when the first women academics in Basel began to build up collections of private scholarly papers as their living conditions began to resemble those of their male colleagues. Here then a too mechanical and restrictive application of the term *private papers* excludes sources instead of rendering them accessible. It is not the required archival techniques that are lacking but the ability to apply them in a manner appropriate to the sources. Similarly, the decision to include a collection in an inventory such as the one mentioned must be based on a due consideration of the historical conditions surrounding its origins and preservation; it is not analytical techniques that are lacking but the will to apply them to material documenting women's history.

The fact that source material for women's history is not usually assessed carefully enough is also due to the way women's sources are preserved. It is not only men who disperse women's papers. Upper-class women in Basel, in contrast to their male counterparts, tend to pass papers on to female friends or relations as souvenirs. During the nineteenth century, women built up collections of papers but often gave their letters and diaries to daughters and nieces. This specific mode of preservation, with its own structure, reflects a motivation completely different from that of male society. Preservation was not institutionalized in the form of archives, as was the case with men, and was therefore much more fragile.

Only through the medium of historically based archival studies can the processors of these family archives acquire sufficient knowledge to identify and appropriately catalog fragments of women's collections found among men's private papers. We first need to know what women's source material exists. This is the only way to determine the extent of specifically feminine paths of transmission and of women's indirect participation in public life, in order to develop systems of categorization appropriate for accessing sources for women's history contained in existing archives. My question as to the standards of evaluation needed to describe and render accessible sources for the history of women and their organizations in general, nonspecialized archives is addressed to both historians and archivists. Only cooperation between the two can lead to a satisfactory scholarly solution of the problem.

The Dutch Women's Thesaurus

The "-W" Option

Marieke Kramer (Netherlands)

INTRODUCTION

The Dutch Women's Thesaurus, published in 1992, was developed for, and in close cooperation with, the Dutch women's information services, to be used as a common system for indexing material on the position of women and women's studies. Because the thesaurus was developed as a system for The Netherlands, not just for one center, the situation in the field of women's information and documentation in The Netherlands must be described briefly.

WOMEN'S INFORMATION SERVICES IN THE NETHERLANDS

With 15 million inhabitants, The Netherlands has about fifty libraries, archives, and resource centers on women; most are members of a formal network. They can be categorized as follows:

- Regional or provincial centers, each having a regional collection and targeted to a regional audience.
- Specialized centers, each focusing on one subject, such as women and law, women and autonomy (or development), or women and sexual violence. In addition, there are the women's studies libraries and docu-

Until February 1995 **Marieke Kramer** was head of the Department of Consultancy and Research of the International Information Centre and Archives for the Women's Movement (IIAV), The Netherlands. She is now Project Leader for Databases and Networking, Databank of Expert Women, The Netherlands.

mentation centers at the universities, such as women's studies in agriculture and women's studies in medicine.
- A national center, the International Information Centre and Archives for the Women's Movement (IIAV), in Amsterdam.

Although this sounds impressive, most of the regional centers have limited funding and most of the specialized centers have only short-term funding. Only the IIAV is publicly subsidized.

In 1985 a national symposium for women's libraries was organized around this question: "Why are these special resource centers necessary?" One answer was the invisibility and inaccessibility of women's information in regular libraries and the importance, therefore, of special-subject indexing systems. That answer led us to our main problem: most centers were not satisfied with their own systems and, moreover, wanted a common Dutch system for better exchange of data.

Accordingly, two steps were taken. The first was a six-month feasibility study, carried out by Gusta Drenthe and Maria van der Sommen to determine whether a system existed in The Netherlands or elsewhere that everyone could use. If the answer was no, what kind of system should be developed? The study recommended constructing a new system, preferably a thesaurus.

THE THESAURUS PROJECT

This new project received funds from the Dutch Bureau for Libraries and Information Services, IIAV, and the Anna Maria van Schuurmancentrum, the Centre for Women's Studies at the University of Utrecht. IIAV and the Anna Maria van Schuurman Centre own the thesaurus.

The following criteria were formulated for collecting terms for the thesaurus:

- Dutch language
- Suitable for both small collections and large bibliographic databases
- Usable in both automated and manual systems
- Appropriate for an interdisciplinary field of study
- Gender-free terms (no "women's education," and so on)
- Focus on women's libraries, regular libraries, and on users

The procedure established was as follows:

- Collect terms from existing indexing systems, women's studies researchers and subject specialists, and women's studies literature
- Arrange the terms
- Discuss the results with an advisory committee
- Classify the terms in categories, and check for completeness

- Ask the participating women's libraries to evaluate the results
- Publish a test version
- Organize a workshop for evaluation
- Incorporate the test results

The project took two years, and the thesaurus was published in March 1992.

Content and Structure of the Thesaurus

The thesaurus contains 2,200 terms, in a hierarchical structure, with notes on term definitions and relations. There are also lists of form codes (bibliography, film catalog, lesbian novel), geographical terms (Austria, BT [broader term] Central Europe, BT Western Europe), chronological terms (Middle Ages, colonial period, nineteenth century), occupational groups (agrarian occupations, creative occupations).

Parts of the thesaurus are very detailed, as in the following example:

Term: mothers
Narrower term: single mothers, surrogate mothers, birth mothers, grandmothers, lesbian mothers, foster mothers, stepmothers

In other respects, the structure does not differ much from that of other multidisciplinary thesauri, although several features make the thesaurus unique.

RELATED TERMS (RT)   The thesaurus uses many related terms, and they indicate ideological connotation: for instance, Dowry, *see also* Killing of brides; or Pornography: RT Sexual violence. Moreover, women's culture is an RT of Culture and not an NT (narrower term); this is done to accentuate its equal value. This use of related terms is one thesaurus solution most criticized by regular users.

AMPLE USE OF SCOPE NOTES (SN)   The use of such notes was necessary because the subject is so new. A scope note may consist of a term's definition, possible use, and redefinition, from a female perspective, as in the following example:

Dormitory suburbs [built environment]
SN Male-defined term, used for suburbs with primary function of living/sleeping: for many women, a place to work; for many men, a place to sleep
BT Suburbs
RT Grass widows

MINUS-W (-V) PRINCIPLE   One characteristic of a women's thesaurus is that many terms are used that explicitly define aspects of women's lives (e.g., motherhood), although many general terms have to be used, but as related to women (e.g., health insurance, midlife crisis). Our thesaurus is unique in that the general terms always apply to women. When the terms are used in relation to men, we use (-v) (the initial of the Dutch word for woman/en) to express this. For information on men, an extra step has to be taken: for example, health insurance (-v), midlife crisis (-v).

This principle is used especially for the names of occupations. The Dutch language uses a masculine and a feminine suffix for many professions. Often in a thesaurus, the male form is chosen because the female form means something different or denotes an occupation with much less status. But our thesaurus uses the female form only when the content of the occupation is in fact different, and it is also used for males in those occupations, with the "(-v)" to indicate that males are meant.

The following examples should make this clearer:

Secretaris (traditionally masculine) is an assistant to the director of an important decision-making position (e.g., state secretary); in our thesaurus **Secretaris** is a female state secretary and **Secretaris** (-v) a male state secretary; **Secretaresse** (the usual female form) is a female typist; **Secretaresse** (-v) is a male typist.

Similarly, **Bibliothecaris** is a female library director; **Bibliothecaris** (-v) a male director. **Bibliothecaresse** is a female library assistant; **Bibliothecaresse** (-v) a male assistant.

Use and Maintenance of the Thesaurus

The thesaurus is now used as a complete system in about ten centers. These centers have for the most part a broad, general collection covering all aspects of women's lives. Two centers use a shorter version, compiled especially for them from the original. Other centers are waiting for special, in-depth adaptations.

At IIAV we started using the thesaurus approximately one and a half years ago. This was a huge operation. We were using three systems: a classification system for the library, subject headings for documentation, and broad categories for our bibliographical journal, *Lover*. They had to be merged and transformed into one new one. We now use the thesaurus for books, periodical articles, historical documentation, and our current research database. Shortly we will index the audiovisual materials with the thesaurus as well.

Maintenance includes adding terms and correcting mistakes. The person in charge of maintenance has regular contacts with all the users. We expect to prepare a supplement by the autumn of 1994.

One major adjustment is needed, however. Although the thesaurus works well in general, it needs to be adjusted to "Black perspectives." It is now a White thesaurus, for White collections. Black women miss terms that describe their lives and ask for different, more inclusive scope notes. The Project Information

Services for Black and Migrant Women (see the article by Tanhya Mendeszoon) will start this in 1995.

CONCLUSION

From the start, the thesaurus has been a cooperative project. After the joint initiative, about twenty-five centers have contributed by sending their systems, commenting on the preliminary results, and testing the first version. This is true not only for the Dutch centers, but also Flemish-speaking centers in Belgium, where the thesaurus is used in three libraries. Cooperation continues through the maintenance procedure and through the user group that has been formed within LOVI, the Dutch network of women's information services (archives, libraries, documentation centers).

Finally, I want to make a recommendation about building a thesaurus as a national cooperative project. Let just two, perhaps three, persons be in charge. This applies to both development and maintenance. The more people and the more centers involved, the longer the discussions about single terms will last! But two or three people will be able to make decisions promptly.

The Lilith Information Network

Italian Feminism in an International Context

Luciana Tufani (Italy)

INTRODUCTION

The Lilith Information Network (LIN) is the first Italian database that collects and provides information specifically on what women write in Italy and abroad. Lilith is connected with other women's documentation centers in Europe; our goal is to link our network with women's centers throughout the world.

Lilith can increase international cooperation in several ways. It makes it easier for scholars to do research on Italian women; it enables us to share with other women's groups our experience of building and managing an independent women's documentation center; it provides research tools for academicians interested in developing comparative women's studies departments at their universities; it is connected with projects sponsored by the European Community to train librarians specialized in women's texts; and it has helped to sustain and spread the cultural impact of independent feminist journals.

WOMEN'S DOCUMENTATION CENTERS IN ITALY

In the late 1970s and early 1980s, women in Italy founded a large number of women's documentation centers; several others have been founded since then.

Luciana Tufani is President of Lilith Information Network and of the Centro Documentazione Donna di Ferrara (documentation center and library). She has been editor and publisher of *Leggere Donna* (a women's review of books) since 1980 and author of *Leggere donna: Guida all'acquisto dei libri di donne* (1994), a bibliography of women's books, and other books.

211

Some of these centers are fully autonomous, both financially and institutionally. Others are linked to, and at times directly dependent on, state funding, mostly in cities with supportive left-wing administrations. It is difficult to estimate the number of centers that have existed or continue to exist, because the situation is always in flux; new ones are founded, others close down, and some undergo crises but are eventually able to continue their activities. A few years ago, a census revealed the existence of about 100 women's centers, documentation centers, bookstores, and libraries in Italy.

THE LILITH INFORMATION NETWORK

In 1984, the Association for the National Coordination of Women's Centers was founded. Almost a decade later, in 1993, ten of those centers and bookstores, which had been working together on several other projects, founded the Lilith Information Network. The ten founding centers are in Florence, Rome, Milan, Ferrara, Bologna, L'Aquila, Cagliari, and Genoa, and all have large, specialized women's libraries with rich archives of material that would be difficult to catalog with traditional (male-centered) cataloging systems.

Cataloging Feminist Material

In order to catalog this feminist material, and thanks especially to the expertise and the commitment of Eugenia Galateri and Piera Codognotto of the Florence women's bookstore, we have been able to develop a computer program (using CDS/ISIS software) that incorporates the specific features of a woman-centered database. For example, we have eliminated the generic masculine in all its forms and have developed specialized feminist search words, which do not exist in male-oriented cataloging systems.

The quickest, most effective way to catalog such female-specific documents and books as the ones we own seemed to be the creation of an index based on a female thesaurus—that is, on a list of keywords derived from the feminist books and documents themselves. The most significant advantage of this indexing strategy is that we can now search not only by author and title but also by *feminist* subject, using keywords that belong to the specific lexicon developed in the context of the women's movement and women's studies.

Creating a Thesaurus

By using a female thesaurus we can also pass on and insert into our everyday language the words and phrases that have emerged from the women's movement and that reflect its history and contributions to many fields of knowledge. All this aims first at preserving a female and feminist heritage that may be lost or forgotten, and second at transforming contemporary reality by popularizing in everyday language a gender-conscious vocabulary that, by its very existence, will help change traditional attitudes and ways of thinking.

For example, the following words are traditionally used to designate women's work inside the home:

Housewife
Domestic work
Family work

These terms suggest the invisibility of such work. But the use of Caretaking as a thesaurus term implies that the work should be redistributed between the sexes.

Some new, more politicized words have been adopted for thesaurus use:

Double labor
Double presence

Using such terms to designate women's work inside and outside the home emphasizes the complexity of women's labor.

From the dichotomies nature/culture, body/mind, woman/man, a woman-centered thesaurus helps women arrive at an awareness of their bodies and their cultural and political implications.

Expanding the Thesaurus

The thesaurus, created by Beatrice Perucci and Adriana Perrotta of the Milan women's center, is being enriched, revised, and computerized. We are also planning to develop a multilingual thesaurus, with the Centro de Investigacion Historica de la Dona (CIHD) in Barcelona; we plan to extend this international collaboration to other women's centers in various nations and continents.

About 4,000 of the 10,000 records in the Lilith database were taken from *Leggere Donna*, an independent feminist literary journal founded in Ferrara in 1980. In Italian, the name contains a pun: "reading women" and "reading as women." The goals of the journal have always been to document, discuss, and preserve women's artistic production. *Leggere Donna* was in fact the first journal in Italy to deal systematically with books by and about women. The multidisciplinary and international variety of texts reviewed since 1980 continue to make the journal an important source of information on women's accomplishments in literature and the other arts. *Leggere Donna* is instrumental to the continual updating of the Lilith database.

CONCLUSION

Since the establishment of the Lilith Information Network, others have joined the ten founding centers in collaborating on implementation of, or in simply using, the database. Other institutions, including public libraries and university research institutes, have applied to become members of LIN. The network is available throughout Italy. We have met with other European women's centers, and we have an active network member (CIHD) in Barcelona. We are collaborating with CIHD on a New Opportunity for Women (NOW) project sponsored by the European Economic Community. NOW projects aim to increase the opportunities for cultural and technological professionalization for women. More specifically, the NOW project connected with LIN focuses on training women librarians specializing in cataloging women's texts. Training includes courses in women's studies, library science, and computer science.

Above all, our goal is to link our network with other women's centers throughout the world. We want to let others know about our activities as feminist librarians in Italy. We also want to learn from and about the activities of women in other countries.

Electronic Graffiti or Scholar's Tool?

A Critical Evaluation of Selected Women's Lists on Internet

Suzanne Hildenbrand (U.S.A.)

INTRODUCTION

Considerable hype surrounds all aspects of the Information Age, including computer-assisted communication. Numerous factors contribute to this exaggeration. In pursuit of profits, the computer and software industries make extravagant claims. The U.S. government encourages people to focus on the marvels of the emerging society rather than on present reality. Internet users, aware of their privileged position and the novelty of what they are doing, make nonusers feel that they have been left behind in the Dark Ages. Finally, and most directly related to computer-assisted communication, is the turn toward a virtual community when many natural communities seem hostile and alienating.

Glossary

The Internet has spawned a certain amount of jargon. The following terms are used in this article:

> ELECTRONIC MAILING LIST. A list of members stored on a computer with appropriate software (see LISTSERV, for example) that permits

Suzanne Hildenbrand has an M.S. in Library Service from Columbia University and a Ph.D. from the University of California at Berkeley. She teaches in the School of Information and Library Studies at the State University of New York at Buffalo. Recent publications include "Promoting Participation: Libraries and Women's Roles in American Society," in *The Role of the Library in the Democratic Process* (forthcoming), and "Women in American Libraries: The Long Road from Contributions to Transformation," in *Leidenschaft und Bildung* (1992). She edited *Women's Collections: Libraries, Archives and Consciousness* (1986).

distribution of messages to the group. Lists are typically formed around a topic of interest; topics range from the more academic, such as those discussed here, to personal help lists to popular entertainment.

FLAMING means sending argumentative, rude, or insulting messages to the list. These messages are a violation of "netiquette," recommended behavior on the 'net.

LISTSERV is a type of software, or instructions, developed to manage electronic mailing lists. Commands such as SUBSCRIBE are standard on all lists using this software. Archives, backfiles of messages, can be maintained and simple statistical data produced.

SURFING means wandering aimlessly on the network, often encountering new and interesting things but sometimes only wasting time. It is similar to browsing in a library or bookstore.

THE NEED FOR REVIEWS

Beginning Internet users are faced with an immense data glut and limited guidance in selecting what they need. While surfing can be fun, many, particularly those with scholarly interests or heavy work loads, have little time for it. In addition, many people must pay for messages; for them surfing is an expensive sport. Furthermore, there is much junk in cyberspace. Librarians have a major role to play in evaluating resources in cyberspace, as they have had in evaluating dictionaries, films, and other resources. Their reviews have helped both users and producers of reference tools. In the area of scholarship on women, the need is especially great for at least two reasons.

Contrary to the hype about democracy on-line, gender hierarchies may be reproduced even on lists devoted to feminist issues. While print reference tools may also show a male bias, the interactive nature of the lists often leads to insults and conflicts, which discourage women's participation. Women are also likely to have less access to and experience with computers than men have, so guidance that promotes efficient use may be especially welcome.

To date few true reviews of any lists can be found. There is no obvious impediment to reviews. Rapid changes in the lists should make no difference in evaluation, since reviews can be stored electronically and updated often. What follows is an outline of some of the information about scholarly electronic lists that would be most valuable.

LIST FEATURES TO BE ASSESSED

Three interrelated features of each list can be assessed: structure and management, membership, and messages or content. Each feature has further aspects that need assessment. Some can be readily ascertained, such as the number of members a list has or the number of messages posted in a given time. Others, such as the appearance of an on-line community, are more complex and harder to judge.

Structure and Management

The following items need to be considered:

BEGINNING DATE   The age of a list is important because it takes time for a list to develop members and a character.

GOALS OR PURPOSE   Like a reference work, an electronic list needs a clear statement of purpose and scope. Typically, new subscribers are automatically sent a welcome letter or message that clearly states the purpose of the list and provides basic commands.

ARCHIVES   The presence of an archives that stores all messages sent to the list is of vital importance to its fullest use. The archives can be searched just as can any database. It also permits study of the evolution of the list.

DIGEST VERSIONS   For lists with heavy traffic, it is important to know whether a digest form exists. Digests provide a brief summary of topics of messages and permit users to select only the messages on topics of interest. In addition, some lists are available on Usenet, which posts messages from lists to a special reader list, and not to the subscriber's electronic mailbox. This avoids numerous postings that clog mailboxes.

ROLE OF THE OWNER/MODERATOR   Most lists have owners; subscribers post directly to the list, and their messages are distributed automatically. Some lists have moderators; subscribers' messages go to the moderator, who determines whether they should be distributed to the entire list. Inappropriate messages are not distributed. Moderators may also group related messages. The moderator seems to have more power than an owner, but an alert list owner can make suggestions of other placements for inappropriate topics and frequent reminders of unacceptable types of messages.

HARDWARE/SOFTWARE   All systems are vulnerable to problems. The women's health list, WMN-HLTH, for instance, was plagued with technical problems that interrupted message flow and had to move to a new machine and different software. As systems improve and the ability to transmit multimedia becomes available, adoption of the necessary software and hardware will be important.

Membership

The matter of membership presents some challenges to the librarian reviewer. First, there is no true equivalent to this category in other media that are reviewed; although membership resembles audience or intended readership, it is different because of the interactive nature of the medium. Second, this feature of computer-assisted communication has been most distorted by InfoAge hype. Exaggerated claims are often made about the allegedly democratic nature of computer-assisted communication and the on-line community. Claims that participants have no established identity or social baggage are enormous exaggerations and the effort to link this to democracy seems misguided.

The reality is that many features of personal identity are obvious on the nets. Few people conceal their gender. The e-mail address itself may give clues to affiliation (although many small institutions access Internet through nearby large universities), and the messages themselves, as well as the fact of access and the level of communication, are indicators of social status.

It seems to be not democracy that is promoted by the allegedly identity-less state on the nets, but rather some less positive aspects of U.S. culture. If African Americans or women of any race must conceal their identity to be heard, that is not democratic. To one observer (Giuseppe Mantovani, "Is computer-mediated communication intrinsically apt to enhance democracy in organizations?" *Human Relations* 47 [January 1994]: 55), the enthusiasm for communication unhindered by social baggage seems antisocial, shifting the blame to society for the "inhibition and frustration" faced by individuals. Is this merely an updated version of traditional American rugged individualism? It certainly suggests the culture of the isolated "intrepid adventurer" that Sherry Turkle found dominated computer training and alienated women and girls (cited in *Women, Information Technology and Scholarship*, edited by Jeanie Taylor et al. [Urbana: Center for Advanced Study, University of Illinois, 1993], p. 18).

While electronic lists do facilitate a sense of community, it seems clear that the community generally exists beforehand; the list thus becomes a valuable tool for building and maintaining a community. This seems to be the case according to various reports of emerging feminist on-line networks. Community is, however, difficult to assess as it is highly subjective.

There is a range of data needed about list members, some of which are easier to obtain than others.

NUMBER   The number of members can be determined from the membership list, usually available with a review command to the listserv.

GENDER   While it is not always easy to determine gender, even on academic lists where there is little reason to conceal gender identity, the number and percentage of women and men are useful facts. Communications research continues to document significant gender differences.

DISTRIBUTION   Geographic and social distribution and academic and professional affiliations are all useful information. Unfortunately it is not possible to determine even geographic location for large numbers of subscribers. Internet addresses show a two-letter code for countries, but they do not provide codes for U.S. states or for provinces or other portions of countries.

PARTICIPATION   It is clear that each list has a large number of members who do not send messages, the so-called "lurkers." New members, especially those new to the world of electronic lists, are often slow to post messages. Gender differences in participation, already mentioned, are significant. One researcher finds that higher-status persons are more likely to refrain from participation than are lower-status persons, apparently the opposite of face-to-face communication, where higher-status persons tend to dominate. In this, as in all areas of computer-assisted communication, more research is needed.

Related to participation is the problematic issue of community development. When researchers investigating Women's Studies List (WMST-L) asked members for the most useful aspects of membership, a high percentage responded "sense of community." Many others said they enjoyed sharing personal experiences. Another potential measure of community is whether members communicated with people previously unknown to them as a result of belonging to the list. Again, more research is needed.

Messages or Content

Content is the reason one starts or subscribes to a list. The data desirable for a review range from simple message counts to sophisticated content analysis.

VOLUME AND PATTERNS   Important variables include (1) the average number of messages in a given period, (2) the average postings by a participating member (a list may be dominated by a few frequent posters), (3) the average length of postings, and (4) when the traffic is heaviest or lightest, and what kinds of messages occur on a seasonal basis. Very high volume causes some people to sign off a list.

TYPE   Many messages on academic lists are what librarians call ready-reference questions, such as bibliographic and directory questions and responses. Some messages are distributed to the entire list by mistake. Other common types are messages from the list owner or moderator in the role of manager and those forwarded from another list. A high percentage of the latter may indicate a sluggish membership.

RELEVANCE   The degree to which the messages fall within the scope of the announced goals of the list is crucial. If irrelevant or peripheral material becomes dominant, the reality of the list will not match its title and stated goals, causing subscribers to quit, misleading potential subscribers, and diminishing the list's value as a source for its discipline.

QUALITY OF DISCOURSE   Some lists maintain a high level of civility; others have an angry, contentious tone. Is there typically much "flaming"? Do individuals acknowledge and respond to each other, and does this response vary by gender?

THE STUDY: SELECTION, PROCEDURES, AND FINDINGS

After following many lists of an academic nature that dealt with women's issues, the author set out to review several women's lists. Several guides to women's electronic lists are available. The most up-to-date, because in electronic form, and inclusive, is maintained by the Women's Studies List owner, Joan Korenman. It is "Gender-Related Electronic Forums," most recently updated in February 1995. (For access directions see Appendix.) Print sources covering major lists include *Electronic Access to Research on Women: A Short Guide* by Judith Hudson and Kathleen A. Turek (Institute for Research on Women, State University at Albany, 1994), and Mary Glazier, "Internet Resources for Women's Studies" *College and Research Libraries News* 55 (March 1994): 135–7. What is reported here is a work in progress.

Selection

Four lists focusing on women's concerns were selected for study. These lists were selected to provide an understanding of the size and scope of academic lists available on women. It is difficult to assess many features without some knowledge of related lists. While WMST-L seems big in the world of women's lists, for example, it is small compared to some professional library lists with memberships of four to five thousand.

The lists selected were WMST-L (women's studies list), WMN-HLTH (health issues), H-WOMEN (women's history), and FEMISA (women's issues in international relations). The selection reflects a need to include lists with archives, a range of interests, and a readily manageable amount of data, and to avoid highly specialized lists. The appendix to this article gives directions for subscribing.

Procedures

Two major files were established, one of messages obtained from the archives and including all those posted for the period April 22–29, 1994. This file contained 399 records. The second file, of the membership lists, was obtained by a review command sent to each listserv and showed a total of 5,055 subscribers to all four lists.

The membership list was coded for gender, and the messages, for gender of sender and for content and form. Care was taken to code gender for the original sender, not for the moderator who re-sent the message. Unfortunately, coding was limited to three letters. Name data were accepted as entered on the subscriber list or message. A rather large number of both subscribers and message senders were coded *I* for indeterminate, owing to gender-ambiguous names or the use of initials.

A simple, homegrown scheme was used for content and form coding. Each message was actually read because subject lines were often misleading or missing. So, for example, a message that dealt with theory, including research *(T)*, and was bibliographic *(B)* in nature was coded *TB*. Many messages were coded with just one letter: for example, a request for a citation or an observation on a topic. As expected, there were many bibliographic and directory messages, announcements, and calls for papers. The *T* code was applied generously to many messages dealing with definitions; electronic lists do not appear to be the place for major discussions of theory.

Findings

Men were somewhat overrepresented in postings on all lists or the percentage of posts by men for the week studied exceeds their percentage on membership lists, although less so on WMST-L and more so on H-WOMEN than on others. On average, on all lists men posted longer messages than women did. The difference on WMST-L was only 6 lines, while it was almost 100 lines on WMN-HLTH, undoubtedly because one man posted an entire issue of *Morbidity and Mortality Weekly Report.*

WMST-L   WMST-L is the largest list, both in membership (2,873) and in traffic for the week (199 messages). An older list with an established character that is highly professional, WMST-L is well managed. Messages covered teaching tips, student evaluations, and sex between professors and students. The only messages coded for theory were posted by women.

H-WOMEN   A relatively new list, H-WOMEN is part of the ambitious H-NETWORK project, which has lists on numerous fields of history. The only moderated list among the four, it showed no error messages for the week. It is large in terms of subscribers (1,024), but was third in terms of traffic for the week (59 messages). It had the highest percentage of men posting messages, approximately one-third. Many messages had nothing to do specifically with women; there were calls for papers for general history conferences. There was a lively discussion on the origin and meaning of the phrase *rule of thumb*, which accounted for many of the messages labeled theory; women posted almost twice as many theory messages as did men. Surprising, after WMST-L, was the lack of any discussion of teaching women's history in separate or in general history courses, but this topic may have been covered previously.

WMN-HLTH   Next in size by number of subscribers (617) but last in terms of messages posted during the week (39) was WMN-HLTH, which brings together a bewildering variety of people, including persons with a disease or physical disability, researchers, and clinicians. While such a grouping reflects a recent trend toward developing a community around a specific topic, it seems ill suited to a field as large and diverse as women's health. Topics covered include diseases and normal conditions such as lactation and menstruation. Many messages dealt with personal experiences; others sought advice about therapy— often alternative—with few bibliographic, directory, or theory and research messages. Only 5 of the 39 messages were posted by men, but the longest post on any of the lists was sent to this list by a man.

FEMISA   FEMISA ranks last in terms of subscribers (541) and second in terms of messages posted (102), and displayed the most controversy, argument, and flaming of the four. It also had the highest number (43) and percentage (42) of messages dealing with the list itself, many with alleged male domination of the list. On any given topic, men's messages averaged twenty more lines of text than did women's. A high number of people (13) leaving the list told the entire list rather than just listserv. While this counts as an error in the coding scheme, it is difficult not to conclude that these members were angry and wanted to let everyone know it. In contrast, only 5 messages dealt with rape issues. Reading the messages was like eavesdropping on a noisy family quarrel.

ELECTRONIC GRAFFITI OR SCHOLAR'S TOOL?

The short answer to the title question is "Both." The scholarly user must learn to be selective or waste many hours hitting the delete key. The hypnotic power of the nets is well recognized, and enthusiastic netters may be signing up only for a front-row seat at a shouting match, even on presumably academic lists. List owners need to realize that focus is not necessarily oppressive and can promote scholarly community. Librarians have a role to play in advising both users and owners through evaluative reviews.

APPENDIX

1. To subscribe to FEMISA send the message
   SUBSCRIBE FEMISA FIRST NAME LAST NAME
   to LISTSERV@CSF.COLORADO.EDU (Internet)
2. To subscribe to H-WOMEN send the message
   SUBSCRIBE H-WOMEN FIRST NAME LAST NAME
   to LISTSERV@UICVM.UIC.EDU (Internet)
   or LISTSERV@UICVM (Bitnet)
3. To subscribe to WMN-HLTH send the message
   SUBSCRIBE WMN-HLTH FIRST NAME LAST NAME
   to LISTPROC@U.WASHINGTON.EDU (Internet)
4. To subscribe to WMST-L send the message
   SUBSCRIBE WMST-L FIRST NAME LAST NAME
   to LISTSERV@UMDD.UMD.EDU (Internet)
   or LISTSERV@UMDD (Bitnet)

"Gender-Related Electronic Forums" is available via e-mail. Send this message
GET OTHER—Lists WMST-L to
    LISTSERV@UMDD.UMD.EDU (Internet)
or   LISTSERV@UMDD.EDU (Bitnet)

Global Organizing

Technology and the Goals of Women's Organizations

Susan C. Mooney (U.S.A.)

INTRODUCTION

The Institute for Global Communications (IGC) in San Francisco, California, operates four networks: PeaceNet, EcoNet, ConflictNet, and LaborNet. The IGC is a nonprofit organization that provides networking tools for international communication and information exchange. These tools include electronic mail, electronic conferences, electronic databases or discussion areas, and full Internet access.

The IGC is the U.S. member of the Association for Progressive Communications (APC), a worldwide partnership of networks dedicated to providing low-cost computer communications services for individuals and organizations working for environmental sustainability, universal human rights, and social and economic justice. APC empowers local, indigenous organizations by encouraging expertise in computer networking. Believing that access to information is a fundamental human right, APC serves more than 20,000 activists in 100 countries. It has been the primary provider of telecommunications at various United Nations conferences and will provide such services at the Fourth World Conference on Women (WCW) in 1995. At the WCW, PeaceNet's women's information desk will facilitate networking and help more women's organizations throughout the United States take advantage of the power of electronic communication tools.

Susan C. Mooney is Women's Program Officer of PeaceNet at the Institute for Global Communications in San Francisco.

THE WOMEN'S NETWORKING SUPPORT PROJECT

At each of its partner networks APC has initiated a Women's Networking Support Project to enhance women's involvement before, during, and after important conferences. APC offers a global forum for women's NGOs to exchange information, coordinate actions, and discuss proposals and positions. It provides an electronic space for electronic conferences, databases, official UN information, NGO documents, women's news services and publications, personal stories, and so on. Particular emphasis is given to increasing information flow to and from areas where access to information is limited.

Women's groups have created international networks on such issues as poverty, domestic and sexual violence, environmental degradation, legal rights, health, education, and other issues that affect women worldwide. APC hopes to enhance these networks by facilitating women's access to computer communications technology. To ensure that as many women's organizations as possible can benefit, APC offers technical assistance for women's groups, training in use of the system, and ongoing information support.

HOW WOMEN ARE USING IT

Women are finding electronic communication a good way to disseminate information without the labor and cost of mailings, faxes, and long-distance phone calls. So it is saving them money and enabling them to reach a wider audience. For example, the Women of Color Resource Center is using a conference to gather information about women's issues as they pertain to women of color. Another organization is launching a project that provides training and use of facilities in radio, video, and computer telecommunications to community women. The idea is to use these media to disseminate women's information. Women's health organizations in various parts of the world share information via e-mail and participate in the electronic conference women.health. In short, women's organizations are using this technology and adapting it to suit their needs.

Organizing around National/International Conferences

An important use of this technology is in conference planning. It provides timely access to critical information and allows women to build international coalitions around issues. For example, on-line conferences have provided a means for physically scattered groups to coalesce their plans, refine their strategies, and collectively produce a set of requests or needs. Local-area networks have been set up during international conferences so that people could exchange information with their countries or offices about conference proceedings.

CONCLUSION

Technology by itself is not a panacea. We must look at how it can enhance our work and adapt it to fit our needs. We must also collaborate with other women's media. And we must always consider those who are not being reached by electronic means and move to fill those gaps.

PART IV

Outside Library Walls

An Aurat Foundation researcher reads a poster to women of the village of Youngsonabad, Pakistan.

Photo: Uzma Khan/Aurat Foundation.

Several speakers made the point that information about and for women, especially in developing countries where literacy is low and resources scarce, must be more than "a collection in a building." The articles in this last part range beyond library walls in various ways.

The first three emphasize oral information, whether the use of radio to disseminate information to women, or oral history as a way to document un- or underdocumented women, or to supplement written texts with information never recorded on paper.

An article from Ukraine on the need for including women in statistics echoes others (e.g., Mbambo) that stress the misleading nature of economic statistics that do not include women's unpaid work; this is an issue everywhere, but especially in countries in which virtually all women's work (including not only domestic but also agricultural work) is omitted from economic calculations and planning.

Another universal issue is health. This subject area is so important that it is the only one that merited its own session at the conference, reflecting the fact that there are documentation centers devoted entirely to women's health. Three articles describe such centers and their efforts to get information to all women who need it.

Two articles from the Middle East, one Palestinian, one Israeli, focus as much on women organizing for mutual aid and political change as on information as such, and so serve as a bridge to Arvonne Fraser's plenary presentation linking information and women's human rights on a global scale. This article and the Information Statement that follows it both look to the Beijing conference as a major concerted effort to make progress on these issues. Beijing will be a culmination but hardly the end of the process. Collecting adequate information about women and getting all women worldwide the information they need will continue to challenge information workers for years to come.

Information for Rural Women via Radio Pakistan

Nigar Ahmad and Uzma Khan (Pakistan)

RURAL WOMEN IN PAKISTAN

The rural population of Pakistan has been estimated at nearly 83 million, about 68 percent of the total population of 122 million. Of the rural population, about 22 million are women (aged fifteen and above), and they make a substantial contribution to their households and the national economy. Women spend enormous amounts of time and energy producing goods and services in their homes, in family farms, livestock care, off-farm enterprises and farm labor, and as producers of handicrafts and teachers. Most of this work is unpaid; women and their families accord it less importance than paid work.

Women's work is considered part of their familial duties rather than as an economic contribution. It is not consciously recognized that this unpaid labor reduces a household's expenditures and enhances its capacity to increase output and income. Almost one-third of the rural population lives below the poverty line; almost one-half of rural households cannot meet their basic requirements. Under these circumstances, women's labor is essential for the very survival of their households.

There is another problem with women's unpaid labor: it is difficult to reflect it in national labor force statistics. If it is not reflected in statistics, then

Nigar Ahmad is co-founder and Executive Director of the Aurat Foundation and Project Director for "Information on Food Production Technologies for Rural Women over the Radio." **Uzma Khan** is Director of the AF's Documentation and Resource Centre and Project Documentalist for the project described in this article.

planners cannot plan for increasing women's productivity or allocate funds for this. Women's economic role becomes invisible, and planners and line departments see women as only dependents and consumers.

The rural population is discriminated against in access to basic facilities. Most recent statistics show the ratio of rural to urban population's access to safe water was 27 percent to 83 percent; to health services, 35 percent to 99 percent; and to sanitation, 6 percent to 51 percent. The rural female literacy rate was 9.6 percent compared to 18 percent for all women. Even though rural women are provided some health and education facilities or social welfare schemes, there are no programs to provide extension, technology, training, or credit to make their labor more productive.

AURAT FOUNDATION'S ROLE

Aurat Publication and Information Service Foundation was established in 1986 in Lahore as a nonprofit, nongovernmental organization (NGO) that would collect, generate, repackage, and disseminate information for women's empowerment. Its major focus has been on women from disadvantaged groups, those who have the least access to information. It was felt that, if women received information that enabled them to make decisions about their daily lives, they would not only have more control of their lives but would also acquire the confidence to make decisions about their families and communities. Another aspect of women's empowerment that concerns Aurat Foundation is providing information to those who make decisions on behalf of women or who can work toward providing more political and social space for women.

Aurat Foundation (AF) has undertaken many projects and begun to establish continuing services for women. The major projects include Information Services, a Documentation and Resource Center (DRC), and an Information Network for Women's Development. In addition, training is provided to enhance the skills of NGOs, community-based organizations (CBOs), and women's groups.

Information Services

The Information Services perform the following functions:

- identifying gaps in information, on the basis of which research and surveys are conducted
- informing the DRC about the information needs of women
- identifying the training needs of women and women's organizations
- disseminating information through channels of communication

Information is disseminated directly to women contacting Aurat's offices, and through the media; participation in the workshops, meetings, and conferences of other groups; information dissemination workshops; networking activities; training activities; publications (posters, calendars, leaflets, pamphlets, booklets, manuals, and postcards); and audiovisual material.

Documentation and Resource Center

The Documentation and Resource Center consists of a Reference Library, a Publications Unit, and an Audio-Visual Unit. It is the repository of information required for clearinghouse functions and provision of resources for and about women. It provides the backup for Information Services. The DRC also develops, through writing, repackaging, and translating, AF's publications and audiovisual output. Publications in Urdu and English have included such subjects as credit and savings schemes for women, basic health care, and legal rights of female factory workers.

Information Network for Women's Development

The Information Network for Women's Development is an ongoing project to build a support network through which NGOs and other organizations can discuss mutual problems, exchange information, and plan joint activities. Networking also provides alternative channels of communication to identify the needs of women and organizations working for women, as well as for disseminating information. Members of this network include welfare, activist, and development organizations; professional, youth, community-based, and church groups; government agencies; and individuals.

Training Workshops

Workshops are held regularly in all four provinces of Pakistan to train NGOs in formulating projects for women's development. Community-level workshops enable women from low-income localities to identify their problems, analyze the causes, and work for solutions. The focus is on creating awareness and motivating women to organize. Training is also provided in participatory methodology for community development workers, a program organized in response to the expressed needs of various NGOs. Training of community health workers is conducted by AF doctors.

By 1990 AF was sufficiently well established to open additional offices in Karachi and Islamabad. It was looking to expand its outreach to rural areas. The initial idea for the project arose from a workshop on "Food Technologies for Rural Women" held in Bangkok. While still considering the feasibility of such a project, AF was invited to hold the First National Conference of Peasant Women in Pakistan, the Haryali Conference.

THE HARYALI CONFERENCE

The Haryali Conference was held primarily to make visible the impact on the lives of peasant women of the degradation of Pakistan's natural resources. It was therefore important to hear directly from peasant women how their livelihood was being affected and how they perceived their lives could be changed. This was the beginning of a dialogue between peasant women and those who make decisions on their behalf at the national level.

This was the first conference of its kind, and there was skepticism about whether peasant women would leave their homes and fields and travel to Lahore to meet similar women. This kind of event is traditionally organized and attended by men. But 103 peasant women came, from Sindh, Punjab, Baluchistan, NorthWest Frontier Province, and the northern areas of Pakistan, escorted by extension workers or representatives of organizations that had helped identify them. The interest, effort, and courage it required for these women to overcome the many barriers to take part in this event can only be appreciated by those who know about their lives.

The specific objectives of the Haryali Conference were to:

- encourage peasant women to articulate their relationship with land, water, and forest resources through their daily work
- enable peasant women to share their experiences and concerns
- provide exposure to women's groups that have made progress because of collective efforts
- provide an opportunity to work together to identify possible solutions to problems
- provide an opportunity for policy makers and public representatives to hear from peasant women so as to reflect their concerns in policies and programs for better management of natural resources to meet rural women's needs

Women's Inaccessibility to Technology

In rural Pakistan women have traditionally had no access to technology. This inaccessibility exists at three levels:

1. Information on technologies that raise productivity in activities that are shared by men and women is usually not provided to women. Male extension agents do not or cannot contact women farmers, training schemes are designed by males who may not be sensitive to the constraints on women's participation, and women lack control over resources.
2. In female-specific tasks, such as household chores or food preparation (which includes collecting firewood and water, making cow dung cakes, and grinding grains and spices), there has been little development of tech-

nology and where there is, little acquisition of it by households. This reflects both the low priority given to women's work and the lack of societal concern about its physical drudgery.

3. Any technology introduced for female-specific operations is immediately taken over by males. Women have the doubtful pleasure of being relieved of not just the drudgery of this work, but also the income they may have earned from it.

The Haryali Conference determined that there was a need for a project that would keep a continuous link with peasant women; build up a critical mass so as to develop peasant women's bargaining power; facilitate women's organization through helping provide links and experience sharing; strengthen support structures, such as local NGOs or CBOs and supportive local political representatives; develop advocacy and links with relevant government agencies and political representatives on a continuous basis to keep women permanently on their agenda; and develop links at the level at which women could deal directly with the services and facilities provided for them by local-level line departments, public representatives, NGOs, and others.

Dissemination over Radio

Given the extremely low literacy rate for rural women, it was decided that radio would be the most appropriate medium for communicating this information. Radio is a mobile medium. The message can be received while the listener is involved in other activities. Radio can be multilingual and still remain more cost effective than any other mass medium, is used even in remote areas without electricity, can provide instruction and entertainment at the same time, is a familiar technology, and easily accessible.

AF's partner in this endeavor was the state-owned Pakistan Broadcasting Corporation (PBC), more commonly known as Radio Pakistan. Through its eighteen broadcasting stations, PBC currently reaches 75 percent of the country's area and 95 percent of its population. According to UNDP (United Nations Development Programme) statistics, the number of radios in Pakistan in 1988 was 86 per 1,000 population, but this is probably a low estimate because of the many unlicensed radios. Surveys conducted by PBC found that 90 percent of the population listen to the radio, although only half are regular listeners. PBC's prime time differs for various segments of society—10 to 11 A.M. is considered prime time for female listeners.

In discussions between AF and producers and staff at the Lahore station, it became apparent that the length and choice of broadcasting time were based not on the needs of the intended audience but on financial resources and policy directives. Although more than 100 hours of information programs are broadcast for farmers every week, there is only half an hour for rural women.

THE PROJECT

The project was funded mainly by UNIFEM (United Nations Development Fund for Women) and work commenced in January 1993. It included the following components:

- Field research to build up agricultural activity profiles of rural women to identify their current agricultural practices and their access to government services.
- Institutional research on methods to enhance agricultural productivity of peasant women and their households through providing information on inexpensive and environment-friendly methods of production.
- Research of literature to identify appropriate methods of production that have been successfully used elsewhere.
- Preparation of a thirty-minute weekly radio program in the national language and four regional languages to be broadcast over two years to provide rural women information on technologies relevant to their roles as food producers.
- Production of simply written, illustrated material (pamphlets, leaflets, posters) and audiocassettes for follow-up dissemination.
- Setting up 500 Supervised Listening Centers where women could listen to the program actively and have access to the accompanying printed materials.
- Providing an answering service as a first line of agriculture extension to women requesting specific information after listening to the program, until their links with the regular services are institutionalized.
- Linking women through Listening Centers and the rural-based NGOs and CBOs with agriculture extension, technology transfer, and credit institutions and facilitating the institutionalization of these links.

Although the program would reach a very large target group, its short duration meant that supplementary activities were essential for continuing impact. A follow-up action plan was formulated to maintain continuity in communicating information, develop two-way communication channels between women and technology institutions, and respond to expressed needs. Specific follow-up activities included repackaging information in printed material, audiocassettes, and the like; dissemination of material by mailing directly to women in the listening center, or through rural-based organizations that are part of AF's network; and arranging for technology demonstrations and training by relevant institutions and agencies wherever rural women express such a demand. The first phase of the project was conducted in northern and central Punjab. The program was broadcast in Urdu, the national language, for six months and comprised twenty-six episodes.

Research

After the researchers had been given an orientation on agriculture and gender issues, areas were selected for field research on the basis of ecological zones and cropping patterns. Correspondence was started with CBOs and NGOs working in these areas so that they could introduce the researchers to peasant women. The results of the field research provided information on rural women's social environment, their work and how it was accomplished, their access to and use of technology, their information needs, their attitudes to and awareness of radio, and their listening time preferences.

Once the field data were analyzed they were compiled to make "standard sheets" showing traditional operations performed for growing various crops. These sheets enabled the researchers to identify the topics for institutional and literature research. Agricultural research institutions, training departments, and extension services were visited for this information. It was then analyzed and repackaged for script-writing, for printing as posters, and as replies to listeners' queries. The sheets also allowed the researchers to discuss plans with agricultural technology transfer institutions for future training and demonstration sessions for peasant women.

Establishing Supervised Listening Centers

Supervised Listening Centers were established on the basis of contacts at the village level made at the Haryali Conferences and through various organizations, institutions, and local government bodies. Each Listening Center would have a supervisor who would be literate, acceptable to the local women, and able to visit and be visited by these women, to arrange meetings where women could hear and discuss the radio program or its recording on tape, to read aloud and discuss the printed material accompanying each episode, and to correspond with the project team both to provide feedback and on behalf of the women in her center.

Production

Since field research showed that the preferred listening time was around noon, AF requested a 12:30 P.M. time slot. PBC granted this request and offered its studio facilities and the services of a producer and two engineers. It was decided to broadcast on November 16th to coincide with the winter planting season. Final scripts were checked by three authorities: the media consultant for dramatic content, a technology expert, and the project director to ensure that the project's objectives were fulfilled.

The program was recorded in the studios of Radio Pakistan Islamabad, and transmitted from stations in Lahore and Rawalpindi, because both technology institutions and peasant women demanded that the program cover irrigated areas (through Lahore) and *barani* or rain-fed areas (through Rawalpindi). The program was received in approximately 75 percent of the Punjab and could be heard by a potential audience of 44 million, about 11 million of them women.

Prebroadcast Publicity

Prebroadcast publicity was started through AF's networking meetings, in information dissemination meetings, and by researchers during their field and institutional research. The forthcoming program was also written up in AF publications: the quarterly newsletter *Aurat* and the news bulletin *Itlaa*.

Peasant women attending the Second National Conference of Peasant Women (the second Haryali Conference), held in February 1993, were told about the forthcoming radio program. Letters were later sent to participants of both Haryali Conferences, informing them about the radio program and asking them about their work. (Their responses were also used in formulating the initial questionnaires used by the field researchers.)

The program was advertised on radio and television. A letter to introduce the program and get help in establishing Listening Centers was disseminated via NGOs and government institutions. A handbill was sent to the Listening Centers already established, to NGOs, and to the Directorate of Agriculture Extension Wing.

The Program: "Mishal"

The radio program was in the form of a soap opera, written by a woman dramatist who had been sensitized to rural women's problems. Its name, *Mishal* ("the light that shows the way"), was the name of the central character, a young woman who uses improved methods of production and is a source of information for the village women. Women are portrayed positively as is the relationship between Mishal and her mother-in-law. *Mishal* also gives information on crop technologies, poultry and livestock care, health, and women's rights.

Once the serial started, feedback from the Supervised Listening Centers was used to respond to the expressed needs of rural women. Desired information was added to the story or to the opening and closing announcements. Two examples of response to expressed needs were the inclusion of a way to protect crops from frost and strategies to counter an unexpected drought in the *barani* areas. The program's health component has also been topical. For instance, pneumonia is the second-highest killer of children in Pakistan, and its incidence was especially high in the winter of 1993; pneumonia prevention and management were therefore included in one episode.

Repackaged Printed Material

In preparing publications to accompany the radio episodes, priority was given to material concerning technologies to increase production (e.g., planting wheat in standing cotton crop) or reduce loss (e.g., maize storage). Because of the low level of literacy in rural areas, it was decided to use the poster format, with large script and clear illustrations. When the amount and nature of the material required it, pamphlets were printed. In both cases, simple Urdu was used and the technical language checked to ensure that rural women would understand it.

Feedback and Monitoring

The project has certain built-in mechanisms for monitoring the radio programs. The establishment of the Listening Centers ensures that a certain minimum number of women actively listen to the program each week. Their comments are communicated to the project team through preprinted postcards and letters. After each episode, the team knew the approximate number of women who heard the program, whether they liked the story, whether the technology was useful and relevant, and listeners' further information needs. To ensure that supervisors' correspondence reflected the opinions and needs of the women in each center, the project team visited the centers. This process continued until the end of the radio broadcast.

Internally, reports are written after each field visit or meeting, and the project team maintains diaries. The team is documenting the project, for itself and donor agencies and as a model for other organizations. Project activities have been filmed and photographed.

Queries from rural women are answered in various ways:

- The supervisor plays the audiotape of the episode so that the women can again hear about the technology that interests them.
- The project team, sometimes after consulting the relevant technology institute, sends answers to the Listening Center supervisor.
- Some questions are passed on to the appropriate institute, which sends its answers back to the project team to be forwarded to the supervisor.
- Links with technology institutes are being formed, so that institutes will reply to the women directly and will provide training to rural women's groups near or in their villages.
- Rural women are encouraged to address their problems directly to technology institutes.
- Questions on nonagricultural topics (such as health, finance, and education) are referred to AF's Information Services.
- Audiocassettes of the radio program are provided to NGOs and CBOs to be used for the rural women they work with.

Letters from the Listening Centers and the community provide much-needed insight into rural women's information needs.

EVALUATION OF THE PROJECT

Feedback and monitoring done until the end of the first phase in May 1994 indicated that at least thirty villages had used the technology and health information provided. In early June, a two-day workshop was held to get feedback from Listening Center supervisors. The supervisors who attended represented on average 2,000 women who listened to the program every week in the Listening Centers as well as the approximately 300 households in each supervisor's village.

The workshop consisted of plenary sessions, including one on health, as well as group sessions in which the supervisors were divided by districts. The results can be summarized as follows:

Listening Centers

- In the initial weeks the women were slow in coming to the center and had to be called personally from their homes.
- As the program progressed, and especially after the posters started arriving, attendance improved.
- News about the program was announced in the village, through personal visits by the supervisor or her family members, and by word of mouth.
- Attendance was not a problem where the women were already organized: for example, in literacy centers or industrial homes.
- Attendance went down during the sowing and reaping seasons or when there was a death or a marriage in the village.
- The women recognized the advantage of getting together once a week. They were able to discuss problems, both personal and work-related, and they made many more contacts with each other than in the past. They also felt they were able to gain useful information.

Radio Program

- The soap opera format was generally liked. Even though most of the women understood Urdu, they had a problem understanding the program in Urdu. The supervisors usually had to translate into Punjabi.
- The favorite characters were the heroine, Mishal, and her mother-in-law, Malkani, because they depicted a positive relationship between a daughter-in-law and mother-in-law.
- The women also liked cousin Bala, a rustic/comic character familiar to those who know rural Punjab. Bala served as a foil to the more knowl-

edgeable Mishal, and the audience was able to learn through his ignorance and his mistakes.

- Some men, generally family members of the supervisors, also listened to the program regularly (usually on cassette).
- The women preferred the radio program over the posters, since it could be understood even by those who were illiterate.

Technology Information

- The supervisors were frequently the first to try out new methods they had heard. Many felt that they could not pass on information unless they had first tried it themselves.
- The information most commonly used was related to poultry and cattle diseases, storage of grain and potatoes, fumigation using *neem* leaves, and simple home remedies.
- There was only one known case in which a loss resulted from trying out a new technique (planting wheat in standing cotton crop). The agriculture expert on site during the workshop was able to discuss this problem with the supervisor.

Accompanying Material

- Accompanying materials were mostly large posters, with some pamphlets. Posters were preferred, as they could be put up and seen by many people.
- Posters were generally put up in places where they could be seen by both women and men: on outside house walls, schools, shops, and mosques.
- The women were not generally interested in the posters when they arrived but came to the supervisor to read them (or have them read) when they had a specific problem.
- The men were more impressed by the program once the posters started arriving. They helped display the posters in prominent places in the villages and encouraged the women in their families to read them, believing them to be useful.
- School children also helped put up posters.
- The paper for the posters was felt to be too thin, since they fell off after the first rain or dust storm. Children were also blamed for tearing down posters.

Communication with Aurat Foundation

- At first preprinted postcards for weekly feedback from supervisors did not reach the Foundation and were returned to the senders. This was because AF's preprinted address and the return address were on the same side. This problem was solved by adding "To" and "From."

- Some supervisors had to buy envelopes and return the postcards in these. Sometimes envelopes were hard to obtain in villages.
- Some supervisors complained that there were not enough posters, that they arrived too late for some farming procedures, or not at all.
- Some supervisors complained of delays in answers to their requests for information.
- Some supervisors complained of delays in receiving honoraria.
- A few village men asked their wives to write through their supervisors for information about problems they were having, such as with their livestock.

Suggestions for the Future

- The program should be in regional languages.
- It should retain the dramatic format but also include question-and-answer sessions.
- It should be in the form of a television drama.
- Posters should be printed on better-quality paper, with larger writing and illustrations.
- Most supervisors felt that they could continue to run the centers through their own efforts.
- It was felt that getting together would bring further benefits to the women in the Listening Centers: gaining and exchanging information and advice, improving interpersonal contacts, and receiving training from agricultural extension workers.

Social Benefits

- The women in one Listening Center together cleaned up the lanes and gutters in their village.
- Women in another village worked to upgrade the girls' primary school to middle level (as the boys' school already was).
- Project field researchers were told by some village women that they were being paid half the daily wage that men were being paid for the same work. This was the first part of a process of consciousness-raising. Some months later the women went on strike, asking for similar wages for similar work. Their demand was accepted.
- The excess land surrounding an industrial home was turned into a vegetable farm by three members of a Listening Center. The teachers and students share in the produce.
- Women in a village Listening Center organized a function for International Women's Day on March 8.

- Four women of a center approached their Agriculture Development Bank of Pakistan (ADBP) branch and obtained a loan to buy a tractor, using land they owned or were given as collateral.
- The children of one village were immunized.
- A health week was organized in another village.
- Women made decorative *changair* (flat straw baskets) and marketed them in Lahore.
- In another village, the women got together to do embroidery and marketed it through a local NGO.
- Women tried different ways of saving money. Some unraveled old knitted garments and sold the wool to be made into *durries* (woven rugs).

END OF PHASE I

After twenty-six episodes, the story of *Mishal* has ended, for the time being. At first it was planned to stop broadcasting until the regional language versions of *Mishal* could be aired in the autumn of 1994. However, because of feedback from the women in the Listening Centers, Radio Pakistan personnel, and agricultural institute experts, all of whom felt the continuity of this program should not be broken, Aurat is continuing to broadcast it under the same name but a different format. Experts in agriculture, poultry, and livestock have been asked to answer women's questions on the air.

Field-level research is being conducted in southern Punjab and the other provinces. Initial institutional research is ongoing and links with technology institutes will be maintained. New Listening Centers are also being established.

It is expected that the project will not only enhance peasant women's productivity and incomes and improve their family health, but also provide them with a window into the larger world outside their village, and raise their awareness of their own vital role in the rural economy and of the services and facilities available to them. The project links the women with agriculture extension, technology, training, and credit institutions, and sensitizes these institutions about peasant women's needs, which, with requisite lobbying, will begin to be reflected in government policies and programs.

Finally, through its networking activities, the project links peasant women with each other, creating a greater awareness of their common problems and the need for group action. This bonding and awareness of possibilities for change will catalyze peasant women into taking control of their lives and communities.

Tribal Women of Montenegro

Zorka Milich (Montenegro)

MONTENEGRO

The mountainous Republic of Montenegro—Black Mountain—is on the Adriatic seacoast of Yugoslavia, with Albania to the east, Bosnia-Herzegovina to the west, and Serbia to the north. In 1990 I conducted a field research project there, wherein I located, visited, and interviewed thirty tribal, illiterate women between the ages of 101 and 115. These previously undocumented women included Moslems, Roman Catholics, and Eastern Orthodox Christians. They are surviving representatives of the fully tribal cultures that once flourished throughout ancient Europe, before they lost their political freedom and tribal identities to the conquering Romans, or later by being incorporated into the various feudal systems that arose in the Middle Ages. It is remarkable that such a people could survive for so long, quite independent of the nation-states and empires that surrounded them. Because of their geographic and cultural isolation for hundreds of years, they were able to nurture and sustain their ways and views, which have changed little to this day, particularly in the everyday lives of the women in this study.

Zorka Milich is Associate Professor of English at Nassau Community College of the State University of New York. She holds a Ph.D. from St. John's University. Her book, *A Stranger's Supper: Oral Histories of 100 Year Old Tribal Women of Montenegro*, is based on the interviews described here and is forthcoming from Twayne Publishers in October 1995.

247

The rugged and almost impenetrable peninsula that the Montenegrin tribes inhabit was the locus of the ancient Illyrian empire; the Roman emperors Claudius, Diocletian, and Aurelian were sons of Illyrian peasants. For more than four centuries the area was part of a mighty Islamic empire, that of the Ottoman Turks. During the late fifteenth century, while other Balkan Slavic peoples quickly submitted to the warlike and politically well-organized Turks, the Montenegrin tribesmen, having resisted the domination of fellow Christian feudal Serbs and in the habit of fighting for their local autonomy, never fully submitted to Turkish domination. In the mid-1800s, they amazed the western world by forming a free nation-state in the midst of the Turkish empire. This was a harrowing and grisly time of hardship and death. Many of the women interviewed said, "It would not be called Black Mountain if it were not black. It is steeped in poverty and death." Roadside atrocities were commonplace, as the Ottoman occupation sought to subdue rebellions by making a spectacle of the penalty. Men were impaled alive on stakes driven into the ground and heads displayed on poles at bridges and military installations. Turkish heads were displayed as a sign of Montenegrin resistance.

WOMEN IN MONTENEGRO

Women of the traditional period of Montenegro's past, the mainstay of the family and sole homemaker and educator of the children, in a family frequently without a father present, have gone totally undocumented and unstudied. They were the foundation of the culture, and their influence is clearly felt to this day. The majority of my narrators were surprisingly articulate and lucid, recalling names, incidents, and minute details of their frequently painful and tragic childhood days, including marriage, childbirth, and deaths. All had survived at least four wars and blood vendettas, and some escaped kidnapping by Turks seeking adolescent females for their harems. Yet each told her story stoically and proudly, accepting her role in an androcentric society.

All marriages were arranged by the respective families, many before the actual birth of the children. Research into the background of a prospective mate went back at least one hundred years, and any evidence of unfitness, either of character or genetics, was grounds for immediate rejection. Evidence of bravery, physical stature, and honor were highly prized. The primary responsibility of the prospective couple was to bear many sons, who were expected to protect and defend their family, clan, and tribe against outside attack, and to uphold the highest moral character, as befitting true warriors. Marriage for love or sexual attraction was seen as unheroic, and discouraged. The primary purpose of all individuals was the perpetuation of the blood line, and defense of the family and culture against all threats, both frequent foreign invasions and local blood feuds between clans and tribes, which could go on for countless decades.

A strict moral code of behavior was enforced. To assure the bride that she would be respected and protected by her new family as though she were a member of their natal family, she was obligated to spend her wedding night with her brother-in-law. If he was married, she would sleep with both him and his wife—all fully clothed. If he made even the slightest sexual overture or gesture, his life was forfeited immediately.

My informants had an average of twelve to fourteen children, many dying in childbirth or in wars. Since most women lived in extended families, with fifteen or more people in one large room, children were conceived and born outside the home: in barns, fields, and so on. The birth of a son was, and still is, celebrated with feasting and gunfire. It was also the mother's "rite of passage." The birth of a daughter went largely unheralded, as she was seen as a future asset to another family, through marriage—"a stranger's supper." She was, however, much loved, and her honor was often defended by male members of the family and community, frequently unto death in blood feuds, perhaps continuing for generations. The dishonoring of a wife, daughter, or sister, either physically or verbally, or the breaking of an engagement was the most frequent cause of ongoing blood vendettas between males of different clans and tribes. Even the suggestion of immorality on the part of one's self or a family member could cause the most severe retaliation, in order to regain one's honor and self-respect. This behavior was encouraged by the females, who saw it as indicative of a good warrior who could be relied upon.

Compared to the rest of Europe, Montenegro has highly infertile soil. It is a rugged and inhospitable place, and even subsistence farming is difficult. Since constant wars, raids, and feuds required a man to be ever vigilant, he learned from early childhood that the survival of the society depended on him. He could never lower his head to work in the field; he must always be in an upright position with his rifle beside him should the enemy attack. Women were therefore responsible for working in the fields and had total autonomy in rearing the children. It was they who taught them to respect and honor family, providing a strong image of brave husbands as good models for their sons. Many women kept the bloodied clothing of dead husbands as daily reminders to sons of the courage of fathers who gave their lives for the preservation of culture and tradition. Males were expected to be brave and moral warriors, females the mothers of warriors. Many of the women I interviewed repeated the old Montenegrin expression, "A house does not rest on the ground; it rests on a woman." Girls and women were expected to carry food and clothing to the males fighting on the battlefront, often many miles from their homes. These were hazardous journeys, on foot, frequently through hostile territory. Montenegrin and northern Albanian tribal law strictly prohibited the killing of a woman, even if she participated in battle, but it did not prohibit the kidnapping of wives, a common practice of the Turks, or their transportation to Turkey as slaves and concubines.

But this danger did not deter local women from fulfilling their obligations. Those I interviewed related such harrowing journeys, many during the Balkan Wars and World War I. Not infrequently, upon their arrival at the battlefield, they found either no trace of their brothers, sons, or husbands, or, if they were fortunate, the tattered remains of their bodies, perhaps enough to bury. The data I collected, all recorded on audiotape as it was told to me, comprise many personal accounts of this nature.

Nikola, king of Montenegro during the early lives of my subjects (prince, 1878; king, 1900–18), has been called the "Father-in-law of Europe," because his daughters married into several royal families: the Romanovs of Russia, the Savoys of Italy (one eventually becoming queen), and, through the Hessian Battenbergs, the British royal family. Nikola's first son, Danilo, was immortalized in the famous operetta "The Merry Widow." The mothers and grandmothers of these notables have never been studied by modern scholarship, and the conditions and culture from which they came have never been properly documented, by any means. One wonders what influence these Montenegrin mountain women, descended from an ancient warrior patriarchy, may have had upon their husbands and children, and through them, on the history of the modern world. There remains a dearth of scholarship on this topic, and until this study there has never been a comprehensive effort to gather data from these tribeswomen. My project was one step toward filling this void.

Archival repositories for audiotapes of these interviews in Serbocroatian, and transcripts in both English and Serbocroatian, are currently under review. Twenty hours of video footage of select interviews by Mark Milich, a filmmaker, are being edited for a documentary. A book on this study, published by Twayne Publishers, will be available in October 1995.

The mere existence of such a population of centenarian women, many of them very active and coherent, bears witness to the likelihood that Montenegro was one of the most successful prefeudal, tribal societies to have existed in Europe. In its isolated location, it has found no necessity to change.

Oral History with Women Geographers

Lynda R. Smith-Bugge (U.S.A.)

INTRODUCTION

The Society of Woman Geographers (SWG) was founded in 1925 by women explorers who had traveled to the four corners of the earth and who felt a need for an association of women to exchange information about their experiences. These women had made history by breaking barriers and pioneering new fields.

The word *society* reflects the collegial nature of the institution; *woman*, used as an adjective, defines the members as different from the vast majority of geographers in 1925; and *geographers* has from the beginning been broadly defined to include allied fields from anthropology and archaeology to zoology.

ORAL HISTORY PROGRAM

Twice in its nearly seventy years, SWG has been strengthened as an institution by an oral history program in which younger members interviewed older ones. In 1973 SWG launched a Society-wide oral history program to interview members who had joined before 1940. More than eighty interviews, each lasting about one and one-half hours, were recorded between 1973 and 1993. The tapes are in the SWG archives.

At the time of the WIF conference, **Lynda R. Smith-Bugge** was Museum and Archives Director of the Society of Woman Geographers in Washington, D.C., and is now a consultant there. She has an M.S. in museum education from Bank Street College in New York and has worked for libraries and museums in New York City and Florida and also at the Library of Congress and the Smithsonian Institution.

The second project was started in March 1993 to reinvigorate SWG's oral history and archives programs. Two foundation grants enabled SWG to hire professional staff, who soon developed guidelines and a standard methodology; these were taught at regional workshops, which resulted in the training of twenty-six potential interviewers.

Selecting members to be interviewed is difficult because so many merit attention. We are still refining our criteria with the help of scholars from different disciplines. In general, we give priority to interviewing the more senior members and those with outstanding achievement in exploration or in their professions, or whose contributions to the society are notable.

Interviewers are SWG members working as volunteers. After training by a professional historian, interviewers are quickly learning to articulate the right questions, to listen, and to guide the interview sessions. In order to ensure the quality of the current oral history program, the transcripts are being reviewed by a professional oral historian.

Having younger members collect oral histories of older ones has led to an interesting byproduct: a new vitality and involvement in the society on the part of interviewees. Because much of their accomplishments and recognition may have happened in the past, they are enlivened by the society's interest in their lives. "After the interviews," wrote one interviewer, "the older members come to life. There is a new sparkle and humor that they bring to SWG meetings. They become involved in a new way."

Many interviews reflect worldwide travel and field work done during various decades. From the 1920s to the present, they reveal unrecorded aspects of life. Many interviewees discuss the differences between the opportunities and difficulties they faced and those faced by women today.

The SWG membership is far-flung. The enthusiasm generated by the oral history program is a way to invest this national constituency in the organization. Besides creating interviews useful for research, the program has produced ideas and plans for future exhibitions, using photographs, documents, and sound recordings uncovered during the interviews.

SWG RESEARCH SOURCES

Oral histories complement written documentation found at SWG headquarters. The policy of SWG is to make not only its library but also its archives, including oral history tapes and transcripts, available to researchers. In the past, due to cramped quarters, limited staff, and a tight budget, the society was unable to make these resources readily available. In 1988 SWG donated files on deceased members to the Library of Congress Manuscript Division; these files are easily available for research. In 1992 SWG acquired a headquarters building of its own, thereby vastly improving the accessibility of the collections. Staff have worked with scholars in a variety of fields and with other archives so that SWG can serve as a clearinghouse of information about where members' papers are deposited.

Members have worked all over the world and have documented their experiences in many forms. The library houses members' publications; the archives, membership files with articles about and by members. The SWG's annual *Bulletin* documents members' professional development. This is especially important for women whose papers are lost. In the *Bulletin*, a researcher can trace a woman's yearly development and read descriptions of her findings. In the oral histories one can hear her talk about her personal motivation and her family and professional expectations.

CONCLUSION

The oral history, archives, and library programs are important vehicles for member involvement. Collecting members' oral histories is one of the most successful tools for investing the membership in the organization. It is a way for members to contribute their stories to younger women and to future researchers.

Data Collection on Women in Ukraine

Svetlana V. Kupryashkina (Ukraine)

In official Soviet statistics women were viewed mainly as a large social group of workers and reproducers. Statistics therefore reflected the main interest of the state: keeping women in both positions. That often meant ignoring other factors related to women as a social group, such as ethnicity, religion, age, and educational level. The social sciences, such as demography and family sociology, have ended up being prescriptive rather than descriptive and cannot supply the emerging gender research in the post-Soviet era with an appropriate methodological apparatus.

DISAGGREGATION AS AN APPROACH

Until the 1970s, mainstream Western research, policy, and planning virtually ignored the economic role of women. Plans and policies were either based on men and then generalized to all people, or they prescribed a picture in which men were assumed to be the only breadwinners and women and children were dependents. The practical outcome of these approaches adversely affected the welfare of many women and was in conflict with the interests of others.

During 1994–95, **Svetlana V. Kupryashkina** was a Fulbright Visiting Scholar at the Institute for Research on Women at Rutgers University in New Jersey. She was Director of the Ukrainian Center for Women's Studies, 1992–94, and researcher at the Moscow Center for Gender Studies, 1991–92, has a doctorate from Kiev State University, and is a founding member of the Ukrainian Association of University Women. Her publications include a translation of Kate Millett's *Sexual Politics*.

There are two main explanations for such an oversight in the planning processes: (1) the main assumption remained that women's participation in development was outside the economic mainstream and (2) there were gaps in the data on what women do and the contribution they make to social and economic development.

The Percy Amendment

In the fall of 1973 the U.S. Department of State held a briefing on foreign affairs, including the proposed International Women's Conference. State Department officials listened to women's organizations' ideas about the issues of the conference. The testimony of Women In Development (WID, an international organization based in Washington, D.C.) was so persuasive that two State Department staff members, Clara Beyer and Mildred Marcy, determined to promote an amendment to the U.S. Foreign Assistance Act of 1973. This amendment, which became known as the Percy Amendment (after U.S. Senator Charles Percy), required that the U.S. Agency for International Development (USAID) "give particular attention to those programs, projects, and activities which tend to integrate women into the national economies of foreign countries, thus improving their status and assisting the total development effort." Later the Percy Amendment was extended to cover programs of other agencies using U.S. funds.

In 1975, at the inauguration of the United Nations Decade for Women, priority was given to disaggregating by sex all national economic and social statistics. The aim was to make two things visible to policy planners: the full extent of women's economic participation, particularly in areas traditionally considered to be dominated by men; and the status of women in terms of their income, health, and education. The process of disaggregating national statistics by gender has been uneven, because the necessary changes are often slow and costly to manage.

Problems with Data

Many problems remain with the newly gathered data. The main problem is that disaggregation by gender does not in itself reveal the whole picture of women's lives and work, mostly because of two common, and unfounded, assumptions.

The first assumption is that all techniques of data collection and measurement are equally valid for men and women. The evidence indicates, however, that women and men experience their economic and social environments differently, and the differences affect their responses to questions about their situation. In this regard, all gender-sensitive questions, with various implications, may produce answers that are seen as right by some respondents and as wrong by others. For example, the Ukrainian Center for Women's Studies recently surveyed households on income and expenses. While most women answered questions precisely, most men seemed to have trouble with elementary questions about family budget; the cost of food, phone, or rent; the school years of their children; and the like. This reflects the gender imbalance in the distribution of labor in the family.

The second assumption is that general conceptual categories hold the same meaning for all people. The concept of work, for example, is often taken to have the same meaning for women and men, and therefore their work experiences are believed to be adequately represented in unisex categories. But for many women work may be largely subsumed within the household and be unpaid labor, whereas for men work is socially visible and economically rewarding.

Techniques of Measurement

The basic requirement of statistical measurement is that an activity or characteristic be susceptible to quantitative measurement. However, quantitative measurement is neither easy nor necessarily a neutral procedure. What is measured by statistics depends on the techniques of measurement, such as the unit of enumeration and the dominant perceptions and attitudes about what is important or relevant information. For example, a number of studies have severely criticized census and national income accounting methods that exclude production outside the marketplace; see, for instance, Luisella Goldshmidt-Clermont, *Unpaid Work in the Household* (Geneva: ILO, 1982), and Lourdes Beneria, "Accounting for Women's Work" in *Women and Development: The Sexual Division of Labour in Rural Societies* (New York: Praeger, 1982). These studies argue that some aspects of informal sector production and production for use within the household must be assessed in economic terms.

This approach holds particular significance for economically developing countries and, in some aspects such as trade and small enterprises production, for the countries of the former socialist bloc, where many of the trade deals, and much of the production and sales, happen outside the infrastructure of the state and even of the private sector. Unofficial estimates for Ukraine, for example, are that 50 percent, and maybe more, of all trade is happening outside the regular infrastructure; this activity avoids banks and taxation and is not accountable. Such statistics could improve the overall vision of the economy and finance of a given country and accessibility of resources to different groups of the population, especially to women.

SOVIET AND POST-SOVIET STATISTICS

The main characteristic of Soviet statistics in regard to women was their extreme paternalism; that is, the state, through its institutions, enforced women's roles as producers and reproducers and itself exercised a caretaking function over women. There were two main purposes for Soviet statistics to remain as they were, an economic one and an ideological one.

First, the state needed to maintain women in their double roles. By making women responsible for both public and family production, the state was relieved of the necessity to develop an infrastructure of social services. Those services that existed barely helped women in their task. The amount of unpaid work at home, by some estimates, amounted to thirty hours a week for the average Soviet woman. The state was able to relocate resources out of the social infrastructure and into military production.

Second, the ideological need was to legitimate the Soviet policy of equality between the sexes. Sex equality has been one of the strongest arguments in defense of the Soviet way of life and for many years was actively used in Communist Party rhetoric. Fortunately, many women were indeed provided with equal access to work and education. But unfortunately, official policy discredited many notions of real equality and feminism, which explains the stubbornness with which many women reject these notions today.

Transition to a Market Economy

Transition from a command to a market economy has left many sectors of the population vulnerable and unprotected against the traumatic social changes that have taken place. The effects of the newly enforced reforms are markedly different on different social groups. Women—previously the main work force and consumers in the heavily subsidized public sector (health care, education, food services, cultural services)—now have almost no access to resources or high-paying jobs and are increasingly tied to their reproductive roles. The gender asymmetry in many spheres of economics, especially in the private sector, is quite visible and has already been noted by such researchers as Nanette Funk; see her "Women and Post-Communism," in *Gender Politics and Post-Communism* (New York: Routledge, 1993). Exclusion of women from economic activity, leaving them in lower-paid jobs, and increasing female unemployment (women comprise up to 78 percent of the unemployed), besides having an extremely negative effect on morale, will result in considerable economic losses. For unemployment statistics, see, for instance, the article by Zoya Khotkina in *Women in Russia*, edited by A. Posadskaya et al. (London: Verso, 1994, pp. 85–108).

Current policy tends to reduce jobs at women's expense and to encourage women's early retirement, prolonged maternity leaves, and similar measures.

These measures are seen as a temporary solution to unemployment, but they may prove inefficient in the long run. The human potential of women—who comprise large numbers of skilled workers, technical staff, teachers, and doctors—could play a crucial role in reconstructing the economy and in development of the private sector.

Toward Gender Disaggregation

Many of these changes remain unrecognized and invisible. The national bureaus of statistics and of census are largely dependent on contracts and are poorly subsidized by the state. As of 1994 no assessment had been done in Ukraine regarding the status of women. In the absence of any statistics, it is doubly hard to emphasize gender disaggregation, but it should be developed, at least as an alternative approach. It might be that foreign agencies interested in assessing aspects of social development in Ukraine will apply some of these methodologies when studying the Ukrainian situation. It might aid a better understanding of various trends in employment, migration, and reproductive patterns, and, in the final analysis, facilitate the adoption of more gender-sensitive social policies.

It should be noted, however, that gender disaggregation does not and will not bring immediate improvement in the lives of women in the former Soviet Union. It is a positive step but no panacea. Real changes in the position of women can happen only when women themselves take an active role.

Regional Information Support on Women's Health

Rita Raj-Hashim (Malaysia)

Interaction and discussion with nongovernment organization (NGO) leaders, key government officials, the media, and international organizations as well as grass-roots women clearly indicate a need for more regional information resources on the latest research, analyses, perspectives, and action on women's issues. Organizations want ready-to-use information in the form of systematic databases, policy and program guidelines, research findings, and news on women from women's perspectives.

PROBLEMS AND NEEDS

One major problem women's groups face in relation to women and development is access to up-to-date and practical national and regional information and resources in order better to plan, implement, and evaluate programs. Often, national organizations are more in touch with international bodies or Western sources of information than they are with countries in their own region that share similar histories, cultures, and levels of socioeconomic development.

With a master's degree in Public Administration, **Rita Raj-Hashim** has extensive work experience in public and private organizations and with family planning, population, and women's development in Malaysia, Asia, and the United States. She is founding director of the Asian-Pacific Resource and Research Centre for Women (ARROW), a regional NGO incorporated in Malaysia in 1993.

261

Women's and development organizations want to know which programs, strategies, and actions in their own region have benefited women the most. They want to know what the success factors were and how they can replicate such efforts. Most research at national and regional levels on women and development focuses on documenting and analyzing women's situations in various sectors but does not include a critical analysis of policies, programs, and organizations aimed at improving the situation. There is a great need for research and evaluation to assist in such strategic planning.

WOMEN'S HEALTH

In Asia and the Pacific region since the late 1980s, awareness has increased that policies and programs related to women's health have often been designed and implemented without the input of women's own perspectives of their needs. Narrow conceptualization of women's roles together with limited understanding of the realities of women's lives has often led to programs that limit women's access to the health services they need, and to services that are inappropriate and inconvenient for women, that regard women as objects or targets. This has a negative effect on women's self-esteem. It diminishes women's right to quality health services and their right to decide about reproductive issues, such as childbearing, choice of contraceptive technology and sexual protection, childbirth practices, and sexuality.

A number of women's organizations, generally NGOs, have begun to advocate for changes in national health programs, using such various strategies as taking part in government health planning committees, organizing awareness seminars, and establishing alternative models for service delivery and education that are women centered. Some family planning organizations, such as the national family planning associations of Indonesia and Malaysia, for example, and the International Committee on Management and Population (ICOMP), are attempting to reorient their services and programs to be more sensitive to women's needs. At the same time, government women's ministries or departments in such countries as the Philippines, Papua New Guinea, India, and Malaysia are formalizing their concern for women in national women's policies and plans, including the area of women's health and more recently the issue of women and AIDS.

Need for Regional Action

Even the experiences of women's and health NGOs are not well known and have not been documented and disseminated nationally or in the region. There is a need for stronger regional articulation by women's organizations of an analysis of population policies and reproductive health programs that is credible, convincing, and well documented.

Regional action is important because in a number of countries population policy is a highly sensitive issue. Women's groups are currently preparing for the preliminary meetings leading up to the 1994 International Conference on Population and Development, the conference itself, and the United Nations Fourth World Conference on Women, with their own meetings on the theme and such special initiatives as Women's Voices 1994 and IRRRAG: International Reproductive Rights Research Group, a collaborative project on the meaning of "reproductive rights" to women in diverse cultures; interdisciplinary teams are carrying out this research in Brazil, Egypt, Malaysia, Mexico, Nigeria, Philippines and the United States.

Making women's voices heard on population policies is imperative for changing policies and programs on the basis of women's perspectives. In order for declarations and agreements made at these meetings and conferences to be acted on, however, women's and health organizations need more practical information resources to support advocacy and implementation of the reorientation of health policies and programs.

Need for Information Program

Although there is some information and research in the region on the general effect of population and reproductive health policies and programs on women, and on such specific issues as gender bias in contraceptive technology, there is little information and few resources on organizational strategies and action to support these initiatives. There is a need for conceptual frameworks, program guidelines, and materials and information on action that has been effective. A sustained information program to support efforts to change health, population, and reproductive health policies and programs from women's perspectives is needed. A regional program based on the experience and perspectives of Asia and the Pacific will help support national initiatives to bring about changes in population and reproductive health policies and programs.

ARROW'S AIMS

The Asian-Pacific Resource and Research Centre for Women (ARROW) aims to close these gaps by providing relevant information, resources, and research findings to enable organizations to plan, organize, re-orient, and evaluate effective programs and activities for women. This is aimed at achieving ARROW's vision of women in Asia and the Pacific region as becoming better able to define and control their lives and acquiring the resources to do this.

ARROW is part of an International Women's Health Documentation Project, which pools information collected by its member organizations. These include the Boston Women's Health Book Collective (U.S.A.), CIDHAL (Mexico), SOS Corpo (Brazil), and Isis (Chile). Thus ARROW has at its disposal the information already collected by this network.

Documentation Center

ARROW is establishing a systematic documentation center on women and development issues that will provide computerized information services, produce innovative resource publications, and engage in action-oriented research and evaluation.

The Dissemination of HIV-AIDS Information to Women

Maria Salet Ferreira Novellino (Brazil)

WOMEN AND AIDS IN BRAZIL

There has been an alarming increase in the number of AIDS cases among women in Brazil. Whereas between 1984 and 1991 the major risk for women was intravenous drug use, from 1992 on transmission through sexual intercourse became prevalent. This cause has, however, been largely ignored in the context of official prevention campaigns.

The real situation of women in relation to the HIV-AIDS epidemic has been played down, hindering an alert to the female population. Dividing the population into risk and nonrisk groups is outdated. Instead, emphasis must be on risky behavior. If HIV is transmitted sexually, then any sexually active person who does not practice safe sex (e.g., the use of condoms) is as a rule adopting risky behavior.

When the epidemic began, it was believed that women but not men could be infected through heterosexual intercourse. This belief, coupled with the concept of risk groups, which included homosexuals, drug users, and sex workers but excluded "nonpromiscuous" women, was a factor in the spread of the virus. Men who practiced mainly heterosexual sex did not protect themselves or their partners, and the latter did not fear being infected.

Maria Salet Ferreira Novellino has a master's degree in Information Science. Formerly coordinator of the Brazilian Interdisciplinary AIDS Association Documentation Center, she is now working toward a doctorate in Information Science.

Today, when monogamous women are becoming aware that they are at risk and want to protect themselves, they face difficulty in talking about sex with their partners—who may not be monogamous—and trying to negotiate safe sex. Issues arise that couples find hard to discuss, such as fidelity, sexuality, and pleasure.

Heterosexual sex is today the dominant means by which the HIV virus is transmitted throughout the world. The number of infected women increases daily. Besides increasing women's morbidity and mortality, this has psychological, social, and economic impact.

PSYCHOLOGICAL IMPACT   A woman's reproductive function is an important component of her personality, whether because of personal desire or social stricture. Given the possibility of perinatal transmission of the HIV virus to a fetus, motherhood represents the perpetuation not of life but of the disease.

SOCIAL IMPACT   On a micro basis, the social impact of AIDS is felt in the dismantling of the family. In general, parents become aware of their own disease when their children begin to show symptoms. In most cases, fathers die first and mothers try to stay alive in order to take care of the children. When both parents die, grandparents (usually grandmothers) assume care of the children, whether HIV-infected or not. Integrating HIV-positive children into society is a problem; schools are not prepared to receive them. Such children are discriminated against by schoolmates, parents, teachers, and school employees.

ECONOMIC IMPACT   Today, women represent 35.1 percent of the work force in Brazil. In a discriminatory society in which women workers are valued less than men, employers are unlikely to be supportive of women who lose time from work, whether because of their own illness or to care for sick relatives.

ABIA

ABIA—Brazilian Interdisciplinary AIDS Association—is a nongovernment organization (NGO) founded in 1986 and aimed at promoting education and information in order to prevent and control the HIV-AIDS epidemic. A nonprofit organization without political, religious, or other links, ABIA has a wide range of information, education, and prevention programs, in addition to producing analyses of the development of the epidemic in Brazil. It also monitors public health AIDS policies, fights against discrimination and prejudice, and stimulates solidarity as a way of confronting the epidemic, in a permanent defense of human rights.

The AIDS, Reproductive Health, and Public Policies Project was developed with the support of the Ford Foundation. The project articulates three major themes related to health in Brazil: AIDS, reproductive health, and public policies, and has three components: (1) analysis of public policies relating to AIDS and reproductive health, (2) organization of a collection of documents and training, and (3) production of publications. The project integrates ABIA's efforts to disseminate accurate information and to define effective communication strategies so as to develop HIV-AIDS prevention activities.

The project comprises seminars, training, and publication of books and bulletins. It aims to contribute to the development of critical analyses of public health policies and of collaborative and cooperative programs with other Brazilian institutions, such as AIDS-related NGOs and organizations concerned with women's health.

THE ABIA DOCUMENTATION CENTER

The ABIA Documentation Center is one of the main reference centers in Brazil for information about the HIV-AIDS epidemic. It collects and analyzes information about the epidemic and organizes and disseminates information to individuals and institutions in Brazil and elsewhere.

Collection and Analysis of Information

This function entails following the evolution of the epidemic and the responses to it by science, government, and the community. The information collected includes documents produced by Brazilian and foreign institutions:

- Educational booklets, brochures, posters, and videotapes used in prevention campaigns (showing historical, regional, and cultural variations in these campaigns)
- Theses and dissertations
- National and international publications with technical or simple information, comprising both scientific periodicals and bulletins for HIV-positive persons, their families, and others interested in opportunistic diseases, treatment, drugs and vaccines, human rights, and other aspects of the epidemic
- National and local epidemiological bulletins
- Newspaper clippings with up-to-date information
- Educational videotapes, both documentary and fictional
- CDs with scientific and epidemiological information

Organization of Information

Since no specialized thesaurus exists for AIDS, one had to be constructed. This is being done inductively, as documents are indexed. A thesaurus is important not only for indexing but also for recovery of data, because an automated bibliographical catalog does not allow cross-references. For reasons of economics and compatibility, ABIA uses the CD/Micro-Isis Program, which is preferred by Brazilian and other Latin American documentation centers and libraries. Taking this software, the center's document holdings, and user needs, databases were constructed: a bibliographic one of the center's collections; and factual ones: a directory of relevant individuals and institutions, and a glossary of AIDS terms.

Dissemination of Information

Information is disseminated not only in response to requests, but to those who need it even if they are not aware of this need. To reduce the level of ignorance and false information that generate both risky behavior and discrimination, ABIA's action strategies aim to reach people through organizations, services, and persons in leadership positions.

These target users of ABIA are persons external to it who are active in the struggle against the epidemic and in its analysis, who develop activities and research, and who are opinionmakers. These persons can rely on the center to support decision making or broaden their knowledge. They are persons with HIV or AIDS; elementary, secondary, college, or graduate students; journalists; and professionals and researchers in social sciences, health, and communications. Institutions and organizations targeted include state medical and social services, private clinics, businesses, unions, NGOs, community groups, educational and research institutions, the press, and other documentation centers.

Information is disseminated in several ways:

- Response to demands from users, whether in person or by mail, phone, fax, or e-mail
- Creation of indexes, bibliographies, and the like that make the center's collection known
- Exchanges with national and international organizations and institutions with similar and complementary interests and needs (this also broadens ABIA's access to information)
- Participation in networks
- Collaboration in other institutions' publications
- Collaboration with the media
- Electronic conferences
- Speaking with Brazilian and foreign visitors—researchers and journalists seeking not bibliographical information but an oral statement about the state of the epidemic and ABIA's objectives, plans, and actions
- Distribution of material produced by ABIA
- Training "multipliers," those who will spread information about the epidemic

THE DOCUMENTATION CENTER AND WOMEN

In the beginning, "nonpromiscuous" (a rather dubious term) women were not considered possible receptors and transmitters of the virus. Many women became infected due to ignorance. Even today, government campaigns are directed primarily to young people, as if mature women do not have an active, and therefore risky, sex life. And feminist organizations have been slow to take an active role in the struggle against the epidemic.

The center aims to alert people to the current profile of the epidemic and to present ways to face it, through communication with women's health organizations, health professionals, and other individuals and groups. It employs instruments and channels usual for documentation centers and also tries to reach large numbers of people through newspapers, magazines, and other periodicals, specialized or not. It even publicizes information about the epidemic in conservative newspapers and periodicals.

A bibliography can be sent to libraries and documentation centers not only of feminist organizations, but also of unions, businesses, and so on, and can even be inserted into an electronic conference. Communications containing epidemiological data and analyses can be sent to house organs and bulletins. Scientific articles can reach women academics.

Women are historically, ideologically, economically, and culturally different from men. Different means and channels of communication must therefore be developed to reach and inform them.

The Vital Flow

Information and Health Networking in Latin America and the Caribbean

Kathleen Vickery (Chile)

ISIS INTERNATIONAL: WOMEN, INFORMATION, AND COMMUNICATION

Isis International was created in 1974 in Rome as a women's information and communication service. It is the brainchild of three women who saw the need to connect the multiple expressions of a women's movement just beginning to blossom in many corners of the world. They saw that the international women's movement needed its own channels of communication. Their initial objective was to gather as much of the information being produced by women as possible and distribute it through an international network. They received support at the First International Feminist Congress, held in Frankfurt, Germany, in 1974, and published the first Isis newsletter in English, Spanish, and Italian in March 1976.

From 1974 to 1984, as Isis International was building an information network and documentation center in Rome, women throughout Latin America were beginning to organize as women. Inevitably, as they joined together around survival issues or to resist political oppression, what we now refer to as gender consciousness began to surface. Women shared their personal lives, discovered the commonality of many of their problems, and began to analyze

Kathleen Vickery is a program assistant with Isis International's Communications Networking Program and a member of the editorial committee of the Latin American and Caribbean Women's Health Network, which is coordinated by Isis International in Santiago.

these in the broader social context. Health and sexuality were raised as primary topics of women's concern.

In May 1984 the Corporacion Mujer y Familia, a Colombian nongovernmental organization (NGO), convened the First Regional Latin American and Caribbean Women and Health Meeting with the sponsorship of the Colombian Ministry of Health, the Pan American Health Organization, and the Pathfinder Fund. Held in Tenza, Colombia, and attended by seventy-five women from thirteen countries, that meeting marked the beginning of a concerted effort toward collaboration among women's health workers and activists in the region. Among their primary demands were greater access to health information, resources, and training. They decided to form a network that would enable individual women and groups working on health issues locally, nationally, and regionally to share their information and experiences and to coordinate activities.

Isis International had recently transferred its Latin American Programs to Santiago, Chile, where it was setting up an Information and Documentation Center. Given its recognized expertise in documentation, communication, and networking, the women meeting in Colombia asked Isis to coordinate the Latin American and Caribbean Women's Health Network from its new office.

THE LATIN AMERICAN AND CARRIBEAN WOMEN'S HEALTH NETWORK

Isis accepted, and the Health Network began with a short mailing list and three major objectives: (1) facilitate contact and communication among women's groups, (2) provide information resources, and (3) provide organizational support for special meetings and events.

Today these objectives define the Health Network's principal activities, of which contact and communication are the most visible. The Health Network coordinator's office is usually the most active place at Isis. Dozens of letters, faxes, and telephone calls come and go daily, many concerned with the organization or content of meetings and events on women's health. Stacks of publications are received regularly, and the editors' desks are piled high with materials being processed. At first glance, the essence of the Network would appear to be this communications dynamic—the channeling of information from a great variety of sources to a broad network of contacts. Essential to this activity, however, is the information resource base provided by the Isis International Information and Documentation Center.

Although there are no formal requirements for membership in the network, virtually everyone involved participates in the ongoing exchange of information. The Isis International Documentation Center receives and processes the printed materials received by the Health Network: self-help manuals and educational materials, newsletters, flyers, calendars, magazines, working papers, books, theses, conference reports, and so on. About 3,000 articles and documents are currently included in the women's health database, and about 200 periodicals are received in exchange for the network's publications, *Revista* and the *Women's Health Journal.*

This material is not just catalogued and filed, however. Members of the editorial team review all the publications and correspondence and select news items and articles to reprint or for internal use as background material on current issues. This ongoing cycle of information best illustrates the network's dynamic: the Health Network recycles information to its members, which range from small, local groups with limited resources to large policy-making bodies such as the World Health Organization and national ministries of health.

REVISTA AND *THE WOMEN'S HEALTH JOURNAL*

The volume and variety of information on women's health and related issues on file in the Documentation Center have grown steadily as the Health Network has expanded. The Network's original newsletter, first published in Spanish in mid-1985, included the names and addresses of 287 groups and institutions in 17 Latin American and Caribbean countries with which it was in contact, as well as 57 groups and 12 national and international networks in other parts of the world. Today, the Latin American and Caribbean Women's Health Network links close to 2,000 groups, individuals, and institutions worldwide through two quarterly magazines, the *Revista* in Spanish and the *Women's Health Journal* in English.

NEWS FROM THE NETWORK

One-third of each magazine is dedicated to women's health groups and their activities, in four sections: "Sharing Our Experiences," "News and Meetings," "Mailbox," and "Groups and Resources." The content of these sections frequently overlaps: news items may be extracted from correspondence, and the letters section frequently contains news.

- In "Sharing Our Experiences," groups describe what they do and how they do it. Groups that have shared through these pages recently have included EMPOWER, an NGO that provides educational support of different types to sex workers in Bangkok, Thailand; the Health Unit of the Instituto de la Mujer, the Women's Institute in Madrid, Spain; Si Mujer, in Nicaragua; and the Women's Health Project of the Union of Palestinian Medical Relief Committees.
- "News and Meetings" contains such information as reports of meetings and workshops, announcements of new publications and networks,

updates on preparations for the Fourth World Conference on Women, and news of the activities of many different organizations.

- "Mailbox" is the letters section.
- "Groups and Resources" includes brief profiles of groups in the network: name, address, and other contact information, and a brief description of objectives and activities. Information is extracted from a database on the individuals, groups, and institutions with which the network is in contact.

Opinions and Perspectives

Another one-third of the magazines' pages is devoted to opinion, debate, and analysis, reflecting the diversity of issues and priorities represented by groups in different countries as well as different perspectives on a variety of controversial issues.

The Campaign

The "hard" information is in the largest single section of the magazine, known as "The Campaign." This section is conceived as a dossier on a specific topic and is designed to provide the most up-to-date information available, from a woman's perspective, for use by all types of network members. According to feedback, this information is widely used for reference, discussion, and training by women's health groups, and requests for reprints are received frequently. Information for this section is usually compiled, written, and edited by the Health Network's editorial team in Isis, working closely with the Documentation Center.

Each issue also includes a bibliography of new materials on health as well as materials related to the campaign topic.

A CENTRAL ROLE OF THE WOMEN'S HEALTH NETWORK

The content of the publications was initially intended to help women become informed, generate their own information, and share it. During the last decade, however, the Latin American and Caribbean Women's Health Network has played a central role in articulating the priorities and concerns of a broad movement. It currently links and informs not only women's and primary health groups, but also training centers, research and development projects, government and health services, and international organizations. Through its networking activities, publications, and participation in a variety of meetings and forums, the Health Network has been a fundamental instrument in gaining representation and legitimacy for Latin American women's views in mainstream national and international arenas and in creating awareness of women's health issues and of women's physical, reproductive, and mental health needs.

One-to-one contact at meetings and conferences has generated multiple ideas for pooling and disseminating information resources. There is now a regular section in the Health Network publications of news from the Caribbean because the coordinators of the Health Network and the Women and Development Unit (WAND) of the University of the West Indies in Barbados agreed there was a communications and organizational gap between the women's health movements in the Caribbean and in Latin America.

The editors and other Isis International staff members frequently attend and cover national, regional, and international events to find both news and collaborators. The Health Network has also sponsored national and regional meetings on health and population issues and has channeled information from these forums back to the network through its publications.

In 1991 the Health Network sponsored a regional work meeting attended by 80 women from 17 countries to discuss priority issues for the regional health movement, approaches, and strategies. Population policy was identified as a key issue about which women felt they were seriously uninformed. Information was seen as the key to being able to determine what policies most benefit women and how to advocate for these.

Given its capacity to channel information and make contacts, the Health Network was designated as the Latin American Regional Focal Point for the NGO Forum of the International Conference on Population and Development (ICPD) held in September 1994. It has been providing women's NGOs throughout Latin America with background materials that inform them about issues relevant to women and health being raised in the context of the ICPD.

THE INTERNATIONAL DOCUMENTATION CENTERS NETWORK

The foundation for all this work is the information base. The volume of available information, the demand for information, and the velocity at which information is being produced and transmitted all require that Isis continuously improve its capacity to select, process, analyze, and distribute information that serves its stated objectives. One step in that direction has been formation of the International Network of Documentation Centers on Women and Health. This network was created in March 1991 at the initiative of the Boston Women's Health Book Collective, with Isis International and four other institutions in Latin America, the United States, and Asia. It was set up expressly to help these organizations make increasingly effective use of new communications technologies for the exchange of documents and information on women's health from around the world; to develop ways of sharing selected holdings of each institution's collection with groups not currently part of this network as well as among the participating institutions; to explore and, if possible, develop and evaluate strategies for improved coverage of women and health issues by the mass media as well as alternative and women's media; to provide useful information to organizations (including the participating institutions), public officials, and the media aimed at influencing public policy affecting women and health; and to promote access to feminist language and analysis on women and health.

Discussion of the "core collection" was also initiated, defined in the first phase as a list of selected documents on reproductive health and related topics. The collection is at the disposal of the participating institutions and other groups working on the subject of women's health.

Controlled vocabulary has been another topic of discussion. Isis distributed to all network members the *List of Descriptors on the Theme of Women*, which includes specific descriptors in the category of women's health.

The potential for this network to improve the collection and dissemination of information on women's health is enormous, although Isis realizes that it must continue to combine technology with services that are accessible to a wider constituency.

Women, Information, and Human Rights

Aida Haddad (West Bank)

The Palestinian woman in the 1990s should not be seen as a Third World woman, tradition bound, conservative, but in the process of modernization. She may be a poet, a mother with sons and husband in prison, a professor, a professional librarian, a political activist, an elite woman, or a vegetable seller in the old city of Jerusalem. Most Palestinian women are educated. Many are graduates of American or European universities, others of Arab universities. Many believe in a secular state, others yearn to see the whole of historic Palestine an Islamic state. The general consensus of the Palestinian women's movement is whole-hearted participation in her people's struggle for self-determination, human and civil rights, and involvement in all aspects of life.

PALESTINIAN WOMEN'S MOVEMENT

The Palestinian women's movement, part of the wider Arab feminist movement, began in the early days of the national struggle in the 1920s. The movement started with humanitarian work by elite urban women; political matters were at first the preserve of men. But in 1920, a mass demonstration comprising 40,000 took place in Jerusalem to protest British and Zionist activities. Most of the

Aida Haddad has a B.A. from the American University of Beirut and an M.L.S. from the University of Wisconsin—Madison (1978). She was Head Librarian at Birzeit University, 1979–89; head of Technical Services, 1989–92; and is currently head of Collection Development and Gift Exchange. Active in the Palestine Women's Movement, she has served on the board and the human rights committee of the YWCA.

participants were women. The following year the first Palestine Women's Union (PWU) was formed, mainly of upper-class, educated women. The PWU did mainly welfare work. Because of loss of land and the threat of exclusion from employment, poorer, less-educated rural women became actively involved in armed rebellion in the countryside, in the first Intifada (1936).

Many charitable societies sprang up after the 1948 Arab-Israeli war, in refugee camps on the West Bank and Gaza Strip, to meet the refugees' relief, social, and educational needs. Women felt that this work was safe as it did not challenge the entrenched prejudices of their society. Many educated women joined Palestinian national movements, however, and in the 1960s activism in support of resistance organizations began.

The General Union of Palestinian Women played an important role in mobilizing women in the refugee camps outside Palestine. Israeli occupation after the June 1967 war was followed by a sharp rise in women's participation in all kinds of resistance. Women's political consciousness also developed rapidly, because the Palestinian popular and political organizations are entirely male-dominated. This has weakened the stand of women, as they emphasized participation in the national struggle rather than social transformation to overcome internal forms of domination.

THE 1980S INTIFADA

The Intifada that began in December 1987 has had positive and negative effects. Mass mobilization, when citizens regardless of sex or age took to the streets, led to the establishment of neighborhood and popular committees. In September 1988 the Israeli authorities outlawed the popular committees and they transformed themselves into underground movements; this led to ideological conflict among Palestinian factions and a decrease in women's activity.

A closer cooperation and coordination among women's organizations started in December 1988 when the Higher Women's Committee (HWC) was established, and several women's conferences have been held during the Intifada. There is partnership with international NGOs, such as the Women's International League for Peace and Freedom, and U.N. agencies. Last and not least is the networking and support from some Israeli women's groups—for example, Women in Black, who hold a weekly silent anti-occupation vigil in cities throughout Israel, and Women's Organization for Political Prisoners (WOFPP), which works to ease conditions for Palestinian females held in Israeli prisons.

Among women's centers and their publications are the following: the Women's Studies Centre (Jerusalem) publishes a newsletter and a journal in Arabic; the Institute for Women's Studies at Bir Zeit University issues a bibliography of books concerning women in Arabic and the centers and universities that hold them; and the Women's Centre for Legal and Social Counseling issues publications in Arabic on legal aspects of marriage, alimony, and adoptions.

Grass-Roots Organizing and Institution Building

The Israel Women's Network

Alice Shalvi (Israel)

The Israel Women's Network (IWN) has published a number of directories, including one on women's health services and another (in Hebrew, Arabic, Amharic, and Russian) on agencies that provide aid and assistance of various kinds. To counter the frequently heard argument that there are no women experts in a variety of male-dominated fields of action or decision making, IWN has compiled a directory of women qualified to serve on boards of directors, commissions of inquiry, government appointment committees, and the like. Similar lists have been prepared for and circulated among media networks, radio and television stations, and newspapers to ensure that women are consulted, presented, and quoted. IWN's spokeswoman has established excellent contacts with the country's print and electronic media, and IWN has learned how to organize and conduct activities that are sufficiently dramatic, novel, or gimmicky to be deemed newsworthy. The results are especially impressive on occasions such as International Women's Day and the more recently initiated Sixteen Days of Protest, which run from November 25 (International Day Against Violence Against Women) to December 10 (Human Rights Day).

Alice Shalvi was born in Germany and holds a B.A. and M.A. from Cambridge University, a postgraduate diploma from the London School of Economics, and a Ph.D. from the Hebrew University of Jerusalem, where she taught for nearly forty years. She is the founding chair of the Israel Women's Network and recipient of several distinguished awards.

RESOURCE CENTER

IWN's Resource Center, initially established as a source of data and information for its staff and members, has grown beyond all expectation. It is a unique collection of press clippings, journals, and research papers—by IWN and others—in Hebrew, Arabic, English, and some other European languages. Exchange of publications with numerous women's organizations all over the world has helped expand this collection. IWN periodically publishes fact sheets on various aspects of Israeli women's lives and status, such as employment, political representation, health, and education. The Resource Center now serves a wide range of users, from Members of Knesset, ministries, and government officials through journalists, writers, and researchers to pupils doing class projects.

Above all, IWN has demonstrated that knowledge and expertise are power and that access to knowledge and expertise is also the key with which to gain access to the *corridors* of power. We now look forward to an era of peace, to a lessening of the centrality of defense and military considerations, and to a social climate that will facilitate the attainment of what, in 1984, so many women incorrectly assumed we already had—namely, equality of opportunity, equality of reward, and equality of status, the equality that in 1948 Israel's Declaration of Independence proclaimed as the ideological basis on which our independent state would be founded. We hope that era will come soon! Meanwhile, Israeli women are doing their best to foster its speedy birth.

Women, International Information Policy, and Human Rights

Arvonne Fraser (U.S.A.)

We are, I believe, in a period of massive transformation, both globally and here in the United States, and women are at the center of that transformation. The recognition in June 1993 at the Vienna World Conference on Human Rights that women's rights are human rights will be looked upon by future historians as a watershed—a shift in policy that recognizes that women are not "the other," but that they have the right to be full and equal citizens. The Vienna World Conference did more: it recognized the universality of human rights and thus kept us on the road toward worldwide democratization.

Human rights are the basis on which democratic processes and democratic governments are built. Under the Universal Declaration of Human Rights, individuals are granted such basic rights as freedom of speech, freedom to associate and organize without government approval, the right to acquire knowledge—that is, to be educated—the right to work, the right to rest and leisure, to found a family, and more. The Declaration states that all these rights are guaranteed only by organized society and by individuals who respect others' rights.

I think that recently people in this country and probably worldwide have concentrated on the "rights" side of the Universal Declaration and have

With a B.A. from the University of Minnesota, **Arvonne Fraser** was U.S. Ambassador to the UN Commission on the Status of Women, 1992–94. She was a Senior Fellow at the Humphrey Institute of Public Affairs at the University of Minnesota, 1982–92; Director of the International Women's Rights Action Watch; National President, Women's Equity Action League (WEAL); and co-founder of the National Women's Political Caucus and the Minnesota Women's Campaign Fund.

forgotten that the other side of the rights coin is responsibility. What is too often forgotten is that the concluding articles of the Universal Declaration assert that human rights for individuals can be guaranteed only if citizens participate in their governments and if society protects those rights. All citizens must be vigilant in protecting everyone's rights in order to secure their own; everyone has obligations to society.

Recently there has been a shift within the women's movement. We no longer see ourselves as "victims" but as "agents of change." I want to pay my respects to Charlotte Bunch and the many others around the world who brought the issue of violence against women to the attention of the public, and thus gained an acceptance of women's rights as human rights. Bunch and others recognized that, once they brought this issue to public attention and provided information about it, traditional human rights advocates would have to acknowledge women's human rights.

The human rights community has traditionally focused on abrogations of human rights by governments, rather than on discussing the broader scope of human rights. It has organized and gained support by illustrating and publicizing how dreadful the denial of human rights by governments can be. Bunch and her colleagues essentially turned the tables on a community that had previously resisted the idea that private matters, such as domestic violence, are part of the human rights realm.

Bunch and her group organized the Women's Tribunal at the Human Rights Conference. The Tribunal heard the testimony of individual women who had been victims of gross violations of their human rights. They were victims of violence, mostly domestic violence. The message was so powerful that the male leaders at the conference could only accede to the demand that women's rights be considered human rights and that the Convention on the Elimination of All Forms of Discrimination Against Women is a women's human rights treaty. The women who had served on the United Nations Commission on the Status of Women since the late 1940s understood this and gradually developed the convention as a human rights document, adopted by the UN in 1979. On the basis of information gathered from commission meetings and from studies in countries all over the world, the women on the commission made their case through the United Nations system.

For the last decade women all over the world have been organizing and disseminating information on the issue of violence and other women's rights issues. They told the world's dirty little secret, about how common women's experience with violence was and is. Most important, they wrote papers and got the attention of the media, and ultimately of governments. Victims of violence have been agents of change. By their testimony they showed that women as a group—no matter how different the individuals—have a common experience and common concerns. This is a powerful example of the effective use of information by women. These women made an impact; they had an effect on governments.

Another example of how women have taken and used power is in the formation of international networks and using the United Nations system to define and claim their rights, including the right to be educated, to gain knowledge, *and* to impart information. This ultimately changed international policy.

By the time of the World Conference on Human Rights in 1993, 130 nations had ratified the international treaty called the Convention on the Elimination of All Forms of Discrimination Against Women. Women in those nations and others had become a recognized political force that demanded attention. Governments do respond to political constituencies, to citizens who have organized. This treaty defines discrimination against women; its sixteen substantive articles spell out the requirements for eliminating discrimination, for guaranteeing women their right to be educated, to have access to health care, to determine the number and spacing of their children, to have legal and economic independence on equal terms with men, and to participate in public life. Only if women gain and exercise their equal right to participate in public life will they cease to be the subordinate half of the human race, confined to serving men and children in the home.

With this treaty in place, and with the convincing argument that violence against women is tantamount to the abrogation of their human rights, the world is forced to acknowledge women as full citizens, entitled to protection and the freedom to exercise their rights.

The women's rights/human rights treaty and the worldwide women's movement rest on four elements that are key to putting human rights policy into practice: (1) literacy for women, (2) organizing by women, (3) an international information policy that works through the United Nations system and through nongovernmental networks and (4) time and space for women to convene on an international level. Women delegates from United Nations member states have used the Commission on the Status of Women (CSW)—and still use it—to meet, exchange ideas and experiences, and hear the results of studies by experts. The documents resulting from these meetings are available for distribution by the United Nations and in many libraries around the world.

The United Nations has in place a two-part process of documenting and promoting improvements in the status of women. First, as a result of implementation articles of the treaty, a worldwide committee of experts—the Committee on the Elimination of Discrimination Against Women (CEDAW)—hears reports from ratifying countries on their progress in living up to the principles of the treaty. Every year several countries submit reports that identify progress in and obstacles to improving the status of women. The committee reviews these reports and issues its own reports concerning the status of women worldwide.

CEDAW reports are a gold mine of information, as are the reports and documents the Commission on the Status of Women has issued in its almost fifty years of existence. These reports are underused because they are not easily available, but they are extremely useful for those who persevere in finding them within the UN or in depository public libraries.

The CSW also serves as the preparatory body for all world conferences on women. It is now preparing for the UN's Fourth World Conference on Women in Beijing, China, in September 1995. Several regional preparatory meetings are being held to review and assess the work of the past ten years, since the third conference, and make recommendations. CSW asks the regions to review what has happened to women in each region and to make suggestions on what should happen in the future to advance women's status.

The Asia-Pacific Conference was held at Jakarta in June 1994. Sixty percent of the world's women live in this huge region, which includes China. There will be conferences in Vienna, Latin America, Africa, and the Middle East. Each will complete a review and appraisal of the last ten years and develop a regional plan of action before the Fourth World Conference.

Also before the conference, the CSW will draft a Platform for Action, considering women's human rights, political empowerment, poverty alleviation, work, and other issues. Work will be an important issue. The traditional tasks that women do are not defined as "work." There is a movement worldwide to redefine work and perhaps to quantify unpaid work. One's status—especially for males—often comes from employment. When one is unemployed, one loses both status and self-esteem. Perhaps work can be redefined to include tasks that maintain individuals, families, and society.

There is also a strong movement to consider the future of girls as well as women. Because education is long-term, and because the CSW was trying to move adult women ahead, we neglected education and girls. It has taken us fifteen to twenty years to realize that, if the women's movement does not focus on girls and the way we educate and train them, we will have to reinvent the women's movement every second generation. We still think of girls as potential wives and mothers and educate them for subservience rather than as active movers and shakers locally, nationally, or internationally. At the same time, we need to educate boys and men to think of women as partners, not as subordinates.

At the regional meeting in Jakarta, there was also discussion of the media's not giving adequate attention to the women's movement and women's concerns, and for their continued stereotyping of women. Censorship was also an issue, as was control of the media and whether they are going to give equal time to women. The Western media, especially television, should look at this Jakarta document carefully because they need to change how they portray and employ women and report news about them.

Are these United Nations documents and meetings important to ordinary women? Yes. From these conferences we gather information about women worldwide and women collectively. Regional conferences collect enormous amounts of background documentation that is useful within the region and globally.

The Platform for Action that will be discussed and adopted at Beijing has two important elements. First, it will review the last ten years and take a global view of where we are now, asking what has changed, what new circumstances are affecting women and all people: essentially, what are the elements of this massive transformation that we are going through. The Beijing document will also reflect other world conferences, such as the one in Rio de Janeiro, where women's role in the environment was discussed, and the Cairo conference on population and development. And it will address the ongoing violation of women's human rights and document what is happening in women's health, education, and other facets of women's lives.

Second, on the basis of a list of critical areas of concern, the Platform for Action will outline the goals and the strategic actions to be taken. The most important questions are: Why are women the majority of the poor of the world? Why is the education of girls such a low priority? How are we going to deal with societies in which employment is not highly structured and where there are few or no employee fringe benefits? The whole question of the restructuring of economies, and women's role in them, will be high on the Fourth World Conference agenda.

An important issue in Jakarta was female migrant labor, discussed between the sending and the receiving countries. It was heartwarming to watch the Philippine women fighting for the rights of their countrywomen who have migrated to other parts of Asia as domestic workers. Many countries derive a great deal of income from the money such female domestic workers send back to their families, but the poor treatment of these women in the receiving countries is a burning issue.

Still to be decided before the Beijing meeting is the role of NGOs (nongovernmental organizations). Those of us who live in the United States take for granted the right to organize to solve a problem. That is not, of course, true in all countries. In fact, some governments have great difficulty accepting the idea that people not only go out and organize, but say what they think when they meet and spread whatever information they like. Some countries cannot understand that people organize their own conferences and set their own agendas. At every UN conference there are two conferences: the government conference and the NGO forum. The latter is the creative part; it is where like-minded people get together and discuss, exchange experiences, and decide what they are going to do on a free and equal basis. The government delegates come representing their governments, instructed as to what official policy is. Many women delegates also come with backgrounds as activist women. I do believe women's conferences are freer. Women are more open; we look for consensus.

NGOs are the free-wheeling, creative associations, advocating for their ideas with the official delegates. But we need new sets of rules for the way women treat each other in public meetings, and the way groups interact with governments and the UN system. These rules should be human rights put into practice, respecting the integrity of the individual, and constructively mediating conflict.

I encourage every woman to understand the world situation and to act as a full citizen, as a part of all humanity. Unless we do, we are not going to solve the problems that face the world. We are slow in applying the information that we gather and in putting forth constructive solutions to problems. Gathering information may make a good historical record, but it is not enough. Information may convince others—that is, the male half of the world or the governments of the world—to do something, but change will not come quickly unless women get involved in the political system.

The women's movement is learning that it can have solidarity without consensus. We do not all have to agree, but if we believe in human rights, we do have to practice solidarity, putting human rights in practice in whatever we do.

THE ARTHUR AND ELIZABETH SCHLESINGER LIBRARY
ON THE HISTORY OF WOMEN, RADCLIFFE COLLEGE

INFORMATION STATEMENT BY "WOMEN, INFORMATION, AND THE FUTURE"
JUNE 20, 1994

WE, the 218 participants from 46 countries and six continents, gathering at the Schlesinger Library International Conference "Women, Information, and the Future" convened at Radcliffe College, Cambridge, Massachusetts, USA, June 17-20, 1994, respectfully offer the following statement for consideration at the United Nations Fourth World Conference on Women in Beijing, People's Republic of China.

RECOGNIZING THAT THE ADVANCEMENT OF WOMEN in their struggle for equal human rights and for sustainable human development depends on access to information essential to their own political, social, economic and physical well-being, and to their families' health and social and economic betterment;

NOTING THAT TECHNOLOGY can facilitate the creation of information systems that enable women to build and maintain networks, and that collection of information for, about and by women also should proceed in communities which do not have access to modern technology;

CONSIDERING THAT WITHOUT DOCUMENTS women have no history, and without history women will be accorded little respect in the present or in the future, therefore collections of archives, family papers, oral histories, and artifacts should be preserved to document and to honor the contributions of women, and information about women should include statistics, directories of women's organizations, and bibliographies of research on women;

RECALLING WITH SATISFACTION that since the 1985 United Nations Third World Conference on Women in Nairobi, Kenya, many nations have set up systems to collect and disseminate information on women;

WE ENCOURAGE the participants in the United Nations Fourth World Conference on Women in Beijing to urge their governments

      1) to make women's access to information and to the means of dissemination a priority
         of public policy;

      2) to expand their collection, dissemination, and preservation of data and documents
         on women;

      3) to take advantage of new technologies and assure women's equitable access to them;

      4) to utilize the skills of women in creating and maintaining networks.

WE URGE ALL GOVERNMENTS to expand people's knowledge of the past and understanding of the present, and to develop policies that will empower women to achieve equal human rights in the future as the world moves toward sustainable human development.

289

Index